Contents

Arts Management

Derrick Chong

 Routledge
Taylor & Francis Group

LONDON AND NEW YORK

First published 2002
by Routledge
2 Park Square, Milton Park, Abingdon, Oxon, OX14 4RN

Simultaneously published in the USA and Canada
by Routledge
270 Madison Avenue, New York, NY 10016

Reprinted 2003, 2004, 2005, 2006, 2007 (twice)

Routledge is an imprint of the Taylor & Francis Group, an informa business

Typeset in Times by
Bookcraft Ltd, Stroud, Gloucestershire

Printed and bound in Great Britain by
MPG Books Ltd, Bodmin, Cornwall

British Library Cataloguing in Publication Data
A catalogue record for this book is available
from the British Library

Library of Congress Cataloging in Publication Data
A catalog record for this book has been requested

ISBN 0–415–23681–9 (hbk)
ISBN 0–415–23682–7 (pbk)

Preface

An observation attributed to Germaine Greer at the end of the twentieth century – that marketing is the principal cultural form of our time – served as a topic of exchange in a major British newspaper (*Guardian,* 27 March 1999). The choice of debaters, the managing director of a major public relations firm and the paper's chief art critic, was suggestive of the links between publicity and oil painting examined by John Berger in *Ways of Seeing* (1972). Following Berger's analysis in the early 1970s, the encroachment of management theory – not least of all associated with notions of consumer sovereignty – into many areas of social activity has been steady. Fear and greed, particularly on the part of middle managers, helps to explain 'Heathrow Organization Theory', the mischievous term coined by Gibson Burrell to characterize the 'philosophical vacuity' underpinning management thinking, which results from 'the fact that most mid-Atlantic managers think with their beliefs than about them' (Burrell 1989: 308, 307).

Yet it is prudent to remember that insider accounts have characterized management gurus as fallible propagandists. *Financial Times* columnist Lucy Kellaway has criticized the management self-help business. By way of illustration, 'F + M = P * R' (where F = Formula, M = Management, P = Pretentious, R = Rubbish) is how she mocks the crude and simplistic pragmatism encapsulated by flow charts to gain scientific respectability (Kellaway 2000: 58). In the same vein, 'bullshit bingo' is a game of lining up management clichés: it accentuates the reliance on a 'piece of verbal wallpaper to cover flaws in argument and gaps in thinking' (leader in the London *Times,* 6 April 2000). This is consistent with the case against management theory – incapable of self-criticism, incomprehensible gobbledegook, rarely rises above basic common sense, and faddish and bedevilled by contradictions – as posited by *Economist* staffers (Micklethwait and Wooldridge 1996).

What is the relevance of art and aesthetics in the practice and study of organizations and their management? How can we better understand the management of creativity and innovation in complex knowledge flows between cultural production and consumption? These are questions posed at the 2001 Critical Management Studies conference, organized by the Manchester School of Management, in the sessions devoted to 'art and aesthetics' and 'the management of creativity and creative industries'. The points of contact between the arts and management are many and complex. We are particularly interested in 'arts management' as an emerging (i.e. post-1960s) sub-discipline worthy of critical investigation. An inter-disciplinary approach is required, given the diverse range of theoretical texts from disciplines that continue to be important on the writing about arts management. As opposed to writing a manual on so-called 'best practice' – there are numerous books on arts marketing, fund-raising, and sponsorship, for example – our aim is to examine some of the main impulses informing discussions in the management of arts and cultural organizations. The desire is to offer assistance to students and researchers in identifying various signposts.

Synthesis has been crucial. Theoretical texts from a diverse range of disciplines – sociology of culture, cultural economics, museology, cultural policy, art history, and management (including marketing, strategy, organization studies, and critical accounting) – continue to have a profound impact on arts management writing. Artists and works of art have been invaluable with imprints dotted throughout. *Arts Management* is informed by certain important cultural commentators including Raymond Williams, Hans Haacke, Pierre Bourdieu, members of the Frankfurt School (namely Theodor Adorno and Walter Benjamin), and Paul DiMaggio. *Free Exchange* (1995), an extended conversation between Bourdieu and Haacke on the potential for the art world to be manipulated by social and political forces, remains an instructive text. Management theorists, from different disciplines and orienta-tions, include Henry Mintzberg, Gareth Morgan, Charles Handy, Michael Porter, Philip Kotler, and Gibson Burrell. Research promoted by the British think tank Demos and the international management consultancy McKinsey has been useful. The writing on arts management has spawned specialist publications like the *Journal of Arts Management, Law, and Society*, the *International Journal of Arts Management*, and the *Journal of Cultural Economics*. AIMAC, an international bilingual (English and French) association devoted to promoting an arts and cultural management conference, was formed in the early 1990s. Different concerns and approaches to arts management have been advanced. Prominent arts manage-ment writers include John Pick, D. Paul Schafer, and J. M. D. Schuster. Fitzgibbon and Kelly's edited collection, *From Maestro to Manager* (1997), offers a Euro-pean perspective which complements the American orientation of Byrnes's intro-duction to the subject, *Management and the Arts* (1999: second edition). Good research-driven texts which widen the perspective to encompass commercial orga-nizations include Richard Caves's *Creative Industries* (2000), which focuses on the theory of contracts and the logic of economic organization; and Harold Vogel's *Entertainment Industry Economics* (2001; fifth edition), which offers a financial analysis of media-dependent and live entertainment firms.

There is much to suggest that various forms of blurring conventional boundaries (i.e. public/private notions of patronage; interactive media to create works of art; market protection versus the marketplace) will continue. Given that the euphoria associated with postmodern arguments for eclecticism has diminished, there is a renewed opportunity to consider the critique of Adorno and Horkheimer, who coined 'culture industry', in 1947, as a derogatory term. In a subsequent work, 'Culture industry re-considered', Adorno refined his position:

The culture industry fuses the old and familiar into a new quality. In all its branches, products which are tailored for consumption by masses, and which to a great extent determine the nature of that consumption, are manufactured more or less according to plan.

(Adorno 1991: 85)

Central to Adorno's critique is the application of capitalist industrialism, namely the profit-motive, to creative activity. Marxist historian Eric Hobsbawn expanded on this theme, namely the decline of the avant-garde and the arts after 1950, in *Age of Extremes* (1994). Moreover, marketing of artists and works of art since the 1960s forces us to look at the mechanics of presentation within the culture industry and to assess the role of the merchandiser. One recognizes that all arts organizations are engaged in expressions of self-promotion, trying to cultivate the 'right' image and identity. Branding, as such, has assumed a mythic importance. Business dealings with the arts have expanded beyond corporate sponsorship to include more complex collaborations involving the enhancement of creativity and innovation 'skills'. Examining the interdependence between the arts and business raises issues concerning aesthetic integrity and the role of artists and arts organizations in contemporary society. As entrepreneurial norms of performance have become social norms of behaviour, a new layer of 'non-artistic' managers (say in marketing and fund-raising) has emerged.

Arts Management is designed to help stimulate interest in the field of arts management by setting something of its basic character in an engaging form. The Association of Arts Administration Educators (AAAE) is keen that arts management be treated as a postgraduate course of study. Arts management for undergraduates, according to the AAAE, should be 'firmly based in a liberal arts curriculum whose objective is the broad development of students as human beings capable of analysis, reasoning, communication and judgment' (Prieve 1993: 69). Basic educational aims of the book for postgraduate and undergraduate readers include the following: to educate existing and future arts managers to assess their artistic, managerial, and social responsibilities; to judge the context and conditions faced by arts organizations in contemporary society and associated management issues; and to understand interdisciplinary approaches to solutions. Substantial citations are used to illustrate the engagement of commentators such as arts managers and artists: what they say is as important as how they say it. This is to suggest that interpreting rhetorical strategies is part of any genuine arts management education. Moreover, works of art communicate: they sharpen our thinking by offering new perspectives.

The text does not serve as a 'how-to' guide to management and the arts, yet it would be idealistic, nay irresponsible, to argue that art as a domain ought to be free from the constraints which now characterize much social activity in advanced western economies. To what extent is arts management an 'academic' pursuit? To what extent is arts management grounded in current application? In order to avoid excluding an entire set of concerns in what can become competing interests, a concerted effort is made in each of the ten chapters to strike a balance between theories espoused by cultural critics, which support a fuller understanding of arts organizations as socio-political institutions, and pressing managerial imperatives as economic organizations; at the same time, problems arise if aesthetic objectives start to fade from view. The literature on arts management has become large and increasingly diverse: one task of the book is to highlight some of the more prominent writers and to suggest sources for more engaged readers.

Arts management is a more complex term than one first imagines, as Chapter 1 sets out to illustrate. Traditional boundaries are being blurred, yet there are highly charged debates when arts managers need to reconcile managerial, economic, and aesthetic objectives. Three commitments – to excellence and artistic integrity; to accessibility and audience development; and to public accountability and cost effectiveness – serve as a loose framework for the text.

The uses and limitations of three key areas of arts research, cross-national comparative cultural policy, economic impact studies, and audience surveys, are discussed in Chapter 2. Understanding how arts research may have an impact on decision-making by managers, policy-makers, and funders is important; moreover, awareness that the terms of reference of any arts research project have an impact on the findings is valuable.

Entrepreneurship is viewed as an advantageous social process with economic benefits; it is actively promoted as instructive and beneficial for all types of arts organizations. In Chapter 3, cultural entrepreneurship is examined as a source of dynamism (helping to make cities hubs of creativity). Impresarios have a long history in the arts; visual and performing artists have also contributed to our understanding of cultural entrepreneurship. The global franchising of a cultural brand raises many of the pressing issues with which arts managers must grapple.

Chapter 4 highlights that collaborations in the arts come in various forms. What is the relationship between private patrons and public institutions? How may contemporary links between corporations and arts organizations be interpreted? Are there lessons that the arts can teach business? Such questions contribute to the growing debate about the role of the arts in contemporary society.

A commitment to excellence and artistic integrity, of foremost importance to all arts organizations, is a theme linking artistic leadership (Chapter 5) and strategic positioning and brand identity (Chapter 6). There is no reason to assume that commercial success must come at the expense of excellence and integrity; on the other hand, even 'high' art organizations cannot avoid what happens in the marketplace. Working with artists and managing creativity are facets of arts organizations raised in Chapter 5. Yet there is recognition of extra-artistic concerns with explicit management issues regarding artistic leadership: these include bifurcated management structures and approaches to organizational change. Chapter 6 is based on a meeting of management strategy and marketing. Strategy as positioning means that every arts organization needs to think about its basic character; communicating what sets it apart from similar organizations draws attention to the value of branding and corporate identity.

'Arts marketing' (or marketing the arts) represents a growing sub-sector of marketing (as initially conceived for highly branded commercial products like cigarettes, automobiles, and perfume). Chapter 7 explores the benefits and limitations of marketing the arts in terms of making a commitment to accessibility and audience development (i.e. widening the socio-economic mix of the audience base as identified in Chapter 2). As an inversion, 'the arts for marketing' helps to focus attention on exchange relationship as a fundamental concept of marketing and marketing challenges faced by arts organizations.

Public accountability and cost effectiveness as the third commitment is addressed in two chapters. Chapter 8 looks at how numbers have a multi-faceted impact on management and the arts: taste can be dictated by surveys and ratings; Baumol and Bowen's 'income gap' is a foundational concept of cultural economics; performance indicators represent a management control technique based on auditing practices; and the contested term restructuring often emphasizes cutting and reducing. Alongside containing costs, arts organizations and artists need to raise funds. Chapter 9 examines distinct sources: the philosophy behind fund-raising (from membership schemes to endowment enhancement); equity financing with reference to theatre 'angels'; and ways artists seek to exploit their property rights.

The 'organization' of arts organizations necessitates a review of issues of power, control, and authority. Four broad areas of organizational analysis are examined in Chapter 10. Who should control the arts organization (Henry Mintzberg)? How does institutional isomorphic change help to explain the homogeneity of organizational forms and practices found in arts organizations (Walter Powell and Paul DiMaggio)? Can the use of images and metaphors contribute to a reading of arts organizations (Gareth Morgan)? What is the potential impact of the new logic of organizing on arts organizations?

Abbreviations

A&B	Arts and Business
AAAE	Association of Art Administration Educators
ABSA	Association for Business Sponsorship in the Arts
ACGB	Arts Council of Great Britain
AGO	Art Gallery of Ontario
AIM	Alternative Investment Market
AIMAC	International Association of Arts and Cultural Management
BCA	Business Committee for the Arts
BSO	Boston Symphony Orchestra
CBAC	Council for Business and the Arts in Canada
ECO	English Chamber Orchestra
EI	Emotional Intelligence
GDP	Gross Domestic Product
IPO	Initial Public Offering
LIFT	London International Festival of Theatre
Met	Metropolitan Museum of Art
MBA	Master of Business Administration
MFA	Museum of Fine Arts
MMFA	Montreal Museum of Fine Arts
MoMA	Museum of Modern Art
NEA	National Endowment for the Arts
OECD	Organization for Economic Cooperation Development
PI	Performance Indicators
PMA	Philadelphia Museum of Art
PSO	Pittsburgh Symphony Orchestra
RIAA	Recording Industry Association of America
RRP	Rembrandt Restoration Project
SOLT	Society of London Theatres
SPPA	Survey of Public Participation in the Arts
UCLA	University of California, Los Angeles
UN	United Nations
VFM	Value for Money

1 Introduction

There is some attraction in the thesis that arts management is an outgrowth of the experiences of arts organizations in the United States during the 1960s. The assumption of a monolithic and universal arts management is based on American hegemony in commercial spheres near the end of the so-called American Century. The 'logic of industrialization' assumes that the goals of arts organizations converge like those of business corporations, with deviations from the 'one best way' eliminated by a process of social Darwinism. But do the facts bear out this 'Americanization' thesis? Once arts management had developed in the USA, was it inevitable that other countries would go through the same process? Do various environmental and institutional factors suggest otherwise? What are the international repercussions of the American model of arts management? Has an American ethos altered the terms of reference by which issues are defined, relationships maintained, and contentions resolved?

Though 1960s' America has been pegged as a starting point for arts management, it is instructive to move the historical marker to developments c.1945, namely the creation of the Arts Council of Great Britain (ACGB). The ACGB provided a model for arts councils which later emerged in other industrialized Commonwealth countries (Canada, Australia, and New Zealand) and the USA; moreover, it played a leading role in initiating arts management courses and encouraging greater business involvement in the arts. The ACGB was incorporated in 1946 as an outgrowth of the Committee for the Encouragement of Music and the Arts, which formed in 1939 as a wartime programme to bolster morale. Prominent features of the ACGB – including an arm's length relationship with government and peer review as a method of adjudication for awarding funds – have served as a model for other national arts councils. The health of arts councils and the debates in which they are involved serve as barometers of wider cultural concerns.

Two other institutional players in the USA, along with the National Endowment for the Arts (NEA), showed an interest in the arts during the 1960s: 'brand name' foundations including Ford, Rockefeller, and Carnegie funded arts research; and 'blue chip' corporations such as IBM, Exxon, Chase Manhattan, and Mobil helped to establish the Business Committee for the Arts (BCA). At the same time, social unrest helped forced cultural institutions to re-examine programming objectives and decision-making processes. Slower at establishing arts councils, the USA has been avid in exploring art and culture as subjects of economic inquiry, encouraging a nexus between business and the arts.

There was an attempt in the USA to learn from the European experiences of arts patronage. This is illustrated in Frederick Dorian's *Commitment to Culture* (1964), which sought to find out what Americans could learn from European patterns of arts patronage. It was recognized that 'private patronage has already been established in our country', but that it 'alone cannot carry the burden' (Dorian 1964: 457, 459). The case for government allocations (or subsidies) to the arts at all levels (federal, state, and local) to complement private sponsorship never established a strong following in the USA. The NEA, which did not exist at the time of Dorian's study, has been subjected to criticisms concerning liberty under government patronage; the notable absence of a 'secretary of state for culture' in the USA is a direct consequence of a distrust of a closer relationship between art and politics (except when seeking to promote American cultural interests abroad).

A dominant motif since the 1960s has been the rise of managerial imperatives. For example, Thomas Raymond and Stephen Greyser, both at the Harvard Business School, and Douglas Schwalbe, an arts administrator at Harvard, founded the Arts Administration Research Institute in 1966; and, in 1970, the trio established the Harvard Summer School Institute in Arts Administration. Yet the emergence of a 'new breed' of arts manager has been depicted as pernicious and regressive:

> Trained by prestigious business schools, they are convinced that art can and should be sold like the production and marketing of other goods. They make no apologies and have few romantic hang-ups.
>
> It is expected that the lack of delusions and aspirations among new arts administrators will have a noticeable impact on the state of the industry. Being trained primarily as technocrats, they are less likely to have an emotional attachment to the peculiar nature of the product they are promoting. And this attitude, in turn, will have an effect on the type of products we will soon begin to see.
>
> (Haacke 1986: 60–1)

Essentially, Hans Haacke was concerned that the commercial language of management would become naturalized in the discourse and practice of managing arts and cultural organizations. He was not alone: John Pick, for example, criticized the adoption by British organizations of 'half-baked Americanised notions of "management" ... . A new breed of arts managers ... make[s] it clear that one should not look for pleasure from the Arts, but market returns' (Pick 1986: 7).

More specifically, Haacke criticized 'arts administration courses taught according to the Harvard Business School case method ... by professors with little or no direct knowledge of the peculiarities of the art world' (Haacke 1986: 61). Haacke was taking aim at the inclusion of his celebrated 1971 dispute with the Solomon R. Guggenheim Museum, which was represented in *Cases for Arts Administration*, edited by Raymond, Greyser, and Schwalbe (1975: 217–22): 'Director of a major museum weighs whether or not to cancel a show by controversial artist'. It goes without saying that the Haacke/Guggenheim controversy was much more complex; it raised questions concerning the idealist concept of the autonomy of art, and the belief that the art museum is a neutral, nonsocial, apolitical institution (for an excellent account of the case, see Burnham 1971). The manner in which the case study method fosters cursory debates and rewards quick and detached decision-making with limited information has been criticized: it encourages 'an approach to the practice of management that is "thin" and "superficial"', according to Henry Mintzberg (1989: 90).

In this introductory chapter, we consider how conventional boundaries defining arts organizations are being challenged. Keywords associated with arts management need to be disentangled and investigated. What is the proper role of arts management? Three commitments applicable to different types of arts organizations – to excellence and artistic integrity; to accessibility and audience development; and to accountability and cost effectiveness – highlight the complexity associated with their management.

Blurred boundaries

Exploring the interaction between managerial, economic, and aesthetic objectives with which all visual and performing arts organizations in contemporary society must confront has gained increasing attention. The following examples illustrate a selection of the changes taking place for all types of arts organizations. Some have been alive with animated and sometimes acrimonious debates to an unprecedented degree.

In his report on *The Future of Lyric Theatre in London* (1998), Sir Richard Eyre recognized that the problems of a high-profile arts organization, in receipt of significant state subsidy, may have wider repercussions:

> as a barometer of the health of the performing arts [the Royal Opera House] has inspired righteous indignation, invited mockery, invoked accusations of irresponsibility, overspending, mismanagement and elitism, and begged questions about the validity of the principle on which all organizations receive taxpayers money.
>
> (Eyre 1998: Foreword)

Even the revered Royal Shakespeare Company, in its bid for £50 million in public funds to replace its current 1930s Art Deco theatre with a 'theatre village', has not escaped charges that such a sum might be better used to help alleviate social deprivation in areas (e.g. ex-manufacturing and ex-mining) that are now struggling. An alternative system, based on optimism and faith in the individual – as expressed in essays by Ralph Waldo Emerson (1803–82) – has taken root in the USA and is complemented by a taxation system (i.e. full taxes on income or testamentary estates devoted to civic or educational purposes are not collected):

> This remarkable delegation to private citizens of the power to spend funds which would otherwise have gone to the government certainly did not assure

taste or even responsibility. But in a huge country with hundreds of thousands of new fortunes arising, and tens of hundreds of private foundations coming into existence, it did assure the richness of calculated cultural anarchy.

(Kingman Brewster in Appignanesi 1984: 7)

It has been noted by an informed commentator that Italy has to address unique cultural issues:

> This first Italian particularity is that of having the largest 'open-air' heritage in the Western world. Other countries, of course, have important museums, famous collections, libraries and archives of great historical importance. No other country, however, is forced to administer so important an archaeological and architectural heritage that is unguarded and unguardable. Almost all our cities have a historical centre with notable traces of Roman and pre-Roman civilisation. Some have preserved, in whole or in part, a circumference of medieval walls often, especially in Italy, embodying Etruscan and Roman elements. All regions have archaeological sites of great historical interest.
>
> In other countries the number of works of art preserved in churches represents a small percentage of what is kept in museums and private collections. In Italy, thanks to the historical role of the Catholic Church, a conspicuous part of the heritage has a double function: it is an object of aesthetic appreciation by visitors and tourists and also an object of worship by millions of the faithful; and as an object of worship it is in practice as far as administration and security are concerned, an 'open-air' object.
>
> (Sergio Romano in Appignanesi 1984: 12)

If all of Italy is considered a cultural warehouse, the weight of history can become unbearable. This helps to account why 'privatization' has raised its head. Most recently, in October 2001, a one-sentence provision was tacked onto Italy's 2002 Finance Bill that authorized the Ministry of Culture to 'assign to private enterprise the full management of services connected to the public enjoyment of cultural heritage'. Directors of the most powerful art museums around the world wrote an open letter to the Italian government expressing their alarm:

> As directors of major international museums, we are concerned by the proposal, contained in the current *finanziaria*, to hand over to private enterprise, *'l'ntera gestione del servizio concernente la fruizione pubblica dei beni culturali'* [the entire administration of services to the public enjoyment of cultural heritage].
>
> While greater autonomy for Italian State museums may have advantages – as the experience of a number of European institutions makes clear – in all cases, these are run exclusively for a public benefit, not for private profit.
>
> Although museums in the USA are not mainly governmental institutions, they are not run as private businesses, nor put, all or in part, in the hands of private enterprise, and are strictly not-for-profit in their management.

We would urge the Italian government, whose cultural patrimony is of supreme importance to the whole world, to discuss this proposal very widely both at home and abroad, and to move with due deliberation before transferring the running of museums to private enterprise.

(published in the *Art Newspaper*, 22 October 2001)

In view of hostility to what 'privatization' could mean, the Ministry clarified that it is about 'private service providers' being awarded fixed-term contracts to manage individual sites of artistic and cultural heritage; control over policy would not be abrogated (see the *Wall Street Journal Europe*, 7/8 December 2001). On closer inspection, the role of private management in Italy's cultural-heritage sector has established roots: the so-called Ronchey Law of 1993 has allowed various services (e.g. ticketing, bookstores, cafes, and merchandizing) to be contracted-out, as well as allowing commercial prices to be charged for tickets. This is the case at Pompeii, the country's most famous and visited archaeological site. Performing arts institutions have not been exempt: in 1997, La Scala was the first opera house in Italy to be 'privatized'. The year before privatization, 60 per cent of La Scala's budget came from the state and the rest from ticket sales; since privatization, the subsidy has fallen to around 45 per cent. One key issue is to avoid privatization becoming synonymous with commercialism (e.g. the latter could include compromises to sponsors over choice of programme and production teams, namely a radical 'dumbing down' in the pursuit of ticket sales).

Moscow's Bolshoi Theatre represents a renowned arts organization caught up in wider political changes. The transition economy following the dismantlement of the Soviet Union has led to big subsidy cuts. In order to address new economic realities, the Bolshoi introduced a new pricing scheme for tickets; and increasing the level of private donations has been recognized as a top priority (see Klintsov and von Löhneysen 2001). The true value of seats for individual performances is addressed in the new pricing structure, in contrast to the older distribution system in which one-third of the tickets (offered to designated categories like artists, theatre managers, and state bureaucrats) found their way to scalpers. Compared to other international theatres like the Royal Opera House and La Scala, the amount of private funding raised by the Bolshoi is miniscule. Fund-raising initiatives associated with American arts organizations are being adopted (e.g. using trustees, as a prime source of generating donations and sponsorship opportunities, and lobbying for increased state support). On a related front, the Bolshoi needs to protect its reputation from 'pirates' trying to capitalize on its international fame (by fraudulent use of the Bolshoi name and logo). Two issues complicate matters: the Bolshoi sends different official tours abroad to earn money; and dancers are allowed on independent tours and to identify themselves as being from the Bolshoi (cited in the London *Daily Telegraph*, 15 January 2002).

The market is hard and pure, according to Giancarlo Politi, the editor of *Flash Art*:

Art has always been peremptorily linked to the market (however much some may plead ignorance of the fact). What was once referred to as 'patronage'

(Lorenzo dei Medici or Leone X), nowadays takes the form of sponsorship, galleries, collectors.

The art produced today is far higher in quality (and quantity) than it used to be. Supply is up and, consequently, so is the climate of competition and the scope for selection. And the market remains the healthiest filter there is for determining the quality of art.

However paradoxical this might sound, the market alone is hard and pure. It is the market that receives all the input from critics, the media, collector culture, distribution. The market has neither a heart nor feelings, but looks to the values established by the art system (critics, museums, media, galleries, collectors).

Who better to judge a work of art than the art system? The whey-faced young critic (immature or mature) at the mercy of his own emotions, friendships, blackmail and a mountain of bills to pay?

Let's be serious.

(November/December 2000)

Politi offers an instructive note on the historical role of works of art as another form of commodity. Indeed, the long-running anecdote that several social classes denoted the only difference between selling fine art and used motors seems to be gaining some empirical evidence. In December 2001, Alfred Taubman, the former chairman of Sotheby's (a retailer who purchased the auction house in the early 1980s), was convicted of price-fixing. (Taubman's opposite number at Christie's, Sir Anthony Tennant, refused to attend the trial; the American–British extradition treaty does not include civil cases.) In exchange for conditional amnesty, Christie's cooperated with the US Justice Department into how the two leading auction houses, in order to limit competition, colluded to fix commission rates. (Sotheby's and Christie's had already agreed to pay former customers over $500 million in damages stemming from the price-fixing scheme; Sotheby's paid an additional fine of $45 million.) Sotheby's former chief executive officer, Diana Brooks, in exchange for leniency, turned on her former boss. Brooks emerged as the prosecution's star witness; Christopher Davidge, Brooks's counterpart at Christie's, also cooperated. The commission-fixing scheme operated between 1993 and 1998, when the Justice Department started its investigation. Luxury brands featured in the court case: Davidge flew Concorde, LHR to JFK, to meet with Brooks; negotiations on common commission rates were conducted in her Lexus. With a good Anglo-American storyline, containing all ingredients of an American 'tragedy' (in the vein one associates with daytime television mixed with *Lifestyles of the Rich and Famous*), a cinematic dramatization was already underway during the trial: Sigourney Weaver, who is to play Brooks, attended the court case. The ordeal was summed up in an apposite manner in the *Financial Times* (6 December 2001): 'the investigation of the art industry and the subsequent trials are a reminder that despite their distinguished pedigrees and the huge sums they spend each year to promote themselves, they are ultimately brokerages'.

Those charged with the stewardship of arts organizations cannot divorce programming decisions from broader ethical concerns and social responsibilities. For example, what is the proper role of Wagner given his links to Adolph Hitler? Father M. Owen Lee believes that it is possible for 'a terrible man to produce art that is good, true, and beautiful'; and that Wagner's works 'are about the healing of the hurt in, the drawing off of the evil in, the integration of the conflicting forces in, the human psyche' (Lee 1999: 3, 20). Using music as a means to heal wounds helps to explain Daniel Barenboim's decision in 2001 to breach the taboo of playing Wagner in Israel:

> I don't think that Hitler and his people should prevent us from playing and hearing Wagner's music simply because they saw in it something that made them what they were. Not playing Wagner has harmed the Israel Philharmonic artistically. There is a vacuum in their music because there are few composers as important as Wagner. I don't see how you can really understand Mahler and Schoenberg if you don't know your Wagner.
>
> (London *Guardian*, 4 August 2001)

In 1999, Barenboim and writer Edward Said conceived the idea of the Divan Workshop for Young Musicians, to close the chasm between Arabs and Israelis. Wagner's *Die Meistersinger* has a special resonance: 'Few operas in my opinion have done so relentlessly detailed a job of literally enacting the way in which music, if it is looked at not simply as a private, esoteric possession but as a social activity, is interwoven with, and is important to social reality' (Said 1991: 61). Young musicians across the Middle East divide are brought together to build personal and cultural bridges; improving one's level of technical ability through hours of rehearsal and performance is followed by discussion.

In the immediate aftermath of the 11 September 2001 terrorist attacks, Nicholas Kenyon, director of the BBC Proms, decided to change the programme to Last Night of the Proms, the country's biggest, most visible classical music event. It is one of the most explicit opportunities of tub-thumping and flag-waving in the UK. Kenyon jettisoned traditional favourites like *Land of Hope and Glory* and *Rule Britannia!*, but retained *Jerusalem* to end the concert. Disappointment was felt by those who appreciate good music by the BBC Symphony Orchestra with a patriotic wrapper. Furthermore, the inclusion of the final movement of Beethoven's *Ninth* was perceived by some as carrying too strong a political message (i.e. it is also used as the 'theme song' of the European Union). Of course, critics of the traditional Last Night feel that it belongs to a period when Britain was a colonial power, and Britannia really did rule the waves.

Defining arts management

The opening paragraph on 'arts administration (arts management)' in the *International Encyclopedia of Public Policy and Administration* (1998) is an instructive place to start our investigation:

> The application of the five traditional management functions – planning,

organizing, staffing, supervising, and controlling – to the facilitation of the production of the performing or visual arts and the presentation of the artists' work to audiences. The administration and facilitation of the creative process and its communication to an audience is common to both public, nonprofit arts organizations (e.g. nonprofit theaters, symphony orchestras, opera companies, dance companies, museums, public broadcasting, and performing arts centers) and private, commercial, for-profit artistic entities (e.g. commercial theater, 'popular' music, private galleries, film, television, and video).

(Martin 1998: 128)

Dan Martin's entry invites two comments. First, Martin, like Byrnes (1999) in his undergraduate book on arts management, stresses an adherence to the contribution of Henri Fayol (1841–1925), arguably the first modern management writer, who remains important for proffering what has become the classical notion of management, namely leading (or commanding), planning, organizing, coordinating, and controlling. But how relevant is Fayol's notion of management, which focuses on the process of management as reflective and systematic, at the start of the twenty-first century? Second, Martin suggests two distinct but related spheres of activity: public, nonprofit; and private, for-profit. Such boundaries may be useful for including commercial firms involved in the arts, which widens the conventional perspective. It also encourages one to think about the historical role of cultural entrepreneurs and arts impresarios in formation of what have become public, non-profit arts organizations and the legacy of private/public collaborations. Paul DiMaggio reminds us that such divisions are constructed: 'Not until two distinct organizational forms – the private or semiprivate, nonprofit cultural institution and the commercial popular culture industry – took shape did the high/low-culture dichotomy emerge in its modern form' (DiMaggio 1986a: 41–2). Furthermore, 'if we look at our high-culture industries today, we soon see that nonprofit organization is not the only form. Indeed, in art, classical music, and even theatre, our museums, symphonies, and resident stages are only the nonprofit jewels in a for-profit crown' (DiMaggio 1986b: 87).

'When most people in the arts industry talk of arts management, they are referring primarily to the purely administrative functions of an arts organization, not the management practices involved in producing the artistic work', according to Martin (1998: 129), who identifies five management departments – strategic planning, finance management, fund-raising, marketing, and facility or physical plant management – in support of the art for which the organization has been established. Moreover, Martin appears to emphasize a positivistic perspective whereby managerialism is applied to arts organizations. Audiences, visitors, or spectators are reconceptualized along mainstream corporate marketing management lines as consumers. As a prominent example, the Solomon R. Guggenheim Foundation has taken a lead from fast-food outlets to engage in global cultural franchising (New York, Venice, Bilbao, Berlin, and Las Vegas) by recognizing that the asset value of its permanent collection can be leveraged as a financial instrument (see discussion in Chapter 3). The line of demarcation between 'purely administrative functions' and 'producing the artistic work', with arts management focusing on the former, means that the insights of artists and cultural critics on the relationship between the arts and management may be sidelined.

A critical perspective on arts management ought to serve as a starting point – even for those interested in the more utilitarian purpose of identifying legitimate areas of managerial intervention. An inquiry into 'arts management', which disentangles constituent terms and related ones, complements Martin; moreover, it introduces some of the decisions which have informed thinking on arts management. First, what is art? What are the arts? Second, what is management? Who are managers? What do managers do? Third, what is the role of consumption and consumers?

In examining the treatment of 'art' it is instructive to include the complementary term 'culture', which Raymond Williams described as 'one of the two or three most complicated words in the English language' owing to its four diverse states: a general state or habit of the mind; the general state of intellectual development in society as a whole; the general body of arts; and, a whole way of life, material, intellectual, and spiritual (Williams 1983: 76–82). Williams drew attention to culture in its current and most widespread use, namely the third state: 'an independent noun which describes works and practices of intellectual and especially artistic activity'. Thus performing and visual arts in the traditional sense – namely art music, ballet, opera, theatre, and painting and sculpture – are included. By extension, there is a concern with the (public, nonprofit) institutions that allow the arts and culture to be put on display. A case against film as art boils down to one or more of four complaints: movies are commercial; they are collaborations, more committee work than the responsibility of a single artist; they are technological products; and they mix genres (Wills 2001: 72).

Related debates of earlier generations remain unresolved. For example, Walter Benjamin's well-known dictum (from the 1930s) that 'there is no document of civilization which is not at the same time a document of barbarism' (Benjamin 1969: 256) is diametrically opposed to that of Kenneth (later Lord) Clark, who is also closely associated with using 'civilisation', in his acclaimed television series (Clark 1969). However, the current focus may be on other concerns: certain mass cultural forms and practices may comprise the most significant 'culture' of our time, precisely because of its 'popular' character. Such a view of culture is framed in terms of Barbara Kruger's whimsical catch-phrase: 'When I hear the word culture, I reach for my cheque book'. Moreover, the rise of the term 'creative industries' expands the somewhat narrow boundaries of 'the arts in the traditional sense' by including design, fashion, pop music, film, video, publishing, and advertising amongst other areas. Whether policy makers will emphasize creative industries, which draw tourists and contribute to export earnings at the expense of performing and visual arts organizations requiring public subsidy, is an ongoing concern.

Williams also included 'management' in his vocabulary of culture and society: 'The word "manage" seems to have come into English directly from *maneggiare*, Italian – to handle or train horses'; he differentiated three groups, civil servants (or bureaucrats), administrators, and managers, as corresponding to public, semi-public, and private concerns respectively (Williams 1983: 189–92). Whereas the 'actual activities were identical', according to Williams, distinctions in tenor were 'received and ideological'. However, the distinctive traditions associated with civil service were giving way to 'management' as a generic function suitable to each and every organization. Indeed a case has even been made that the 'manager' – as represented by popular management writers such as Peter Drucker and Charles Handy and in journals like the *Harvard Business Review* – was promoted as the cultural hero of the twentieth century.

The continuing relevance of the classical notion of management associated with Henri Fayol has been raised by Henry Mintzberg (1973), a particularly virulent critic, who has depicted managers working at an unrelenting pace, such that their activities are marked by brevity, variety, and discontinuity; in addition to handling exceptions, managerial work involves performing a number of regular duties, including ritual and ceremony, negotiations, and processing soft information that links the organization to its environment.

> The pressure of the managerial environment does not encourage the development of reflective planners, the classical literature notwithstanding. The job breeds adaptive information-manipulators who prefer the live, concrete situation. The manager works in an environment of stimulus-response, and he develops in his work a clear preference for live action.
>
> (Mintzberg 1973: 38)

A leading arts manager has characterized the contemporary balance of skills and competencies as scholar, aesthete, and connoisseur on the one hand; fund-raiser, publicist, and diplomat on the other (Hoving 1992). Greater attention is being accorded by arts organizations to individuals who can clarify achievable overall missions and goals and practical targets, resolve conflicts and priorities that are always going to exist, and manage business information flows as they get more complex. This is largely consistent with the accepted roles of corporate chief executive officers, as identified by the Harvard Business School: an *organizational leader* is responsible for planned results, which include integrating specialist functions; beyond formal structure and policy, the skills of persuasion and articulation are required to be a *personal leader*; and, finally, an *architect of organizational change* has the intellectual and creative capacity to conceptualize the organization's purpose and the dramatic skill to invest it with some degree of magnetism (Bower *et al.* 1991: 13–23).

The term 'culture industry' is regressive, according to John Pick; and former (British) politican George Walden, writing in the *Times Literary Supplement*, is of the opinion that 'arts industry' represents a solecism:

> [It] is also frequently invoked by ministers as a major tourist attraction and export earner. Appeals for more investment in the arts are now made on the same premise as for investment in the infrastructure. Seen as a commitment to

the arts themselves, such calls are attractive to politicians suspected of congenital philistinism. The philistinism implicit in the notion that more cash produces more and better goes unnoticed.

(26 September 1997)

In many respects, Pick and Walden are developing ideas advanced decades earlier by Theodor Adorno. Central to Adorno's critique is the application of capitalist industrialism, namely the profit motive, to creative activity: 'the total effect of the culture industry is one of anti-enlightenment. ... It impedes the development of autonomous independent individuals who judge and decide consciously for themselves' (Adorno 1991: 92). Mass culture is identical and the lines of its artificial framework begin to show through: 'The customer is not king, as the culture industry would have us believe, not its subject but its object' (Adorno 1991: 85).

Adorno's criticism of the manufacture of mass culture – as kitsch versus the genuine art of the avant-garde – is part of a political Left critique (see, for example, the early writings of art critic Clement Greenberg); at the other end of the political spectrum, popular culture is a bugbear of conservative journals of criticism like *The New Criterion* and *Salisbury Review*. That the market economy corrupts culture is an argument Tyler Cowen seeks to counter: he sets out 'to encourage a more favorable attitude towards the commercialization of culture that we associate with modernity' (Cowen 1998: 1).

Consumerism, according to the conservative philosopher Roger Scruton (1982), is a label that is beginning to be applied to political outlooks that see acquisition and consumption as the principle ends of existence. 'I shop therefore I am', goes the Krugerism. Under such circumstances it is more or less standard to view consumerism as a term of abuse. Williams's bone of contention was that the term consumer, during the latter half of the twentieth century, gained widespread and overwhelming extension into traditionally non-commercial fields including politics, health, education, and the arts. The realignment of relationships with 'consumer' as the preferred term to describe virtually all human exchange served to negate distinctions in relationships; moreover, social human needs 'are not covered by the consumer ideal: they may even be denied because consumption tends always to be materialist as an individual activity' (Williams 1980: 188). This fits Adorno's view that the spectator is offered only the illusion of choice by the culture industry:

> The customer is not king, as the culture industry would have us believe, not its subject but its object.
>
> The entire practice of the culture industry transfers the profit motive naked onto cultural forms.
>
> The total effect of the culture industry is one of anti-enlightenment ... It impedes the development of autonomous, independent individuals who judge and decide consciously for themselves.

(Adorno 1991: 85–6, 92)

What is the proper role of arts management? This question has been posed for at least several decades. In a special section, 'Administering for the Arts' in *California Management Review* (Winter 1972), the editor Ichak Adizes, an assistant professor of managerial studies at UCLA, sought to identify a new area of study: 'Art as an area of human activity – in its organizational aspects and managerial functions – has been relatively unexplored. Training for the administrative side of artistic organization has been neglected'. Almost a generation later, in 1988, Joan Jeffri acknowledged that her discipline 'is still decried ... for being soft, undisciplined, not rigorous enough', in her capacity as an editor of the *Journal of Arts Management and Law* (Spring 1982). Such criticisms were echoed in the mid-1990s by Carol Phillips, vice-president of the Banff Centre, with particular reference to books on the management of museums:

> Where is the theory, where is the investigation which supports the values and principles imbedded in museums? ... What is required are original and inventive methods for managing cultural service, but what is proposed yet again in these books is the device of lay governorship as authority for the non-profit corporation, dependency on largesse and the public purse, and hierarchies of professions and pallid versions of corporate practice.
>
> Critical theory, feminist intervention and in-depth analysis flourish within those disciplines that inform museums, such as the humanities, the arts, social and other sciences. How is it then that these bodies of knowledge have not affected in any significant ways the management of the institutions that encourage the research and application of ideas to the meaning of objects and experiences?
>
> (Canadian Museums Association's *Muse*, Spring 1994)

Two divergent views are discernible: arts management as a sub-discipline within MBA studies (following Adizes's route) with attention to application; or arts management as a zone of contact for various intellectual lines of analysis to be pursued (as intimated by Phillips and pursued by those interested in 'critical' management studies).

Is what appears to be a growing divide inevitable? Certain applications of concepts from the business world have been disappointing, but does that discredit the notion of application? There are benefits to be gained by broadening the base of discussion and investigating the possibilities available from different perspectives, however, 'multidisciplinary' approaches can become a prop to compensate for academic deficiencies. For example, if the use of 'theory' is overwhelming, disciplined observation gives way to irrelevance and tedium.

It is beneficial to consider the interventions of artists and cultural critics when examining the relationship between the arts and management, even if one is conducting an exercise to identify legitimate areas of managerial intervention in the name of effectiveness and efficiency. Not unlike the tactics adopted by the Guerrilla Girls to expose imbalances in the art world, there can be virtue in pragmatism:

One can learn a lot from advertising. Among the mercenaries of the advertising world are very smart people, real experts in communications. It makes practical sense to learn techniques and strategies of communications. Without knowing them, it is impossible to subvert them.

(Bourdieu and Haacke 1995: 107)

Even for those who are not interested in subversion, there is the added value of sharpened awareness. It helps to expose how language serves different interests. John Tusa, director of the Barbican Centre in London, has asked for a balance to be struck regarding the use of the language of management by arts organizations:

It is not that any of us want to buck the currently predominant managerial culture – we do not. It is not that difficult to learn – it isn't. We in the arts above all have a pressing need and obligation to use the little money we have as well as we can. But managerialism should be a tool rather than an end; a method rather than an absolute; a rule of thumb rather than a tablet of stone; a system of analysis rather than a panacea for every problem. If applied without discrimination, it threatens to swamp the very activity that it is, overtly, intended to support. It is the servant not the master. It is a necessary part of our lives but it is not sufficient in itself to make a good arts centre or to allow great art to be created. Even once that assumption is accepted, once managerialism and consultants, the high priests of the doctrine, are put in their rightful place, the questions we as organizers of the arts centres must answer in the next century are legion.

(Tusa 1997: 38)

Three commitments

The classical industrial economy is represented as a three-stage process from *production* to *distribution* to *consumption*. This is analogous to how some perceive the basic elements of a performance or exhibition: the creative raw material and a person or persons to interpret the material (production); a place to present the material (distribution); and an audience to witness the performance or view the work of art (consumption). Indeed, consumption has taken on greater importance due to current attention devoted to identity; individuals as consumers may look to the products they consume to affirm their overall identity. Marcel Duchamp, no doubt with his own case in mind, recognized that the artist (producer) and the spectator (consumer) represented the two poles in the creation of art:

In the final analysis, the artist may shout from all the rooftops that he is a genius; he will have to wait for the verdict of the spectator in order that his declarations take a social value and that, finally, posterity includes him in the primers of art history.

(Duchamp 1973: 47)

The making of a work of art is often restricted to the figure of the individual artist, yet as Duchamp has argued, the spectator completes the art work through an aggregation of interpretations.

It is instructive to consider that all types of arts organizations need to address three mutually supporting commitments: to excellence and artistic integrity; to accessibility and audience development; and to public accountability and cost effectiveness. First and foremost, an arts organization needs to make a commitment to *excellence* (international, national, or local) and *artistic integrity* in performance or display. A distinctive style must be protected and nurtured. The institution must make attempts to communicate its identity and image to a wide range of audiences, specialist and non-specialist. Artistic integrity needs to be maintained to avoid 'plastic apples'; namely falsifying the arts. This is to suggest that merely offering the public what it wants is an abdication of responsibility – arts organizations should be in the business of helping to shape taste, which suggests leading rather than merely reacting.

Second, a commitment to make the arts organization more accessible (particularly as measured by socio-economic variables) strikes at the heart of genuine *audience development*. There can be an uneasy relationship between artistic programming and audiences. For too long, audience development has been constrained within the confines of a marketing discourse. Arts marketing has been useful in areas like attendance stimulation, membership development, fund-raising, crisis management, merchandising, awareness building, and business sponsorship. Popular exhibitions which treat 'culture as event' and 'art as entertainment', provide benefits to visitors, host institutions, and corporate sponsors. But is it all win-win? What about sustainability and the longer term impact on audience development? According to the NEA:

> The challenge is to reach out to the majority of Americans who currently have no direct involvement with the professional, nonprofit arts, to expand the nation's cultural palette to include a full range of participatory activities, without losing sight of the standards of professional excellence that still have a role in providing benchmarks of achievement. The opportunity is to build a much larger, more inclusive base of support for the arts, one that gives all Americans a stake in the preservation and transmission of our cultural legacy.
>
> (Larson 1997: 163)

Barriers to first-time visitors are actual and perceived. Education, touring, and electronic media represent ways audiences can be grown. The political mantra of 'education, education, education' is used to justify increased state funding. A wider geographic scope is offered by touring activities – bringing art to audiences. Traditional broadcasting (television and radio) continues to offer opportunities; even more dramatic changes to reach wider audiences involve digital technology and the Internet.

Third, in order to maximize the benefit from available funds – which is not the same as minimizing costs – an arts organization needs to make a commitment to *public accountability* and *cost effectiveness*. Efficient management structures, not least at the level of the board of trustees, can help to secure financial stability. Revenue enhancement, which often means diversifying the revenue stream (or plural funding) is necessary, yet to be successful, an arts organization cannot be guided by money. This is not to suggest that quality and profitability are mutually exclusive – indeed such a tandem should not be viewed with hostility. Securing financial stability is a necessary starting point to allow the aesthetic programming to take place. In many respects, the adoption of a managerial orientation is about presentation: the smart and savvy arts organization is concerned with safeguarding core aesthetic values, but recognizes and appreciates that prudent financial stewardship and corporate governance are viewed by existing and potential funding bodies (both public and private) as a signal of institutional sustainability.

What is the role of arts management? Taking action and conceptual thinking appear to be two sides of the same coin when addressing the interaction between managerial, economic, and aesthetic objectives. Thus, skilled arts managers need to contemplate the complexities such as associated with 'privatization' of cultural institutions in Italy, or performing Wagner in Israel. Any definition of arts management confronts various classifications: high/low, public/private, and nonprofit/commercial. Examining constituent and related terms like art, management, and culture industry is a way also to highlight the various and sometimes conflicting positions adopted by prominent commentators including Henry Mintzberg, Raymond Williams, Paul DiMaggio, the Frankfurt School, Pierre Bourdieu, Hans Haacke, John Pick, and the Harvard Business School. Three commitments – to aesthetic excellence and integrity; to accessibility and audience development; and to cost effectiveness and transparency – serve as an introduction to the challenges facing different types of arts organizations.

2 Arts research

Skilled arts managers are better equipped to make decisions if they have an under-standing of the main types of arts research. Cross-national comparative studies, economic impact studies, and audience surveys can be used for 'lobbying' purposes, even though these three areas of arts research have differing origins. First, cross-national comparative analysis is largely possible because national bodies, like arts councils and ministries of culture, collect and disseminate primary data on various provisions made for the arts; arts researchers and policy makers use these various forms of cultural statistics as the basis for analysis. Second, economic impact studies presuppose that 'the arts' can be viewed as an industry. A typical study is in the form of 'the economic impact of X number of arts organizations (or a particular arts event) on the economy of Y city'. Third, audience surveys (as distinct from arts participa-tion surveys) highlight the difficulties associated with diversifying the 'profile' (e.g. educational attainment, social class, race) of arts 'attenders'. Such issues, related to making a commitment to accessibility and audience development (which support the arts marketing discussion in Chapter 7), are outlined.

No research agenda is 'neutral'. Quantitative approaches (e.g. surveys) are not more objective than qualitative methods (e.g. long interviews). The American Sta-tistical Association is right to identify some issues which shape the administration and communication of surveys:

> People are accustomed to seeing results of surveys reported in the daily press, incorporated in advertising claims, and mentioned on numerous occasions by political analysts, social critics, and economic forecasters. Much less fre-quent, however, is any discussion of the reliability of these surveys or what is involved in carrying them out. The wealth of reported information may easily lull the user into assuming that surveys are easy to undertake, and to overlook the many steps involved in a properly-conducted survey. If technical issues are recognized, there is a frequent tendency to assume that they should be safely left to the survey expert. In fact, many of the surveys that appear in the daily press are conducted under great time pressure and with insufficient allowance for the many different aspects of the process that need to be controlled. Yet, unless the reader of these survey results is aware of what is involved in a survey, and what quality controls are needed, s(he) is unable to

form any opinion of the confidence to be placed in the results, and usually is not even in a position to know what questions to ask about such surveys.

(Ferber *et al*. 1980: Preface)

Cross-national comparative studies

The interest in comparative analysis among social scientists is an 'intellectual repercussion' of the Second World War and its aftermath. An essential feature of comparative analysis is highlighting and explaining commonalities and differences in the content, formulation, and implementation of policies. One wants to develop concepts and generalizations at the level of the nation (e.g. what is true in all nations? what is true in one nation at a particular point in time?). Comparative research contributes to the development of a relevant knowledge base which can fill gaps in our understanding of how countries deal with similar situations. Identifying the differences among various national approaches to management and policy problems can highlight different kinds of constraints: structural, institutional, and cultural.

Cross-national comparisons help one to answer certain types of questions. Is the logic of a particular process the same across nations? Are the effects of policy interventions homogeneous across (or even within) nations? A sophisticated research methodology is required when making comparisons across different political and social systems: comparative studies run the risk of passing too lightly over the particularities of national cultures, surely one of the most significant factors, both ideologically and contextually, in the establishment of arts organizations. Note that the selection of countries for comparative arts research remains highly concentrated on G7 members (i.e. United States, Canada, United Kingdom, Germany, France, Italy, and Japan); other advanced western European economies (like Austria, The Netherlands, Belgium, Denmark, and Sweden), and Australia and New Zealand. Though acknowledging that 'the arts are everywhere subsidized', economist Mark Blaug noted that 'the level of subsidies varies enormously between countries and between different types of artistic activities within countries' and 'the ratio of private charity to public subsidy likewise varies enormously from country to country'; he continued by questioning whether 'it is conceivable that neither subsidies themselves nor their variations between countries can be explained on economic grounds: they may simply reflect custom and historical tradition' (Blaug 1976: 13–24).

For example, Arthur Schlesinger has summarized the case against the public role of art in the USA: public subsidy lacks constitutional authority; public subsidy endangers the autonomy of the arts by making artists and arts organizations dependent on government and thereby vulnerable to government control; public subsidy represents a net transfer of income from the poor to the high-income and educated classes; and public subsidy represents a paternalistic effort to dictate popular taste, which is to say that if a cultural institution cannot please consumers and earn its way in a free market, then it has no economic justification, and if no economic justification, no social justification (Schlesinger 1990: 4). Yet this national identity of cultural capitalism underpins a muscular American theme of the globalization of culture. As suggested by the likes of Serge Guilbaut (1983) and Duncan and Wallach (1978), any narrative account of New York's Museum of Modern Art (MoMA) cannot avoid its role in a wider ideological battle with communism.

On the other hand, the redrafting of the (then West) German constitution following the end of the Second World War made education and culture strictly state (*lander*) and local matters. This highly decentralized system was established as a means to deter the worst aspects of fervent nationalism. (Exporting German culture abroad is severely limited to organizations such as the Goethe Institute.) Post-unification Germany has sixteen *landers*. Municipalities compete for civic stature via the arts: each claims to be the most *cultural*. One result of this competition is a widespread distribution of museums, orchestras, theatres – all kinds of arts activities throughout the nation.

Cross-national arts research has distinct political motives. In the absence of a theory on the 'right' or 'correct' level of public subsidy (or government support) for the arts, the level of arts funding in other countries continues to be used as a yardstick against which one's own country should be compared. As an example, advocates for greater state support in the USA look across the Atlantic:

> The European numbers have to be high enough to be worth working toward, but not too high so as to be completely out of reach. The American figure has to be low enough to indicate that something is going on, but not very much. The ensemble has to coincide with the popular mythology of relative government generosity *vis-à-vis* the arts.
>
> (Schuster 1987: 5)

For example, as a young nation, the American ideals of freedom and individual initiative, built on a strong suspicion of central authority, underlie the formation of arts organizations in the USA following the Civil War, as private organisms managed like business corporations. On the other hand, in Europe 'a cultural continuity has provided unchanging unity in the individual histories – support for things which endure in spite of crucial changes' (Dorian 1964: 433–4); the principle of government patronage is an outgrowth of royal patronage in maintaining a commitment to culture.

'What can be done?' is a related issue. Though commendable, at its worst, 'this type of research is the search for the extraordinary and makes little attempt to learn from the ordinary' such as

> the awkward juxtaposition of arm's length arts councils on top of highly centralized government structures, the implementation of matching grants in situations much more constrained than those where matching grants have been most successful, and the adoption of tax incentives in systems where there is little tradition of private support and little reason to believe that these incentives will have much impact.
>
> (Schuster 1987: 6)

Defining conceptual boundaries of the field one is proposing to study is a critical decision in cross-national analysis. Some of the perceived variation in arts support can be explained by differences in the structure of arts support. At the same time, part of the variation in funding reflects real, fundamental differences in arts policies. It needs to be added that the consideration of arts policy via a single funding structure (e.g. comparison of funding levels of the central, government-funding agency in each country) is not uncommon and problematic.

The per capita comparison has become the *sine qua non* of comparative arts policy research. One can readily understand why per capita comparisons are made: large numbers (such as total expenditure) are made comprehensible (by dividing by the population of a country); and the calculation is the first step to comparative analysis because it scales the result of expenditure calculations to control for the relative size of the country. The political process also demands a *number*, which provides a focal point – possibly an attractive headline figure. In short, 'a per capita calculation is certainly a powerful summary: a simple, easy-to-understand, portable distillation of a multidimensional problem into a single measure' (Schuster 1987: 24). However, care needs to be taken in making and interpreting per capita comparisons. First, how are the numerators and denominators defined? It may be possible to alter what is included in order to obtain a more favourable result. For example, per capita gross domestic product (GDP) is a recognized figure used in cross-national analysis. As a headline number it is used to indicate the level of wealth and economic prosperity the citizens of a nation share. Other league tables – the United Nations Human Development Index is possibly the most visible – have emerged to incorporate 'quality of life' attributes of a nation not captured by GDP/capita, such as forms of unpaid labour, the level of disparity between the richest and poorest sectors of society, and level of democratic participation available to citizens; moreover, the United Nations' (UN's) index views universal health care and the absence of capital punishment as positive. Second, per capita measurements, as *indices*, are often better at measuring change *within* a country over a period of time; this is distinct from the 'static snapshot' of measuring differences across countries at one particular point in time.

Economic impact studies

We are aware of John Maynard Keynes's interest in the arts, yet John Kenneth Galbraith astutely recognized that the most prominent economist of the twentieth century 'was not especially concerned to build bridges between economics and the arts. [Keynes] lived in two worlds; he didn't try to merge them' (Galbraith 1987: 145). The situation has changed as some economists now attempt to apply the tools and concepts of what strives to be the most mathematically precise of the social sciences to the arts. Such endeavours are not without controversy. In a stinging rebuke, political scientist F. F. Ridley argued that 'the values reflected in the literature do not encourage one to recruit many cultural economists as spokesmen in the interest of culture' (Ridley 1983: 1).

Public support for the arts and economic impact studies are closely linked topics. 'Finding a rationale and guiding principles for government support of the arts was one of the major areas of concern of the earliest post-war writings in cultural economics and these issues have continued to recur in the literature ever since' (Throsby 1994: 20). For example, by the mid-1970s, enough worthy essays had been published to justify an anthology of readings, *The Economics of the Arts* (1976), edited by Mark Blaug. The discussion, in the main, focused on two concerns: the rationale for public subsidies to the arts; and evaluating public expenditure on the arts. The former was advanced in four ways: 'efficiency' analysis of the causes of 'market failure'; 'equity' arguments; positive arguments involving the actual mechanisms by which tastes and preferences are formed; and the 'merit goods' argument that the arts possess intrinsic value (Blaug 1976: 13–24). Owing to the political climate in Anglo-American countries throughout the 1980s, the evaluation of public expenditure came under greater scrutiny. The spillover effects of the arts garnered attention. Economic impact studies became a major preoccupation and have remained an important part of the arts management firmament. Alvin Toffler recognized, at the birth of cultural economics in the 1960s, that 'the very idea of measuring the arts is abhorrent to many' (Toffler 1967: 142); yet he believed that the arts as an important determinant of the quality of life in post-industrial societies made measurement incumbent.

Economic impact studies are highly utilitarian; they help to emphasize the economic value of the arts to the economy. Such studies seek to quantify the total financing consequences of arts-spending on a community. Major quantifiable benefits may be summarized as direct, indirect, and induced. Direct benefits, or the first round of spending initiatives, result from the expenditures by an arts organization to host the event (e.g. salary bill, cost of supplies). Indirect benefits result from the multiplier effect of spending by an arts organization (i.e. direct benefits) as these spill over or ripple through the economy. Induced benefits result from spending incidental to an arts activity (e.g. exhibition, concert, festival), other than the entrance charge. Much of the impact produced by the arts is associated with these extra-artistic activities (e.g. purchases in the gift shop, food and drink, transport, stays in hotels, etc.). All these activities, which are said to have been stimulated by the decision to 'consume' an arts event, generate revenue.

Quantification in monetary terms has been used to show that the arts are not 'deficit-ridden spongers'. For example, it is increasingly common to discuss the relative economic impact of the arts in revenue, numbers of persons employed, and wages and salaries *vis-à-vis* other industrial sectors. That discussions of the arts quickly turn to the tourism benefits no longer startle. The 1979 Tutankhamen exhibition at the Art Gallery of Ontario was notable for its attendance figure of 800,000 and generating at least C$20 million in visitor expenditures in Toronto; more recently, the 1995 Barnes exhibition at the same institution had an attendance

> so high that the [Ontario] government loan was paid off, the Gallery's deficit was reduced, and the economic activity from tourism in the region that was generated by the exhibition amounted to more than C$130 million ... the gift

shop at the AGO alone did some C$6 million in sales .... [indeed it would seem to go against the grain not to] suggest that a real opportunity for using the arts as a source of economic advantage may be found if we encourage more commercial cultural tourism ... but also to the great, less-visited nonprofit arts institutions.

(*Art Newspaper*, July/August 1995)

The case that public funding for the arts can lead to concrete and enormous economic benefits has been commissioned by funding agencies; for example, *You Gotta Have Art!* is a 1997 report prepared by consultancy firm McKinsey for the New York State Council on the Arts and New York City's Department of Cultural Affairs (see Bales and Pinnavaia 2001).

But to what extent is genuine benefit to urban regeneration outpaced by such rhetoric of event planners and developers? The general limitations of economic impact studies have been posited:

The economic impact studies of the 1980s, which attempted to measure the economic importance of the arts, have now been largely discredited. The data on employment was highly misleading. The relationship between the arts and tourism was never proven. And the contribution of the arts to inner city regeneration was exaggerated .... Indeed, it is arguable that the economic impact studies have in fact done a great disservice to those seeking greater public expenditure on the arts. Firstly, these studies have had the effect of trivialising and commercialising significant aesthetic and valuation issues. Secondly, the economic judgment of the arts against economic criteria. ... the advocates of economic impact studies, by failing to see the intrinsic weakness of their own position, will have scored a spectacular own goal.

(Bennett 1995: 24–5)

More specific weaknesses have also been identified (see Mulcahy 1986: 33–48):

1   the multiplier effects are often overstated;
2   the reliance on the multiplier limits the discussion and invites other industries, which may possess more robust multipliers, to be promoted;
3   it cannot be inferred that the economic effects identified would not have occurred had the arts institutions involved not existed;
4   it is often difficult to identify a single event or attraction as the only reason for a visit to a metropolis;
5   the long-term induced impacts, arguably of greatest significance, need to include a qualitative dimension.

Yet political imperatives require that quasi-artistic aims, such as addressed by economic impact studies, are considered when applying for large grants such as to support capital projects. There is no reason why economic benefits cannot be supplemented by qualitative (or non-quantifiable) ones. As a basis for innovation in an economy, arts-programming is viewed as making a contribution to wealth creation and improving the overall quality-of-life of the community. According to Raymond Williams:

> It is in fact the great cities of Europe which have been the most successful promoters of cultural policy. This again is a contemporary fight to preserve the necessary powers of cities, but it is one in which there is the possibility of relating cultural policy to an actual community rather than to a relatively abstract and centralized state.

> (Appignanesi 1984: 5)

This sentiment served as an organizing motif for prosaic studies produced throughout the 1990s on the importance of cities (e.g. Worpole 2000; Hall 1998; Rogers 1997; Worpole and Greenhalgh 1996; Landry and Bianchini 1995; Bianchini 1993) with examples culled from around the world, stressing the role of architecture and aesthetics as part of a revived interest in urban renewal (e.g. Barcelona is a prime example, with the 1992 Olympics serving as an impetus for infrastructure development including the creation of a large number of small, interlinked public spaces).

Audience surveys

Arts participation studies are different from audience surveys (see the National Endowment for the Arts-supported document by AMS Planning and Research 1995). Each has different purposes and methodologies. Arts participation studies focus on the general population; both users and non-users of all types of arts programmes are included in the sample; and the research is often to aid policy development. The most well-known example is the Survey of Public Participation in the Arts (SPPA), a nationwide survey in the USA conducted by the National Endowment for the Arts, to gauge participation rates for arts and non-arts activities; time series data is available (surveys have been conducted in 1982, 1985, 1992, and 1999). On the other hand, audience surveys concentrate on known attenders, and are often limited to a sole arts organization; as such, attention is paid to a marketing agenda (e.g. to assess audience satisfaction levels or alternative subscription packages), or to measure the expenditure made by audience members as part of an economic impact study.

The tradition of audience surveys among arts museums is more entrenched than for any other type of arts institutions, according to Schuster (1993). Pioneering work in arts research by the French sociologist Pierre Bourdieu, for example, focused on the art museum. In many respects, the art museum serves as a proxy for arts organizations in the conventional sense. The art museum is rightly viewed as among the most complex, powerful, and successful of modern socio-political institutions. Art museums help to shape public perceptions concerning the meaning and role of art, and have been characterized as one of the most broadly resonant metaphors of our time.

The sociological approach to the understanding of the predisposition to art and cultural consumption – which is at odds with the standard Kantian aesthetic philosophy in which the purity of aesthetic contemplation derives from 'disinterested pleasure' – owes much to Bourdieu and Darbel's *L'amour de l'art* (1969; translated in 1991 as *For the Love of Art),* based on a series of visitor surveys at various French art museums in the 1960s. The work challenged the 'myth of innate taste'; it set out to define the social conditions which made this experience – Kant's phrase that 'the beautiful is that which pleases without concept' – and the people for whom it is possible (art lovers and so-called 'people of taste'). 'Free entry is also optional entry' or a 'false generosity', according to Bourdieu and Darbel, as it is 'reserved for those who, equipped with the ability to appreciate works of art, have the privilege of making use of this freedom' (Bourdieu and Darbel 1991: 109–13). That cultural consumption, such as visiting art museums, is closely linked to educational level (whether measured by qualifications or length of schooling) and secondarily to social origin remains an important conclusion.

Bourdieu's *La Distinction* (1979; translated in 1984 as *Distinction)* continued the general thesis – as the book's subtitle, 'a social critique of the judgement of taste', suggests – of the earlier text (in terms of formal education and the family). 'To the socially recognized hierarchy of the arts, and within each of them, of genres, of schools, or periods, corresponds a social hierarchy of the consumers. This predisposes tastes to function as markers of "class"' (Bourdieu 1984: 1–2). A three-zone model of cultural taste, representing a hierarchy of tastes and preferences which correspond to education and social class, is proffered: legitimate (e.g. the *Art of Fugue* or the *Concerto for the Left Hand,* or in painting, Breughel or Goya); middle brow (e.g. minor works in the major arts such as *Rhapsody in Blue,* or, in painting, Utrillo, DubSuffet or even Renoir); and popular (e.g. choice of work of so-called light music or classical music devalued by popularization, such as the *Blue Danube,* and especially, songs totally devoid of artistic ambition). Moreover, according to a British commentator:

> It was clear by 1900 that the higher arts were perceived by the middle class as a kind of cultural duty – a form of work which was necessary to maintain status – and that art of any kind was barely perceived at all by the working classes. Therefore, not only was the relation between education and pleasure problematic, but also the boundaries of what properly constituted pleasure.
>
> (Greenhalgh 1989: 86)

Bourdieu's work on the sociology of cultural consumption is more important for some sections of society than others: 'It is, however, within the dominant class, the bourgeoisie, that symbolic struggles are most apparent and most severe. It is here that the definition of cultural legitimacy is fought over' (Jenkins 1992: 142).

The science of taste and cultural consumption is examined by Bourdieu with the following postulate in mind: 'A work of art has meaning and interest only for someone who possesses the cultural competence, that is, the code, into which it is encoded'. Two biographical accounts are instructive. First, near to the end of *The*

Sacred Grove (1969), Dillon Ripley offers some impressions of his early experience with museums:

> My own philosophy of museums became established at the age of ten one winter when we were living in Paris. One of the advantages of playing in the Tuileries Gardens as a child was that at any one moment one could be riding the carousel, hoping against hope to catch the ring. ... Another moment and one could wander into one of the galleries of the Louvre. I still remember one day I found the ship models ... Then out to the garden again where there was a patch of sand in the corner to build sand castles. Then back to the Louvre to wander through the Grand Gallery.
>
> There was no essential difference in all of this. The juxtaposition was natural and easy. No threshold of tiredness and lack of concentration was reached. It was as easy as breathing in and out.
>
> (Ripley 1969: 140)

Second, not unlike Ripley, Tim Millar (aged 6) is being introduced to the arts – and letter writing to national newspapers – as a natural part of his social life:

> My dad read the article on Rebecca Horn ... and took me and my brother to see her exhibition at the Tate Gallery. I was very cross and disappointed to find that the hanging piano wasn't working. But I loved the guns.
>
> (letter in the London *Independent Magazine,* 15 October 1995)

Ripley learned the code as if it were play; master Tim is being taught it in a similar manner by his father. Yet not everyone is so fortunate:

> A beholder who lacks the specific code feels lost in a chaos of sounds and rhythms, colours, and lines, without rhyme or reason. ... Thus the encounter with a work of art is not 'love at first sight' as is generally supposed ... [rather] the art-lover's pleasure presupposes an act of cognition, a decoding operation, which implies the implementation of a cognitive acquirement, a cultural code.
>
> (Bourdieu 1984: 2)

Successful mastery of the code to gain artistic competence, according to Bourdieu, requires use of scarce resource time. First, there must be economic means to invest in educational time; this marks differential class access to different levels of education. Second, the development of cultural practice and artistic production has become more complex in its coding; the requirement that one is *au fait* with a wider and wider range of cultural references – because much contemporary art is self-referential – has meant that one needs to devote more and more time in order to remain competent, or use money to recruit advisors who can supplement one's own taste and time commitment. The following exchange between two friends in the play *'Art'* (1996), by French playwright Yasmina Reza, emphasizes that conditions exist for the aesthetic appreciation of so-called legitimate art:

Marc: Are you going to have it framed?
            Serge laughs discreetly.
Serge: No! ... But, no ...
Marc: Why not?
Serge: It's not supposed to be framed.
Marc: Is that right?
Serge: The artist doesn't want it to be. It mustn't be interpreted. It's already
            in its setting. (*He signals Marc over to the edge.*) Look ... you see ...
Marc: What is it, Elastoplast?
Serge: No, it's a kind of Kraft paper ... Made up by the artist.

(Reza 1996: 24)

As another example of cultural competence and consumption, consider the inten-
tionally provocative comment by the occasional opera director Jonathan Miller: 'If
you perform *Il Trovatore* with Pavarotti, and you attract an audience of the sort that
applauds when the curtain goes up, then you know that you've committed a deeply
vulgar opera' (London *Guardian,* 6 August 1998). Both incidents reinforce
Bourdieu's point that mastery is required to appreciate a work of art; moreover,
money alone is not enough to acquire taste and aesthetic acumen.

The general thrusts of *For the Love of Art* and *Distinction*, in terms of schooling
exerting a determining influence and social inequities of inheriting cultural capital
from one's parents, have been validated by researchers in Anglo-American countries.
(This addresses a main criticism of Bourdieu's thesis that it was particular to French
sensibilities of the 1960s.) Sociologist Paul DiMaggio has been at the forefront, in
examining the role of the arts in the USA. DiMaggio and Useem have considered the
factors at the root of one's disposition to the arts and cultural participation:

> Although there were variations between several fields of the arts ... the pattern
> of high educational attainment being linked to attendance held for every field
> of the arts we studied. (Visitors to science, history, and natural history muse-
> ums were noticeably less well-educated, although they were more similar to
> the arts audiences studied than to the public at large.) Art attenders were much
> more well-educated than the public at large whatever the art form, whether
> performances took place indoors or outside and whether admission or tickets
> were expensive or free.

(DiMaggio and Useem 1980: 59)

Furthermore, 'a substantial amount of evidence indicates that educational attainment is strongly related to the arts and cultural involvement and that education is a
better predictor of such involvement than are occupation and income' (DiMaggio
and Useem 1980: 62). Schuster corroborates the chief findings of DiMaggio and
Useem: 'The audience for the arts [in the USA] was more highly educated, was of
higher occupational status, and had a higher income than the population as a
whole'; and he adds that 'while short-term changes in the audience profile may be
attained through very visible and popularly attractive exhibitions or programs, it is

much more difficult to sustain these changes over a longer period of time' (Schuster 1991: 2, 43).

Race has always been a more prominent issue in the USA, which makes the research of DiMaggio and Ostrower enlightening. The consumption by black Americans of so-called 'European' cultural products is lower than for whites, with the proviso that the 'effects of race on these activities, however, are dwarfed by those of educational attainment and are often less than those of income, gender, or place of residence'; more importantly, their study supports 'the applicability of the notion of capital, as developed by Bourdieu in research on historically unicultural France, to multicultural United States' which confirms 'the utility of viewing patterns of artistic taste and consumption as quasi-rational responses to incentives for investment in capital culture, and of interpreting cultural capital as symbolic information about social membership required by persons with complex and extended social networks' (DiMaggio and Ostrower 1990: 130, 131, 132). The research conducted by John Falk into museum attendance in the USA reveals that race is not the key factor:

> African-American leisure behavior is very similar to European-American leisure behavior, though tremendous differences in leisure behavior exist within the African-American community. Whereas black–white differences exist, and there are some, race does not emerge as the best variable to explain them.
>
> (Falk 1998: 40)

Falk, like Bourdieu, highlights social origins:

> One of the best predictors of whether an adult will go to a museum is whether he was taken to museums by his parent when he was a child. … Historically, many minorities, recent immigrants, and the economic under-class had less opportunities to visit museums as children than the more affluent majority population.
>
> (Falk 1998: 41)

Briton Nick Merriman has criticized Bourdieu's exclusion of psychological factors in preference for sociological ones; however, Merriman concluded that Bourdieu's shortcomings were less problematic in certain cases when considering the situation in the UK:

> A contributory factor must be Bourdieu's concentration on art galleries where, we have seen in the case of the Tate Gallery and the Victoria and Albert Museum, visitors are much more highly educated and of a higher status than in more general museums, and where arguments about cultural and class divisions are easier to make.
>
> (Merriman 1991: 82)

The classification of museums by subject matter has invited a hierarchy. Though museums of archeology and natural history were prominent at first, the present situation is marked by the art museum as the 'paradigm of the museum experience' (Jordanova 1989: 24). This illustrates a class structure of museum objects and museums themselves. In theatrical productions, a similar ranking takes place with musicals ranked lower than dramas in terms of artistic merit and intention.

It has been suggested by Nicholas Penny, a prominent art scholar, that Bourdieu and his adherents 'smugly explain away the complex relationship with the past which great collections and the museums of the [nineteenth] century reveal' (*London Review of Books,* 21 December 1989). Even those in sympathy with Bourdieu's position have deliberated in public:

> There seems to us (and this is very much a question of tone, nuance and attitude) to be a functionalist/determinist residue in Bourdieu's concept of reproduction which leads him to place less emphasis on the possibilities of real change and innovation than either his theory or his empirical research makes necessary.
>
> (Garnham and Williams 1980: 222)

Due to the constraints of individual arts organizations to respond to the conclusions provided by demographic profiling at the macro-level, many have turned to individual psychology to better understand the behaviour of attenders and non-attenders. For example, lifestyle analysis (or psychographics) is based on the assumption that marketers can plan more effective strategies if they know more about their target markets in terms of 'attitudes, interests, and opinions'. Entrance fees may be viewed as a *subjective* barrier to visiting museums, according to research conducted in Europe: 'Conscious lifestyle choices represent *actual* barriers to museum visits, not the amount of entrance fees. This agrees with Bourdieu and Darbel's analysis' (Kirchberg 1998: 9; my emphasis). This is consistent with findings on arts consumption in the UK that 'as a barrier to attendance price appears to have only a limited influence; there are many other factors which affect the decision to attend' (Feist 1997: 261). From an American perspective, it has been noted that 'most studies have shown the demand for attendance at the live performing arts to be price inelastic' (Heilbrun and Gray 1993: 94). This means that consumers of such services are not especially sensitive to changes in price. On its own, the decision to re-introduce 'free' entry to the permanent collections of the designated 'national museums and galleries' (based in London) is not enough to entice a socio-cultural mix that replicates the UK population at large. Many non-attenders are rejecting 'arts and culture' prior to a consideration of price. What other barriers exist? How are they being addressed? At the same time, many existing attenders who can afford to pay an entry tariff – say even £10, which is comparable to a London cinema ticket and much less expensive than attending a Premier League football match – are being subsidized.

From an American perspective, Marilyn Hood (1983) is interested in why people do or do not attend museums, and how to attract people who do not already attend. She identifies five profile attributes of pleasurable or satisfying leisure experiences: the opportunity to learn, social interaction, the challenge of new experiences, participating actively, and feeling comfortable in one's surroundings. 'Such characteristics are shared by people of all races and ethnicities, incomes, education levels, and ages, regardless of sex', according to Falk, who contends that Hood's first point, the opportunity to learn, is consistent with Bourdieu's findings:

> The primary reason most people attend museums, whether by themselves or with their children, is in order to learn. That is a major reason why museum-going correlates so highly to a level of education. That is not because one needs a college degree to think learning is important. It is because individuals who think learning is important are more inclined to pursue higher education than those who don't. Individuals who value learning seek it in many forms – through higher education; by watching educational television; by reading books, magazines, and newspapers; and by visiting museums.
>
> (Falk 1998: 40)

Hood added that ambiance and atmosphere provide physical and psychological comfort. With research interests similar to Hood, but working in the UK, David Prince believes that non-attenders are 'a legitimate part of the potential audience' and that their perceptions of arts organizations as both 'social institutions and visit destinations' need to be considered (Prince 1990: 166). Prince, like Hood, stresses that 'attitudes and life values are more useful analytical devices for understanding the problem' of non-participation; however, he is more willing to concede that attitudes and life values 'are themselves mediated by class factors ... peer group and culture self recognition and allegiance' (Prince 1990: 166). Prince concludes on a sombre note:

> Seeking a more representative audience base is therefore a complex problem that needs to be addressed by museums, bearing in mind that the continued, successful communication of their roles and aspirations to the general public is likely to be successful in this regard.
>
> (Prince 1990: 166)

In the UK, visiting museums is a phenomenally popular pursuit as noted in the aptly titled *By Popular Demand* (Davies 1994), with the total number of visitors toppling 100 million; yet the Museums and Galleries Commission publication conceded that there may be relatively little that individual museums can do to attract infrequent visitors (and those who do not visit) from all socio-economic groups in large numbers. Moreover, the habit of visiting museums is not evenly distributed throughout the population. Recent visitor studies have indicated that 'up to 40 per cent of the Tate's visitors come to the Gallery because of a recommendation made by a friend or relative'; and as such, the institution has noted that 'clearly word-of-mouth is a key marketing tool which brings in a third of the Gallery's audience' (*Tate Report 1992–94*). This is consistent with the situation in the USA:

Most American museum-goers say word-of-mouth recommendations arc the single most important factor affecting their decision to visit a museum. The more friends and family one has who are museum-goers, the more likely one is to go to a museum.

(Falk 1998: 41)

Research in the USA tends to support the notion that art museum attendance remains the preserve of a limited spectrum of society: approximately 20 per cent of the population (see, for example, Schuster 1991; Hood 1983). Moreover, 'when modified to account for sociohistorical context, Bourdieu's theory can be used to excavate social class differences in contemporary American consumption' (Holt 1998: 22). Hence, arts managers interested in broadening the audience base are confronted with a truism, 'Change in audience composition is a slow, resistant process'.

There is a strong supposition in the political culture of many societies that institutions in receipt of public funding ought to provide opportunities for all sectors of the population to make use of them. The desire is to dismantle barriers to effective access. A lack of knowledge of the art form – an intellectual barrier – may mitigate against seeking entry. But there are also emotional barriers such that the institution is perceived to be unwelcoming and threatening. Effective arts managers need to be cognizant of existing accessibility barriers (both real and perceived); what the institution is capable of doing on its own accord to stimulate audience development, and the specific areas that require government intervention and support.

Three areas of arts research have been examined. First, cross-national comparative studies are popular (such as figures like arts spending per capita), but can be constrained by limitations. They run the risk of passing too lightly over the particularities of national cultures. Second, linked to urban regeneration and cultural tourism, an economic impact study has become an accepted facet of bidding for capital project funding and as one way to gauge the success of an arts programme. This reflects the growing importance of economic measurements in validating the arts. Third, the research associated with Pierre Bourdieu on the sociology of art identifies factors (education and social class) that help to predict participation and consumption of arts and cultural products. The general thrusts of Bourdieu's findings have been substantiated in Anglo-American environments. This suggests that attempts to widen participation will be a slow process given that the barriers to non-attendance are various and deep-rooted.

The value of arts research may be viewed in complementary sources of value: knowledge-value, decision-value, and creative-value. First, arts research may contribute to a fuller understanding of your arts environment. Intuitive knowledge may be strengthened; 'new' issues may be raised. Second, more informed decisions regarding programme selection, resource allocation, and facility development, for example, may arise from using arts research. Research results may be used to provide crucial direction and momentum to planning efforts. Third, creative ideas might surface during the analysis of data.

3   Cultural entrepreneurship

Alexander McQueen (b. 1969) featured in the 2001 V&A exhibition, 'Radical Fashion'. At the age of twenty-six, he became chief designer of Givenchy. McQueen's shows have been described as 'images of beauty heightened with suffering':

> 'There's beauty in anger. Anger for me is passion. If you don't have passion for something you shouldn't be doing it in the first place' [according to McQueen]. He cites the Marquis de Sade and Stanley Kubrick's film *The Shining* among his inspirations. The sensational eroticism of his shows, built on a combination of exquisite, androgynous tailoring and fantastical creations, defined late twentieth-century fashion.
>
> (from didactic panel accompanying the exhibition)

McQueen's success is based on the multi-layered complexities associated with the fashion world. The industry is driven in the main by financial imperatives; however, crucially, this edifice depends upon the vision of the designers. Moreover, fashion design at the highest level, as an incubator for experimentation, is the starting point for a diffusion process which has an impact on 'high street' fashion.

Themes surrounding entrepreneurship are raised in the McQueen example: pervasive entrepreneurship can be a source of economic dynamism for national economies, according to the Organization for Economic Cooperation and Development (OECD 1997); at the same time, entrepreneurship is also being promoted as an admirable social process, making it suitable for all types of organizations. As an example of cultural entrepreneurship, McQueen has links with the likes of Rembrandt and Rubens, who were comfortable with artistic creation sitting alongside commercial activity. More robust entrepreneurial activity is evident in the cases of visual artist Mark Kostabi and the Guggenheim Foundation. Kostabi illustrates the artist as marketer. Learning from the likes of Disney and McDonald's, the Guggenheim seeks to establish a cultural brand with global reach.

Entrepreneurship as social process

'At its most general, entrepreneurship can be defined as the dynamic process of identifying economic opportunities and acting upon them by developing, producing, and selling goods and services. As such, it is central to the functioning of market economies', according to the OECD (1997: 151). The focus is not on the 'small business' sector, which can be risk-averse and not a good proxy for entrepreneurship; rather, attention is devoted to entrepreneurs 'as important risk-takers, or as essentially innovators' (OECD 1997: 152).

A historical lens can be used to remind us of the entrepreneurial initiatives underpinning the establishment of what we now readily accept as high cultural institutions. Examining the 'process by which elites forged an institutional system embodying their ideas about the high arts' is an interest of Paul DiMaggio (1986a: 42). He focuses on Boston in the nineteenth century: namely on the city's 'Brahmins', and how they went about creating the Boston Symphony Orchestra (1881) and the Museum of Fine Arts, Boston (1860). 'Cultural capitalists' is a term used by DiMaggio (1986a: 43) to denote entrepreneurship as foundational to the creation of institutional high culture. Boston Brahmins, as an example, are capitalists in the sense that their wealth came from management of industrial enterprises from which they extracted a profit. They are cultural capitalists in that they invested some of these profits in the foundation and maintenance of distinctly cultural enterprises; DiMaggio acknowledges what Pierre Bourdieu labels 'cultural capital' (as socially-valued knowledge that can confer prestige upon those who have mastered them). The BSO and the MFA were similar innovations in structure:

> Each was private, controlled by members of the Brahmin class, and established on the corporate model, dependent on private philanthropy and relatively long-range financial planning; each was sparsely staffed and relied for much of its management on elite volunteers; and each counted among its founders wealthy men of considerable scholarly or artistic credentials who were centrally located in Boston's elite social structure.
>
> (DiMaggio 1986a: 58)

The institutional founding of the V&A, as the Museum of Manufacturers, was based on the success of the 1851 International Exhibition, which was spearheaded by the commercial flair of Henry Cole and royal patronage of Prince Albert. The Museum had a clear didactic purpose of improving the standard of British designers, inculcating better consumer taste, and providing an educational resource for members of the working classes. Likewise the Tate Gallery, as an offshoot of the National Gallery, came to fruition due to the persistent benevolence of sugar magnate Henry Tate, who desired the nation to have an institution devoted to British and modern painting and sculpture. Continental neighbours were points of reference for both museum projects. The importation of high quality goods from France, at a time of growing mechanization, was viewed as leading to a decline in the standards of design and production, and served as an impulse for the Museum of Manufacturers. Not unlike the way the National Gallery was viewed as the British response to the Louvre, reference to the Luxembourg Museum in Paris was made in connection with the Tate Gallery. Both cases, thus, reflected dual needs: the need to address national audiences (i.e.

representing the nation to itself); and the need to address international audiences (i.e. representing the nation to other nations).

Fast-growing firms, known as 'gazelles', may be a good indicator of entrepreneurial activity. How is it possible for firms to start small, prosper, and become large firms? Reasons for the prevalence of entrepreneurial activity in the USA include 'culture' and 'institutional set-ups'. First, American culture emphasizes 'a free-market economy, a relatively small role for government and the social importance attached to self-reliance have made entrepreneurship a respectable, indeed admired, attribute' (OECD 1997: 159). Second, the institutional framework in the USA stimulates entrepreneurial activity in a systematic approach including the ease of firm creation and closure, availability of risk capital, patent protection, taxation and regulatory burden, flexible labour markets, and government programmes aimed at facilitating enterprise start-ups and development (OECD 1997). America's pro-entrepreneurial culture – a can-do attitude – is now being encouraged in other countries, '[y]et other countries striving to promote entrepreneurship should be aware that any attempt to replicate only a part of the US system is likely to be inefficient and ineffective' (OECD 1997: 172).

Entrepreneurial modes of behaviour are being promoted as essential for *all* types of organizations. Charles Handy (1999) uses the term 'alchemy': the historical reference to the transmutation of baser metals into gold is adopted as a metaphor for how visionary people seek to make something out of nothing. Like Handy, the think tank Demos has attempted to broaden popular perceptions of entrepreneurs (as buccaneering and male): 'We suggest that *most people* will benefit by adopting the basic set of entrepreneurial practices in their working lives and applying them to the social institutions they have inherited from the past' (Flores and Gray 2000: 30; my emphasis). Entrepreneurs follow a two-step process: they notice that there is something not quite right, anomalous, or in conflict; and then they discover practices for resolving the anomaly. Furthermore, collaborative entrepreneurship focuses on partnerships or teams of people combining different skills to realize ideas.

Entrepreneurship is viewed as being critical for a successful, modern society: 'A society that seeks to foster entrepreneurship must foster the culture that feeds it: openness, meritocracy, democracy and adaptive institutions' (Leadbetter and Oakley 2001: 12). The 'social' entrepreneur, as a form of social innovator, is interested in promoting health, welfare, and well-being (e.g. Aids, mental health, joblessness, illiteracy, and crime and drugs); there is a recognition that the so-called 'new social welfare' environment leads to the blurring of conventional sectors of the economy (Leadbetter 1997). Not unlike entrepreneurs engaged in commercial ventures, social entrepreneurs need to cultivate forms of social capital (i.e. networks of relationships built on a culture of cooperation, fostered by shared values and trust). The nature of 'wired' (i.e. fast, globally-networked, and project-centred) activities fosters 'cultural' entrepreneurs, who are viewed as 'new independents' (involved with multimedia, computer games, and the internet, for example) following earlier waves marked by architectural and design partnerships, and then producers in radio and television broadcasting (Leadbetter and Oakley 1999). Even given the wider agenda of Demos's researchers, there is some convergence with the OECD: 'What enterpreneurship amounts to in an economy in which the genera-tion, application and exploitation of distinctive know-how is fast and becoming the prime source of wealth creation (Leadbetter and Oakley 2001: 17).

Diverse impresarios

'Impresario' has a particular resonance with the managers of operatic or concert companies; the impresario is a promoter. However, manipulation is a historical connotation associated with the character of Svengali, a hypnotist, in George du Maurier's *Trilby* (1894). Trilby, the heroine, is an artist's model under the influ-ence of Svengali; under his hypnotism she becomes a great singer, but loses her power when Svengali dies. The divide between entrepreneurial risk-taker and crass manipulator may be quite thin. For example, P. T. Barnum (1810–91) is one of the most recognizable names associated with the organizations of public enter-tainments. To the average person, his name is linked with the Barnum & Bailey circus (billed as 'the greatest show on earth'), self-advertisement, and the apocry-phal statement, 'there's a sucker born every minute'. 'You pays your monies and takes your chances' is another one of Barnum's dictums, which is invariably used to add credence to the role of the 'sovereign' consumer in making decisions. This is the type of language a new commercial television station may use to compete in a crowded metropolitan market (e.g. Channel 5 in London and Citytv in Toronto), with a tabloid format of sports, soft-core porn, made-for-television movies, and low-cost shows (including interactive formats).

The British have been particularly good at producing impresarios: the name Malcolm McLaren (along with that of clothes designer Vivienne Westwood) became synonymous with 'punk' music, and the musicals of Cameron Mackintosh and Andrew Lloyd Webber are watched by millions worldwide on a scale compa-rable to that of the most successful Hollywood movies. First, 'Impresario: Malcolm McLaren and the British New Wave' was the title of an exhibition mounted by New York's New Museum of Contemporary Art in 1988. McLaren 'didn't invent punk. All he did was envisage it, design it, clothe it, publicize it, and sell it', according to the curator (Taylor 1988: 12). Characterized as the 'Svengali of Punk', a master manipulator, and a 'peddler of people and ideas' (Taylor 1988: 12), McLaren managed the Sex Pistols between 1975 and 1979 (the dates bracket the band's initial appearance and the death of Sid Vicious). On the one hand, the Sex Pistols are characterized as sophisticated hype run amok; on the other, the band is viewed as representing a so-called true voice of a disenfranchised genera-tion. What seems clearer is the observation that 'originally cheap, punk became an expensive fashion ticket' (Taylor 1988: 17) takes on greater significance with the Sotheby's auction in 2001 of Sex Pistols memorabilia (including Johnny Rotten's 'Anarchy' shirt). (One might view Alan McGee's Creation record label, with bands like Oasis and Primal Scream, as representing some of the defining moments of 'Cool Britannia'; following the sale of Creation to Sony, McGee started a new record label, Poptones, in 2000). Second, producer Mackintosh and composer Lloyd Webber are pioneers of the international mega-musical: for example, their second co-production, *The Phantom of the Opera* (which premiered in 1986), has a global attendance figure of over 50 million and takings are in excess of £1.5 billion. The other musicals (e.g. *Cats, Les Miserables,* and *Miss Saigon*) helped to promote the two impresarios as the marketing geniuses behind global brands. A willingness to back his own taste is crucial to Macintosh:

> Although theatre is utterly collaborative, it is impossible when the producers are a group of people. You've got no one definite batting for the production team to go against. Although of course I value other opinions – and if I have to overrule someone it usually means there is something wrong – but in the end it's got to be my taste. When some of my backers once started to say 'We'll back but not this one' I said, 'Well I think you should go off and pick your own'. If they feel they have their own taste they should go off and produce themselves, not back me. Whether one agrees with it or not I've got a strong sense of my taste. I have always gone for what I like.
>
> (London *Guardian*, 23 October 1999)

'Stylishly common' is how Mackintosh goes on a label of his sense of taste.

Even the most talented art music composers have engaged in entrepreneurial activity. For example, it is said that enterprise and industry characterized the family life of Johann Sebastian Bach. In addition to his Herculean efforts as a composer, he was engaged in lucrative work as a consultant on the building and voicing of new organs, and acted as agent for the sale and rental of various keyboard instruments. The case of George Frederic Handel, very much an international composer, is enlightening. Handel left a deep impression on English music – for example, *The Messiah* was still described as part of the average Englishman's religion at the start of the twentieth century – and he remains an English institution, yet this German came to England, in 1710, as an upholder of opera, a purely Italian art. (Henry Purcell, 1659–95, was the first important English composer, but his efforts to make opera in the tradition of English drama had not succeeded). Though remembered mainly for his oratorios, Handel started a long tenure in England as a composer of opera and engaged in the activities of an arts manager and speculative impresario. In 1718–19, a joint stock company called the Royal Academy of Music (no relation to the current educational institution of the same name) was organized by about sixty aristocrats to present operas to the London public (at the King's Theatre in the Haymarket). Handel and two Italian composers, Giovanni Buononcini and Filippo Amadei, were engaged as artistic directors. The Royal Academy of Music flourished from 1720 to 1728; following financial difficulties, not least due to the phenomenal success of John Gay's *The Beggar's Opera* (1728), the Academy decided to cease operation in 1729. Handel decided to take over the theatre in the dual role of composer and promoter. Competition emerged from the Opera of Nobility, a rival venture with Buononcini as principal composer. In 1737, after years of struggle and alternating fortunes, both opera companies had to close. It was only then that Handel began to compose an oratorio, *Saul*. The invitation to write *The Messiah* for Dublin in 1741 committed Handel to this new kind of composition, the oratorio, in English, which could be put on at less expense and for which moreover there was a potentially large middle-class public that had never felt at home with the aristocratic entertainment of opera in Italian.

(Grout and Palisca 1988: 524)

The role of the studio offers examples of entrepreneurial activity in fine art. First, Giorgio Vasari's *Lives* (first published in 1550) is indispensable to art historians interested in the Italian Renaissance, yet it is recognized that he is not providing straightforward kinds of evidence. He believed in the superiority of Florence as a creative centre; the first edition of *Lives* (which is a blend of theoretical discussions and biographies) ended with Michelangelo as the only living artist accorded such an honour. The mystique which has since grown up around the so-called 'Great Artist' owes much to Vasari. He promoted the roles of individualism and conflict: 'Renaissance art seen as a series of dramatic rivalries between passionate egoists is one aspect of art history's inheritance from Vasari' (Sheard and Paoletti 1978: xv). Yet, it may be more appropriate to view collaborative efforts amongst artists in the creative process of painting and sculpting in Italian Renaissance art: the most straightforward has two artists working on the same object or contributing to a single project; and there is the relationship between teacher and pupil whereby a top-ranking 'master' with a large shop would attract highly competent assistants (see Sheard and Paoletti 1978).

Second, it is said that Rembrandt van Rijn was not an artist, but a studio:

Rembrandt's studio was an unashamedly commercial operation. As well as apprentices and paying pupils, a steady stream of young qualified painters passed through and painted under his guidance, sometimes in style closely resembling the master's and sometimes with more individuality. It is clear that Rembrandt signed other painter's works as his own, and it is this fact, together with the inevitable similarity in materials and techniques, that makes attribution of some works associated with him problematic.

(Christopher Brown cited in Turner 2000: 289)

The adoption of his forename as a signature for works of art from 1632 onwards is in imitation of Italians like Leonardo, Michelangelo, Raphael, and Titian. The so-called Rembrandt Restoration Project (RRP) was established in 1968 with an aim of studying – above all from a technical point – and re-cataloguing all paintings by the artist. It goes without saying that the categories used by the RRP – 'A' for authentic works; 'B' for those whose genuineness could be neither accepted nor rejected; and 'C' those certainly not by Rembrandt – are contested by the owners of Rembrandts.

Third, Peter Paul Rubens combined a diplomatic career alongside painting and managing his Antwerp studio. Throughout his working life as a painter, Rubens used assistants such that his studio (which included a picture gallery) is considered an outstanding example of artistic organization. Indeed, assistants are crucial to the artist's overall output: 'rather slick execution of Rubens's studio assistants without whom he would have been unable to produce a great number of works and public commissions that he did' (Alpers 1995: 5). A work's essential value, according to Rubens, starts with its original concept, so that he viewed his preliminary sketch or cartoon as central to the creative process. Direction of skilled assistants by the 'master' was viewed as an operational matter, less important than the original design concept. Yet Rubens did realize that if more work was done by his own hand – the imprint of the artist – the finished work was more valued by collectors, hence a higher selling price: 'It was Rubens's usual practice to touch up the painting by his studio assistants. ... But, in a reversal of Rembrandt's enterprise, perhaps some of what looks like to be by his studio might be by Rubens himself' (Alpers 1995: 158–9).

Art as entrepreneurial process

There is a case that artists have always been self-promoters. Premonitory artists Marcel Duchamp and Andy Warhol confronted technological change, and questioned the role of the artist in society. From an aesthetic perspective, Mark Kostabi operates in an environment influenced by Duchamp and Warhol, yet the commercial world is much changed. There is a greater degree of cynicism and despair. Opportunism is rife.

Duchamp pulls an industrially-produced bicycle-wheel from its accustomed stream of function and places it in a totally unfamiliar, artificial context as a work of art. An introduction to the Schwerin Marcel Duchamp Collection (in Germany) remarks on the artist's general stance:

> The main emphasis lies on the basic concept and attitude as well as on the methods of the painter, who had the remarkable ability to remove everyday items from their context. Duchamp aspired an attitude of sceptical easiness, both in life and work. As regards the visual material of his art and its motifs, he drew inspiration from advertisements and billboards as well as from technical installations. His 'ready-mades' overcome the dictate of purpose and the artist was able to create the necessary distance of the conscience and of freedom in order to interlace things in a new manner. His main motif is the categorical dependence on time of all works, in other words their expiry date.
>
> (von Berswordt-Wallrabe 1995: 9).

Furthermore, in doing so, he was recognizing the revolution in the manufacture of goods taking place in the USA: there was a move away from the manual crafting process towards industrial-scale factory mass-production; moreover, this change in production resulted in a shift in consumption patterns. Duchamp's ready-mades (from 1913–15) represented a fundamental departure from the traditional conception of the creative process of making art (i.e. mental and manual act of creation which generates a unique work of art). (Duchamp exhibited *Nude Descending a Staircase, No. 2* (1912) at the International Exhibition of Modern Art, the celebrated

Armory Show of 1913. The 1917 exhibition of the Society of Independent Artists was likened to a reunion of Armory Show artists; however, Duchamp's urinal submission was not accepted.) The ready-mades – objects which are finished when you buy them – were vehicles of an artistic strategy on subverting and dismantling what had been considered unchangeable. Duchamp is a pioneering 'conceptual' artist, one who remains seminal to appreciating contemporary sensibilities towards visual art. According to contemporary art curator, Achille Bonita Oliva:

> Art becomes a process which goes through the endless manufacture of objects produced, new or used, exhibited or forgotten, in which the artist intervenes to rescue the object from the first chain of *ordinary consumption* and to put it into a higher chain, that of *aesthetic consumption*. The shifting of the object presupposes the recognition of an enduring present of industrial production, capable without the drama of transforming nature into culture, into a processed item.
>
> (Oliva 1988: 40; my italics)

Warhol, as a leading proponent of the Pop Art movement of the 1960s, reproduced the visual trappings of American commercialism (e.g. Campbell's soup cans, Coca-Cola bottles, and portraits of Marilyn and Elvis). These images advertise or embody consumption, or are dedicated to commercial mass entertainment. Warhol recognized that the triumph of the mass market was, in some profound ways, based on satisfying the spiritual needs as well as the material needs of consumers. (This is examined as 'manufacturing glamour', by John Berger (1972: final section). Contemporary advertising practice recognizes the importance of appealing to the 'head' and the 'heart' when promoting a wide range of goods and services.) Mass-produced techniques used in the manufacture of Warhol's works are discussed in terms of his multiples concept. Opinion was divided about Warhol's output during his lifetime. He 'remains central, as an artist who was able to elevate serial products to the status of the uniqueness of art, founding a *snobbism of the masses* with the clear classicality of the great artist who accepts the unavoidability of technology and the deprivation of reality that it causes', according to admirers (Oliva 1988: 40; emphasis in the original). Cynical observers, on the other hand, saw his aesthetic methodology 'merely as another packaging idea that exploited the limited-edition / signed / investment-opportunity impulses that are characteristic of just those decadent lineaments that have ruined modern art' (Battcock 1973: 25); Warhol pretended to proffer opportunity for so-called high art available to all, but it was nothing more than an extension of elitist and condescending aspects of capitalist culture.

A central image in works by Kostabi is the humanoid figure, a faceless individual often wielding a toilet plunger. (For an indicative work see, for example, *Upheaval* (1988): war breaks out between boardroom members.) One may read his compositions as relevant and witty critiques of a technological, manipulative society. Yet Kostabi's engagement with cultural and social issues seems almost incidental:

Question: Do you celebrate the loss of authenticity and critical representation in today's society? If so, do you believe art has triumphed as a
commodity and sign?

Kostabi: I never think about stuff like this, I simply commodify my signs
and sign my commodities

(from the column, 'Ask Mark Kostabi', at www.artnet.com)

Kostabi is a tireless self-promoter, recognizing quite clearly that he – as the artist –
is the brand. A business executive like Steve Jobs, in his second coming at Apple,
wants to be viewed as chief aesthetic officer; Kostabi, on the other hand, positions
himself as a 'mass communications industrialist':

> My painting mimics the industrial process and I'm the chairman of the board.
> Just like Walt Disney I also devolve responsibility to my subordinates to come
> up with the goods. I just guide things in terms of supervision and public rela-
> tions, in terms of manipulating the media, in terms of communicating what my
> corporate image should be.
>
> (Shanes 1989: 37)

There is a trickster persona on display, which is underscored by deliberate references to being raised in Whittier, California, home of Richard Nixon, the disgraced
American president.

Kostabi has taken both Duchamp's and Warhol's diffidence about how a work
of art is made, and their ironic view of the cultural purpose it serves, to even greater
extremes. To understand Kostabi as an artist, one needs to understand that it
involves an entire system. In 1988, Kostabi World – references are the European
tradition, with Warhol's Factory being a more recent model – was established as a
studio, gallery, and office complex in New York. According to art critic Thomas
McEvilley:

> A Kostabi picture openly asserts the complex memory of the process of its
> production. The structure of Kostabi World, its hierarchies of relationships,
> and the formative project of working these relationships out in the hard, high-
> contrast lighting of capitalism – all this hangs invisibly suspended around
> each picture.
>
> (Kostabi 1996: Foreword)

Kostabi's method is to employ assistants – a means of creation that consciously
parallel the production lines that form the basis of manufacturing plants – to create
works in his name. 'It does not necessarily matter when Kostabi's assistants finished painting, nor who they are, and so on, since it is Kostabi's meaning that sus-
tains their result as his art work' (Bailey 1989: 226).

'Cash in on passion' is one of the slogans proclaiming the thoughts of the artist on
display at Kostabi World to encourage workers (Shanes 1989: 35). Kostabi World
emphasizes commodity production, artist–assistant relationships, and raises questions

regarding originality and authenticity: a painting not painted by Kostabi may be a work of art by Kostabi. Economic value is assigned to his works by a self-referential art market system (e.g. artists, dealers, critics, collectors) with its hierarchies of relationships. Not unlike other owners of 'aspirational' brands, Kostabi relies on customers who crave new products, customers–collectors who want to be cultural pioneers. Kostabi – in a *Flash Art* (January/February 2000) advertisement – recognizes that a closer relationship with the artist can be charged at a higher rate:

> It is true that I charge 100 times more for a commissioned work done entirely by my own hand but not because I believe it is necessarily worth 100 times more. I believe any painting priced 100 times more than any other should actually be 100 times better. But if a collector is willing to dole out the extra for 'the aura of the master's hand', I'll do my best to make a masterpiece. The truth is, frequently I can paint a better painting than those of my assistants but sometimes theirs are better, because we all experiment at Kostabi World.

Fine art, as Kostabi knows better than most of his contemporaries, offers its owner social capital. To capitalize on this, Kostabi realizes that he should never detract from his corporate image.

Global franchising of cultural brands

Globalization in art may be seen to have certain parallels with what is going on in economics. In the post-cold war environment, arts organizations, like fast-food conglomerates, need satellites and franchises to make a profit, hence the need to invade 'empty' cultural spaces. Are there 'imperialist' ambitions behind an attempt to establish a global brand? Does art become more closely linked as a handmaiden of cultural tourism?

Though the Solomon R. Guggenheim Foundation was established in 1937, the emergence of the Guggenheim brand really dates from 1959, when Frank Lloyd Wright's 'spiral' building was opened as the Solomon R. Guggenheim Museum. In 1979, the Peggy Guggenheim Collection – which had been established in 1951 in Venice – came under the control of the Guggenheim Foundation. The Guggenheim SoHo, representing a secondary New York site, was opened in 1992. The early 1990s also marked initiatives by the Guggenheim Foundation to pursue additional global sites. Fruits of such ambition were realized in 1997: the Guggenheim Bilbao represented funding by the Basque government with management and art provided by the Guggenheim; and the Deutsche Guggenheim Museum, a more modest proposal, was realized in partnership with Deutsche Bank. Advantages of global cultural production, namely transplants, by using the Guggenheim's permanent collection as trading capital – assets deployed to expand institutional presence and enhance financial stability – were identified. Rosiland Krauss (1990) has criticized the leveraging of art works from the permanent collection (not selling but moving it to the credit sector), with particular reference to the Guggenheim under the directorship (since 1988) of Thomas Krens. Her analysis is informed by changes that have taken place as a result of the free-market spirit of the 1980s: 'The notion of the museum as a guardian of the public patrimony has given way to the notion of the museum as a corporate entity with a highly marketable inventory and the desire for growth' (Philip Weiss cited in Krauss 1990: 5).

New York is to remain the Guggenheim Foundation's hub for its glittering 'constellations' throughout the world. The site in Bilbao, a formerly depressed area undergoing a process of revitalization and transformation via architecture and regeneration, is represented as a significant development: it is a powerful metaphor for the contemporary way to do cultural business, namely by becoming an international tourist destination. Indeed, the exposure of the Guggenheim brand name is about attracting global audiences: 'Our attendance figures are measured globally now, and each exhibition is measured in terms of its global impact rather than its local impact. The Guggenheim's mindset is that of a global institution' (Guggenheim official cited in *Flash Art*, January/February 2000). For example, its online project is billed as a virtual museum, a natural extension of the satellite museum sites, with an objective to enhance the value of the Guggenheim as a brand. Indeed, a mid-1990s slogan on the cultural ambitions of the Guggenheim, as competing for the mind of Europe, seems too modest with hindsight.

Amongst various issues that the Guggenheim's Bilbao project foregrounds, two are highlighted. First, will having an art museum at the centre of an urban renewal project work? Critics point out that the overall renewal plan may be more beneficial to corporate interests than people in the local area. Some will interpret the four 'brands' on display at the opening – the Guggenheim Foundation, architect Frank Gehry, corporate sponsor Hugo Boss, and a majestic, lawn ornament *Sky Puppy* by artist Jeff Koons, who also works as a Hugo Boss model – as representing the tragic nature of cultural franchising. In an effort to develop a greater presence in the USA, Hugo Boss, a German fashion label, signed a sponsorship arrangement with the Guggenheim. Other relationships with corporate funders have been conducted by the Guggenheim: in a form of product placement, BMW contributed several motorcycles to the exhibition, 'Art of the Motorcycle'; and owners of Nokia mobile telephones were offered a two-for-one admission tariff to visit 'China: 500 Years'. Moreover, the notion of works of art making up the permanent collection being treated as working capital is not restricted to the Guggenheim. For example, a museum building in Nagoya, integrated as part of a hotel complex, was opened in 1999 as a joint venture between the Museum of Fine Arts, Boston and the Chamber of Commerce of Nagoya – art from the MFA in return for Japanese cash. This is a good example of how international patterns of economic wealth have an impact on the identity of museums. The MFA views this alliance as the first in a series of international satellites; indeed it is one of the few art museums in the USA possessing a sufficiently large collection to consider multiple outposts. Employing the permanent collection in such a manner sidesteps deaccessioning; moreover, it allows the institution to argue that more of its art works are on display to larger audiences.

What is suggested by the Guggenheim's first new site of the twenty-first century: Las Vegas? Central to the Guggenheim project is 'The Venetian Resort–Hotel–Casino' complex. On the former site of the Sands Hotel, 'legendary' home of Rat Pack performers like Frank Sinatra and Dean Martin, Sheldon Adelson, chairman of the Venetian, seeks to establish the world's largest resort and convention centre under one roof. Both the Guggenheim Las Vegas (focusing on travelling exhibitions) and the Guggenheim Hermitage Museum (in partnership with the State Hermitage Museum in Russia) are attached to the Venetian; access is through the Venetian *only*. Not unlike the strong architectural statements made by Frank Lloyd Wright and Frank Gehry, Rem Koolhaas (recipient of the 2000 Pritzker prize for architecture) was selected by the Guggenheim to create a museum building that would not be overlooked alongside the aggressive visual congestion of 'The Strip', the city's main artery. Las Vegas continues to upgrade its image; this transformation into a so-called 'world class' destination resort relies on rivalry among the city's elite casino owners.

In the late 1990s, Steven Wynn, chairman of the Mirage Resorts, used works of art from his personal collection (including works by Renoir, Van Gogh, and Picasso) as another selling point to entice 'high limit' gamblers (an elite consumer segment). It was a clear example of using 'fine art' to enhance a casino's brand reputation:

> Any work of art 'quoted' by publicity serves two purposes. Art is a sign of affluence; it belongs to the good life; it is part of the furnishing which the word gives to the rich and beautiful.
>
> But a work of art also suggests a cultural authority, a form of dignity, even of wisdom, which is superior to any vulgar material interest; an oil painting belongs to a cultural heritage; it is a reminder of what it means to be a cultivated European.
>
> (Berger 1972: 135)

The Venetian experiment is grander and more ambitious than that accomplished by Wynn. It is the only significant collaboration between an art museum and a casino-hotel in the USA. Assumed European connotations of 'good taste' and 'distinction' are explicit: as suggested by its name, the resort–hotel–casino complex positions itself as 'Las Venice' by reproducing the 'cultural' features (e.g. Campanile di San Marco and the Rialto Bridge over Grand Canal, including gondola rides) found in the Italian city-state. According to a spokesman for the Venetian:

> Culture is here to stay. People are finding that Las Vegas reinvents itself – in dining and in shopping and retail – it's now gaining a worldwide reputation as a place where you can actually seek culture, away from the typical stereotypes that have plagued Las Vegas for a long time.
>
> (Kurt Ochida cited in the *Reno Gazette-Journal*, 14 July 2000)

Yet the treatment of art and culture envisioned by the Guggenheim–Venetian collaboration has raised concerns. For example, according to Frank Gehry, 'I'm worried about this kind of context. There may be a way to do it, but the fear is that it would all just become another theme, whether you like it or not' (*IonVegas*, 20 October 2000).

With the latest Guggenheim project, the role of the Hermitage should not be minimized as a minor partner. Hermitage director, Mikhail Piotrovski, recognizes the need to generate income (to supplement the state subsidy which covers 45 per cent of the operating budget); he also knows that sending masterpieces from the permanent collection around the world may assist. Apart from the Guggenheim deal – it could be worth $1 million per annum for the Hermitage and offers access to American patrons – a joint project has been initiated with London's Somerset House; Amsterdam is the Hermitage's third target destination.

The Guggenheim appears to be adopting the lead of the Walt Disney Company in developing a 'diversified' brand (see Court *et al.* 1999). The initial brand platform can be leveraged to move into other opportunities. Diversified brands attempt to cultivate a so-called 'golden thread' (e.g. Disney is about 'wholesome fun' for all ages), building 'high credibility' personalities (e.g. Mickey Mouse), and leveraging aggressively (e.g. multiple theme park sites tied to feature films, hotels, and other merchandising). Under the directorship of Thomas Krens, the Guggenheim has recognized that opportunities exist to change the ways in which art museums compete. By museum standards, the Guggenheim is noted for aggressive brand leveraging: it is the first museum brand to establish global credentials under its (current) 'one museum, five locations' banner. Establishing a reputation based on one location – as with the Louvre, the British Museum, and the Prado, for example – is difficult to replicate for second-movers (with the Getty Museum being a well-endowed exception). Celebrity endorsers come in the form of respected superstar architects (Gehry and Koolhaas) and flamboyant artists (such as Koons). National (New York and Las Vegas) and international (Venice, Bilbao, and Berlin) scale helps to offer presence. Signature pieces of architecture, a dominant feature of the brand from the start, may enhance the Guggenheim's personality. The Guggenheim relationship with visitors may be likened to pilgrimages: historically, one thinks about the Piero della Francesca trail; Disney's multiple theme park sites may offer a better role model for the Guggenheim. But what is the Guggenheim's golden thread? It is not obvious that the theme of one museum with multiple locations fits the bill. Moreover, it is difficult to accept at face value the Guggenheim's response to critics that a motivation for multiple sites is to make its collection accessible to a broader audience.

Entrepreneurship has strong commercial connotations, yet Paul DiMaggio reminds us that 'cultural capitalists' have been important in the establishment of elite institutions dedicated to art music and the visual arts. Composers such as Bach and Handel and painters such as Rembrandt and Rubens had highly visible entrepreneurial engagements. Moreover, there is a current emphasis to promote entrepreneurship as a social process, linked to the widening boundaries of creativity, making it appropriate for 'most people' working in a diverse range of organizations. Mark Kostabi is much more aggressive than Duchamp and Warhol in self-promotion. His signature style, cultivated at Kostabi World, simultaneously delivers the Kostabi brand name. The global franchising ambitions of the Guggenheim – using works in its permanent collection as a form of financial leverage – may be a harbinger of things to come.

4   Collaborations in the arts

Claims of status and privilege can be expressed and further enhanced through support and patronage of the arts. New York socialite Nan Kempter, representative of the 'social x-rays' in Tom Wolfe's *Bonfire of the Vanities* (1989), is an iconic figure in the arena where fashion is promoted as art:

> I give away a tremendous amount. [My husband, Tommy] thinks it's hysterical, because he used to think it was extravagance, and it now turns out that I was an art collector, because every museum in the country, and in Europe, seems to have costume institutes. And they all scream and yell and come and ask me for clothes all the time. And there are also charity auctions. Can you imagine? Isn't it funny? I thought I was just putting feathers on, as if it was a love-and-comfort blanket, and I now discover that I'm a big art collector!
>
> (London *Observer Magazine*, 12 August 2001)

Competition from the likes of the V&A and the Met extends beyond Kempter's clothes to her future commitments as a major patron.

Collaborations come in various forms. Patronage is an ambiguous term in the history of taste. In the broad sense, patronage needs to be viewed in relation to the interests and activities of a ruling elite (which itself changes over time). As institutions become more important in understanding business and the arts, the public dialogue between Pierre Bourdieu and Hans Haacke is instructive and informative in highlighting the complex nature of such relationships. They distinguish between 'the traditional notion of patronage and the public relationships maneuvers parading as patronage today' (Bourdieu and Haacke 1995: 17). First, the legacy of patronage needs to be addressed. How have terms prescribed by private patrons determined what public organizations are able to do in the present and the future? Second, the nature of contemporary corporate support is examined with reference to initiatives launched in the 1960s by the Business Committee for the Arts. Why is it considered to be in the long-term interests of commercial organizations to support the arts? Critics identify the business–arts relationship as an 'exchange of capital: financial capital on the part of the sponsor and symbolic capital on the part of the sponsored' (Bourdieu and Haacke 1995: 17); and corporations understand the commercial value to be gained by an association with cultural capital (Bourdieu 1984). Third, unlike the traditional perspective of what the arts can learn from business, Charles Handy is interested in the things that the theatre and the arts teach all of us. It is important to evaluate Handy's quasi-spiritual thesis regarding the role of the arts in contemporary society. In doing so, issues about creativity in the corporate workplace, which underpin initiatives supported by Arts & Business (A&B), are reviewed. The overall thrust is to contribute to the growing debate about the transformative value of the arts, and the institutionalization of creativity.

Private patrons and public institutions

A link between elite (such as church and royal) patrons and traditional culture has been a dominant motif in the interpretation of the development of the arts. Patronage 'is inherently an issue of human relations and the result of human motivation on all its levels. It is determined by values and standards, and it represents choices on the part of an individual, of a group, of a country' (Dorian 1964: 6; my emphasis). The role of elite patrons and public institutions is an old and familiar theme. For example, the Accademia degli Invaghiti sponsored Monteverdi's *Orfeo* (1607); there is the case that the academies, houses of oratory and versification, would have appreciated the rhetorically based language of the late madrigal. Monteverdi's highly aesthetic, poetic cognoscenti patrons are different from the Barberini popes, and this helps to account for the more overtly theatrical elements of Zuigi Rossi's *Orfeo* (1647) they commissioned.

In a secular world marked by democratic elections, Bourdieu recognizes that the invitation for the corporate man to assume the role of the sage is enticing:

> Today, an increasing large fraction of owners and upper management throughout the world graduate from the best schools. Although they may not be great intellectuals, those who dominate the economic world, the owners of industry and commerce, are no longer the narrow-minded bourgeois of the nineteenth century. In the nineteenth century, artists such as Baudelaire and Flaubert could oppose the 'bourgeois' as ignorant or dim-witted philistines. Today's owners are, often, very refined people, at least in terms of social strategies of manipulation, but also in the realm of art, which easily becomes part of the bourgeois style of life, even if it is the product of heretical raptures and veritable symbolic revolutions.
>
> (Bourdieu and Haacke 1995: 41)

The example of Charles Saatchi is illustrative of the broadening base of patronage beyond an aristocratic elite (see, for example, Hatton and Walker 2000). What links Saatchi to Prime Minister Thatcher, the Tate Gallery, and the international art market? Charles and his brother Maurice, who was made a life peer in 1996, were co-founders (in 1970) of Saatchi and Saatchi, the advertising firm that was crucial to the electoral success of the Conservatives under Thatcher in 1979. At the time, Charles, an assiduous collector of contemporary art, was an active member of the Tate's high-level support group, Patrons of New Art, and trustee of London's Whitechapel Art Gallery, a public institution. *Taking Stock (unfinished)* (1983-4) was Haacke's attempt to raise concern that Julian Schnabel, a 'hot' artist for much of the

1980s, had an exhibition at the Tate in 1982. Organized by the Patrons of New Art, nine of the eleven paintings on display were owned by Saatchi. A main point was an ethical one dealing with conflict of interest; Haacke wanted to make the various relationships more transparent. Victorian values were cited by Haacke. The main image in *Taking Stock (unfinished)* is a portrait of Thatcher; oil paint as a medium and the choice of frame were based on Victorian era works in the Tate Gallery, as a way to mimic her promotion of nineteenth century conservative policies at the end of the twentieth century. 'Of course, in their own way, the Saatchis are also Victorians. They match the young bourgeois entrepreneurs of the nineteenth century, relatively unfettered by tradition, without roots in the aristocracy, and out to prove themselves to the world', according to Haacke (Bois, Crimp, and Krauss 1984: 24).

Having learned from the world of entertainment, the value of so-called event pictures, a term first associated with *The Exorcist*, a film noted for attracting 'money reviews' (i.e. reviews that attract a cycle of attention in which people read about it and do not want to be left out) and developing 'legs' (i.e. strong popular appeal so that it has box-office longevity), the 1997 'Sensation' exhibition at the Royal Academy of Arts exhibited works from the Saatchi collection of 'young British artists' (such as Damien Hirst, Sam Taylor-Wood, Gillian Wearing, and Tracey Emin). 'Influences such as Saatchi's in the art world is not new. He belongs to a long line of civilised entrepreneurs whose collections form the basis for today's "educated tastes"', according to Lisa Jardine (London *Daily Telegraph*, 19 November 1997). More revealing in Jardine's interview with Saatchi is the relationship between his early professional success in advertising and aesthetic choices:

> From the beginning he felt 'pretty' confident with visual images and their manipulation and that made him relaxed about saying what he liked and following that up with purchasing. He acknowledges that some people consider his advertising man's eyes a weakness. It is true that he instinctively picks the kind of work that plays vigorously on rapid audience reception, and that he has a preference for artists who are likely aware about the interaction between themselves, their work and the gallery goer.
>
> (*Daily Telegraph*, 19 November 1997)

This represents an example of mass media shaping fine art (which is a reversal of the conventional case of learned culture exerting an influence on popular culture).

It is not difficult to see links between Saatchi, a 'big league' collector of contemporary art, and public institutions. Saatchi has already donated art valued at £500,000 to the Arts Council of England. There is a strong likelihood that at least some of the work from the Saatchi collection will enter the permanent collection of the Tate. Thus Saatchi's donations to public institutions will form a historical record for future generations of British art production of the 1990s. Contemporary patronage is a topic suggestive of further research in order to decode more fully the relationship between personal taste and the public perception of (national or 'official') artistic production.

Yet it is important to recognize the complexities associated with private collectors and public institutions. Montreal collectors between 1880 and 1920 (such as Sir

George Drummond, R. B. Angus, Lord Strathcona, Sir William Van Horne, Charles Hosmer, and James Ross) were the product of the industrial boom associated with the building of the transcontinental Canadian Pacific Railway, one of the most ambitious infrastructure projects in Canadian history. They formed a new category of collector: middle class by birth and aristocratic in fortune. Before the social and psychological effects of war and the more direct impact of income tax put a halt to the boom period of collecting, these Montreal collectors 'had created the greatest private collections yet seen in Canada', according to Janet Brooke (1989: 14). She added that 'the dispersal by auction houses overseas of several of the most significant of them' is one reason why the history of collecting in Montreal is 'not merely an aspect of [the Montreal Museum of Fine Art's] institutional history' (Brooke 1989: 15). She attempts to account for why there was not a closer mapping of private collecting and the MMFA's history: tax laws in Canada at the time made gifts of art extremely onerous on the donor and his family, whereas gifts of cash were not affected by tax laws.

Business patrons and the arts

Arts patronage during the latter half of the twentieth century was marked by the emergence of business corporations. The American-based BCA – the first national, business-supported, not-for-profit organization that encourages business to support the arts and provides them with the services and resources necessary to develop and advance partnerships – was founded in 1967 as an initiative of David Rockefeller, chairman of Chase Manhattan Bank, who advocated business understanding and involvement in the arts:

> The modern corporate has evolved into a social as well as an economic institution. Without losing sight of the need to make a profit, it has developed ideals and responsibilities going far beyond the profit motive ... .
> The public has come to expect corporations to live up to certain standards of good citizenship.
>
> (Gingrich 1969: xi; see also www.bcainc.org)

The BCA was answering calls put forward in the Rockefeller Panel Report (1965) that collective corporate action was needed to stimulate support in the arts. *Business and the Arts* (1970), essentially a publicity document, provided a means for the BCA to communicate its message. From the outset, the general gist of the BCA has provoked criticism. Thomas Guback interpreted corporate sloganeering as 'the good community-minded citizen hid[ing] the ultimate nature of its policies', namely that profits may be counted 'in dollars as well as goodwill'; furthermore, he voiced concern over the formalization of a nexus in which 'the same men are running both spheres':

> While no sphere in society can remain entirely insulated from or insensitive to others, there is a difference between independently-activated response and the kind of cooperation bred and initiated by power and control. Especially now it is untenable that one institution should further extend its influence in monolithic fashion.
>
> (Guback 1970: 132, 134)

The BCA provided the model for like-minded organizations in other countries: the Council for Business and the Arts in Canada (CBAC) was established in 1974; and, in the UK, the Association for Business Sponsorship in the Arts (ABSA) – now called Arts & Business (A&B) – was established in 1976. Both the Canadian and British organizations have missions and membership requirements that are similar to those espoused by the BCA. Yet it is important to remember that CBAC, though viewed as a Canadian version of BCA, was established after a conference sponsored by the Canada Council. The founding director of ABSA, Luke Rittner, based the British initiative on elements of BCA and CBAC, with some variation. Unlike the American corporation which feels an obligation, almost a duty to support the arts and cultural life, business firms in the UK were pitched the sound commercial sense of supporting ABSA. Due to higher levels of state patronage, arts organizations in the UK were less dependent on corporate sponsorship; indeed the ACGB was highly suspicious that initiatives by ABSA would encroach on public funding. ABSA distinguished itself through an interventionist role by administering government schemes designed to increase the level of business sponsorship. ABSA's recent name change to Arts & Business reflected a desire to signal that the organization was involved in promoting collaborations beyond business sponsorship.

The most significant impact of the BCA, CBAC, and ABSA (A&B) in promoting business alliances has been to inculcate the current 'arts industry' environment: big business feels comfortable supporting the arts; arts organizations deem support by big business as an essential ingredient for financial success; and target audiences are made aware of the corporate contribution to cultural life. For example, the BCA estimated total American business sponsorship of the arts in 1967 at $22 million; thirty years later the figure was $1.2 billion.

At its inception, the BCA articulated to Fortune 500 firms, the advantages of closer business dealings with the arts: improving corporate image, increasing sales, aiding recruitment, and attracting industry to an area were cited as direct benefits; at the same time, indirect business benefits to employees, the community, and society as a whole were also perceived. Social benefits came under the broad banner of corporate responsibility (e.g. helping to alleviate the problems of the under-privileged and the plight of the inner city). The seemingly diverse range of benefits reflected concerns being voiced during the 1960s and the US Business corporations, like many established institutions, were criticized for being removed from the economic and social crises plaguing larger urban cities. Equally, there was a conspicuous wane in the confidence in American business. Arts sponsorship was presented as one relatively inexpensive way of regaining public support. Furthermore there are often undisclosed personal benefits to the senior executives who make decisions about business support to the arts such as accumulating social prestige and displaying 'good taste' (e.g. Bourdieu and Haacke 1995).

Altruism and enlightened self-interest are two general positions that may be discerned in statements made by the BCA. The altruistic stance addresses social benefits by recognizing that corporations have 'assumed a central role in industrial society that the military organization or the religious community has occupied at other times and in other places' (Strum 1985: 158). Corporate power must be used to pursue profits to ensure economic viability. However, corporations do not exist by divine right: 'The corporation like the Sabbath, was not made for its own survival. Its legitimacy depends on whether its meaning is truly representative of the meaning of life itself' (Strum 1985: 158). With an enlightened self-interest perspective, the firm garners more tangible benefits without necessarily forfeiting broader societal concerns, since 'increasing sales and spreading goodwill will no longer be mutually exclusive objectives but can be goals which complement each other' (Mescon and Tilson 1987: 59). For example, 'museum-goers tend to be affluent, well-educated, upscale consumers … the very audience that corporations want to target' (Lorraine Glennon in the American Association of Museum's *Museum News*, January/February 1988). According to Arnold Edinborough, founder of CBAC, the link between corporate sponsorship and marketing is strong: 'It is the marketing aspect of sponsorship which has brought business to the fore again in the arts. It is, in fact, the success of sponsorship which makes people believe business is involved as never before' (cited in *Canadian Speeches*, December 1987). On the other hand, a donation is a voluntary transfer of property without consideration such as setting aside a prescribed percentage of total revenue to be donated to a charitable organization. Yet philanthropic initiatives by corporations have been criticized: neo-conservative economists led by Milton Friedman view any business involvement beyond narrowly prescribed parameters of maximizing shareholder wealth as not only fiscally irresponsible, but potentially harmful to society.

The links between corporations and large, metropolitan-based art museums are well established. For example, the inaugural meeting of the BCA, in January 1968, under the chairmanship of C. Dillon Douglas was convened at the Met, where he was a trustee. Given the Met's stature, it attracted the most socially prominent and financially powerful individuals in New York. It is not surprising that the Met established the first 'Corporate Patrons Program', in the mid-1970s, a most visible venture under the auspices of its Business Committee. 'The business behind the art knows the art of good business' was the pitch for the Corporate Patrons Program which served to promote the benefits of membership:

> Many public relations opportunities are available at The Metropolitan Museum of Art through sponsorship of programs, special exhibitions and services. These can often provide a creative and cost effective answer to a specific marketing objective, particularly where international, governmental or consumer relations may be a fundamental concern.
>
> (from Met pamphlet, n.d.)

Whereas art museums in the USA have been hustling to attract corporate money, the sponsorship of temporary exhibitions is a relatively recent activity at most British arts institutions. For example, the Tate Gallery's first example of exhibition sponsorship did not occur until 1982 (with support from S. Pearson and Son for an exhibition by the popular Victorian-era painter, Sir Edwin Landseer). Prominent sponsors of the Tate – British Petroleum (for New Displays, the annual rehang of the permanent collection, started in 1990) and British Nuclear (for the Turner Scholarships) – represent an accepted pattern of museum-corporation relations as they have developed in the USA since the 1960s:

> In an era of heightened consciousness of public relations, image building is the most powerful incentive behind corporate museum patronage. Since sponsorship of temporary exhibitions provides the most exposure, it's not accidental that, historically, the biggest funders have been those with image problems.
>
> (Glennon in *Museum News*, January/February 1988)

In practice, arts organizations seldom refuse corporate sponsors based on the corporation's business activities. The director of the Tate during the ascendancy of corporate sponsorship, Alan Bowness (1980–8), included the following comment as part of a debate on arts sponsorship: 'We have only discriminated against sponsorship by tobacco companies partly because the government itself takes a different attitude to this form of advertising' ('What price arts sponsorship?' unpublished transcript edited by David Coombs, 1986).

Hans Haacke is interested in exposing what he feels to be an unhealthy alliance between the arts and multinational enterprises. Haacke's critique complements Erik Barnouw's *The Sponsor* (1978), and has much in common with what sociologist Herbert Schiller describes as 'the corporate takeover of public expression' (Schiller 1989). Haacke's work adopts a media-savvy orientation, as he readily acknowledges in a public dialogue with Pierre Bourdieu:

> One can learn a lot from advertising. Among the mercenaries of the advertising world are very smart people, real experts in communication. It takes practical sense to learn techniques and strategies of communication. Without them, it is impossible to subvert them.
>
> (Bourdieu and Haacke 1995: 107)

Since the cancellation of a proposed solo exhibition at the Guggenheim in 1971 – viewed by many as an act of censorship by the museum – Haacke has devoted himself to exposing what he feels to be an unhealthy alliance between the arts and multinational enterprises:

> In the 1960s the more sophisticated among business executives of large corporations began to understand that the association of their company's name – and business in general – with the arts could have considerable and long-term benefits, far in excess of the capital invested in such an effort.
>
> (Haacke 1981: 56)

He discusses patronage as 'a tool for the seduction of public opinion':

> I think it is important to distinguish between the traditional notion of patronage and the public relations maneuvers parading as patronage today. Invoking

the name of Maecenas, corporations give themselves an aura of altruism. The American term *sponsorship* more accurately reflects that what we have here is really an exchange of capital: financial capital on the part of the sponsors and symbolic capital on the part of the sponsored. Most business people are quite open about this when they speak to their peers. Alain-Dominique Perrin, for example, says quite bluntly that he spends Cartier's money for purposes that have nothing to do with the love of art.

(Bourdieu and Haacke 1995: 17–18, 17; emphasis in the original)

Haacke seeks to highlight the contradictions inherent in the business–arts nexus, issues those most involved in forming alliances and collaborations feel are unimportant, or are quick to gloss over. According to Bourdieu, Haacke has 'a truly remarkable "eye" for seeing the particular forms of domination that are exerted on the art world to which, paradoxically, writers and artists are not normally very sensitive' (Bourdieu and Haacke 1995: 1). Two works are highlighted which seek to offer an intervention, as Haacke puts it:

The more the interests of cultural institutions and business become intertwined the less culture can play an emancipatory, cognitive, and critical role. Such a link will eventually lead the public to believe that business and culture are natural allies and that a questioning of corporate interest and conduct undermines arts as well. Art is reduced to serving as a social pacifier.

(*Art in America*, May 1990)

On Social Grease (1975) was Haacke's attempt to emphasize the extent to which initiatives by corporations in the arts originate 'from the public relations department of a company that wants to project an image of modernity, optimism, efficiency, and reliability' (Sheffield 1976: 122). Integral to the work, and framed as a plaque, on an august corporate edifice, was a pronouncement attributed to Robert Kingsley, an Exxon executive, 'Exxon's support of the arts serves as a social lubricant. And if business is to continue in big cities, it needs a more lubricated environment'. Haacke used *MetroMobiltan* (1985) to draw attention to unease he felt with a specific relationship, namely that between the Mobil Corporation and the Met. Nuanced references were made to the brochure distributed by the Met's Corporate Patrons Program and Mobil's activity in supporting recent exhibitions at the museum, including a show of ancient Nigerian art (1980) and works by New Zealand tribal artists (1984). At the same time, Haacke included as part of the piece the justification proffered by Mobil to opposition demands to terminate petroleum supplies to the South African police and military:

Mobil's management in New York believes that its South African subsidiaries' sales to the police and military are but a small part of its total sales ... Total denial of supplies to the police and military forces of a host country is hardly consistent with an image of responsible citizenship in that country.

(text from *MetroMobiltan* 1985)

From Haacke's perspective, there is the sense that multinational enterprises use the arts as a qualifier of character, hoping that symbolic associations with well-known arts institutions will be more important than the pragmatic description of what the firm produces, and its commercial relationships.

Business learning from the arts

'Liberal humanism has dwindled to the impotent consciousness of bourgeois society, gentle, sensitive and ineffectual', according to Terry Eagleton (1983: 199). As a Marxist literary theorist, Eagleton was taking aim at Northrop Frye, then still alive, and F. R. Leavis. In particular, Eagleton was questioning two related points: the transformative powers attributed to art; and what it means to be a 'better person' as the result of art. Can a similar charge be made against Charles Handy who, like Frye, seeks to nurture spiritual wholeness in a hostile world? Yes, according to Gibson Burrell: 'Handy pocket theory with all its superficiality, ease of travel, liberal humanistic stance, technobabble language and fundamentally conservative political leaning ... [and] all that consultancy-speak' (Burrell 1997: 27).

In trying to look beyond capitalism, Handy advocates 'Proper Selfishness': this 'search for ourselves' is an 'optimistic philosophy' based on the belief that 'we are ultimately decent people' and 'we best satisfy ourselves when we look beyond ourselves' (Handy 1997: 9). Art is central to this journey of self-discovery, according to Handy (1996), who believes that business can learn from the arts. Handy is not alone. The 'staff and organizational development' benefits through partnerships between business and the arts has grown significantly, according to the creative director of Arts & Business:

> It has been driven, we believe, by an increasing awareness that creativity is one of the key differentiators of future business success. This growing realization has led many companies to explore ways of fostering and encouraging creativity and innovation in their staff.
>
> (Tim Stockil in Hadfield 2000: Foreword)

These themes are explored in *A Creative Education* (2000), a report commissioned by A&B to promote arts and creativity in MBA and executive development programmes.

Given Handy's populist appeal to the managerial classes, we contend that he is not a strawman or soft target; at the same time, we do not intend to ridicule or demonize him. One is able to recognize Handy's desire to reverse the accepted sequence such that the arts provide new insights for corporate managers. A similar plea is made by Peter Drucker, who proffers 'a changed human-being' as the product of a not-for-profit organization (Drucker 1990: x). Arts & Business, like Handy, is not located at the margins of corporate life: it remains a lead lobby group in the UK, engaged in 'the promotion, exploration and development of all partnerships between business and the arts' (Stockil in Hadfield 2000: Foreword). The first 'Arts & Business Week', as featured in the *Financial Times* (5 March 2001), focused on 'the idea that the creators of wealth and the creators of culture share ideas and experiences with the aim of precipitating more joint projects': 'Business guru Charles Handy will lecture on the importance of creativity in business, and executives will be encouraged to visit companies that have effectively used artists, from actors to dancers to painters, to improve productivity'. There is a decided accent on the utilitarian nature of the exchange, particularly learning how 'generators of culture' can help to unleash the latent creativity of corporate managers, which raises the productivity level of corporations.

Meditations on organizations and the nature of managerial work have been a long-standing theme for Handy. Adopting an increasingly self-referential perspective, Handy's recent texts – namely *The Search for Meaning* (1996), *The Hungry Spirit* (1997), and *The New Alchemists* (1999) – focus on the importance of the arts in times of structural transformation. To contribute (i.e. by making a difference to the world in some way) is, according to Handy, at the apex of his three-step approach to the search for meaning in life. But before one can start to contribute, one needs to find oneself. Handy believes that the arts provide a way to find oneself. This is a central theme in *The Search for Meaning*, which was first delivered as a keynote London International Festival of Theatre (LIFT) lecture in 1995:

> For me the theatre is a window on the world, as are all the arts. One does not have to be an expert in the theatre or any of the arts in order to get meaning from them. All you have to do is to sit, look, listen and, above all, think.
>
> (Handy 1996: 16)

Two points seem to be implied in Handy's introduction: the unique individual (as spectator) is the focus of attention; and art, through its innate qualities, has the capacity to make one a better person. That works of art can perform a self-help role, or offer a guide to living, is pursued as a theme: 'We need a new dream of society where everyone is enabled to be an artist in this great game of life' (Handy 1996: 66).

This process of self-discovery is based on the notion that everyone is in some way a special artist. Consider the following passage, redolent with spiritual comfort:

> For me the *Resurrection* [by Piero della Francesca] carries a metaphorical meaning rather than a conventional religious one. I am free, goes that message, to break free from my own past and to recreate myself. If I do so, I will be stronger and more sure. Even if my life up to now is counted as a failure by many, as was the life of the man in the painting, the best is yet to come. ... The best is always yet to come if we can rise from our past.
>
> (Handy 1997: 236–4)

There is no need to question the sincerity of Handy's sentiments; however, there is an emphasis on some of the worst excesses of contemporary society. An overtly self-referential perspective is adopted, and based on a simplified solace of immediate self-improvement. What appears to be a return to the mystical power of art might be challenged as a reactionary position; at best, it needs to be viewed with scepticism. Handy can be much more subtle and discerning in his treatment of works of art.

A somewhat quotidian rhetorical ploy is used by Handy to support his desire to see business and the workplace becoming more like theatre. Handy cites the admiration of a corporate manager following a performance by Cirque Plume: "'Why do we have to bribe our people with so much money to work as well as this. Are we missing something?'" (Handy 1996: 72). Many management gurus, as Gibson Burrell notes, use a similar rhetorical trope to identify with the desire of upper management to channel and retain enthusiasm, skill, and adrenalin in the workplace; it is about seeking pleasure in the organization as a means to control producers (Burrell 1992: 69).

What is behind the current experiment in business education with corporate managers learning from the arts? The past few years have seen the growth of slick, multimedia shows, such as Cirque Plume, Cirque de Soleil, De La Guarda, and the Shaolin Wheel of Fire, in which technology is matched with acrobatics to create a new sophisticated form of circus, starring human beings instead of animals. But does Handy idealize the teamwork of arts organizations, and the notion that artists show great skill in the game of life? Two points are raised when one looks below the surface. First, is the principle of the performance fundamentally sound? This is essentially an issue of authenticity and a commitment to aesthetic integrity. Handy's corporate manager may well have made his comments in reference to the Shaolin Wheel of Fire: members of the troupe also perform extraordinary feats with flair and precision. Yet concern has been raised about what is perceived to be an uneasy mixture of ancient tradition and contemporary spectacle. Is there more to the Shaolin monks than circus tricks? Second, participation in making decisions has been challenged as a facet of all arts organizations: 'An orchestra is not a democracy but a dictatorship. The interpretation and presentation of this complex repertoire cannot be pieced together as a kind of consensus among the musicians', according to Henry Mintzberg (1979: 370).

A&B commissioned *A Creative Education*, which seeks to highlight that 'the arts provide rich and varied ways to complement management learning' (Hadfield 2000: 24). The general emphasis is that creativity is not only something creative people do, thus it is a matter of looking at new ways to foster those talents. Several strands of involvement are cited. First, business schools in the UK, including LBS, Cranfield, Henley, and City (Hadfield 2000: Appendix 2), have started to incorporate the inculcation of so-called softer skills, including those associated with the arts and creativity as a means to encourage students to 'think outside the box'. Notions of the leader as performer or conductor emphasize enhancing teamwork roles which are identified with successful companies. Second, in illustrating 'the practical applications of the arts in business' (Hadfield 2000: 13–22), attention is devoted to so-called high culture pursuits (with the inclusion of jazz being a noticeable exception), with generators including institutions of culture (like the Royal Shakespeare Company and the Royal Academy of Arts) and individual artists (e.g. musicians, actors, and poets) operating freelance consultancies. Corporations are represented by businesses associated with A&B (e.g. Orange, Starbucks, and Ernst

& Young). Third, participants, according to examples, are 'senior executives', 'top middle managers', and 'promising employees' (Hadfield 2000: 22, 21, 16); in other words, workers with so-called elite identities.

Creativity needs be applied by the worker to strengthen the commercial objectives of the sponsoring organization. The case study of Halifax working with A&B is revealing:

> Halifax plc are keen to prepare *promising employees* for promotion. Under its Succession Planning Partnership Initiative, these employees, working in partnership with a personnel team, assess their developmental needs against ten *core competencies*. They then participate in project work and study programmes to facilitate their development. They are able to take time from their current roles, but have to demonstrate a *return on investment* through:
>
> • presentation to their Regional General Manager to share their learning;
> • *enhanced performance* on returning to their existing roles.
>
> A programme was developed with Richard Hahlo and Geoffrey Church, from the Royal National Theatre, who use their theatre skills to facilitate this learning.
>
> (Hadfield 2000: 16; my emphasis)

As the Halifax example demonstrates, selecting employees to attend creativity workshops may be viewed as a retention tactic; it also represents a way for the firm to make better use of the intellectual capital and expertise of workers, which is controlled on an individual basis.

That knowledge is now viewed as a primary source of economic productivity offers a partial explanation for the current attention on the arts as offering solutions to business. The theory associated with Howard Gardner (1983), that individuals are made up of multiple intelligences, is viewed as offering a conceptual framework. Gardner is cited by Handy (1996: 60–3), who signals out the importance of 'interpersonal intelligence, the ability to get things done with and through other people', which is to suggest that creativity is linked to managerial leadership. The overall thrust is that intelligences may be developed or improved, hence the case Handy makes for the arts in enhancing and interpersonal intelligence. Daniel Goleman (1996) is credited with coining the term emotional intelligence (EI), an emotional dimension that extends beyond interpersonal skills. He suggests that it is a determining factor in the effectiveness of leaders. As one progresses to more senior levels, emotional intelligence rather than rational intelligence (i.e. raw intelligence as measured by IQ and technical expertise) marks out the successful leader. What still needs to be asked, though, is why 'softer' skills like sensitivity, self-awareness, and integrity are deemed to be wanting in corporate managers. The underlying belief that business is too cold, remains to be addressed. From a more critical perspective, the coercive aspects of emotional intelligence have come under scrutiny (Fineman 1993). Does EI represent another disciplinary mechanism, one that focuses on the social engineering of emotions?

It is not too harsh to view emotional intelligence as yet another management fad. What seems more significant is how the arts have been co-opted to perform a role in staff and organizational development. In particular, there is the implied link between the arts (read as arty-ness) and emotions. This ought to be challenged. It is based on weak and sentimental beliefs regarding the therapeutic value of the arts. For example, consider the responses of literary critic Harold Bloom to an interviewer from the *Harvard Business Review*:

> *Question:* One of the most vexing topics in business is change. What can you learn about change from literature?
>
> *Bloom:* Business people are fooling themselves if they believe that the self can change easily. ...
>
> *Question:* Are you suggesting that through change you become a better person – perhaps more caring, or even more productive?
>
> *Bloom:* No, not at all. ... At the same time, I believe that literature does have a fundamental truth to teach in regard to change: change always arises out of the unexpected. ... By reading great literature, you can prepare yourself for surprise and even get a kind of strength that welcomes and exploits the unexpected.
>
> (Coutu 2001: 67)

Bloom seems to suggest that change from reading literature is not direct; it cannot be exploited in a mechanistic manner as associated with accounting techniques, or guides to good living from pop psychologists.

There is an assumption that the arts are oppositional to sports and science. The arts represent a feminine response, in contrast to other – namely masculine – activities used by management to enhance productivity, including outward bound weekends, and elite athletes on leadership, motivation, stress management, and team dynamics. Whereas the arts are viewed as soft and easy, science is viewed as serious, challenging, and difficult – but not creative. Of course, this represents a fundamental misunderstanding of the artistic process, and minimizes the creativity associated with scientific work.

It is acknowledged that the 'High Aesthete' notion that the glory of art is in its utter uselessness has long gone. Utilitarian mandates are an important part of most aspects of society. From a conventional perspective, capitalism's reverential hat-tipping to the arts – say in the form of building a corporate art collection or by becoming a corporate sponsor – offers a public relations benefit to the commercial enterprise. (Of course, one is able to understand the pressure of arts organizations to chase plural funding sources, and it is an economic necessity of many working artists, musicians, and actors to supplement their artistic incomes.) There is the case that the corporate manager was the cultural hero of the twentieth century. But in many respects, this is not enough. Many corporate managers at the start of the twenty-first century desire to be viewed as cultivated men and women. But is it going too far to expect the arts to actually work for business?

But what are the ties that bind? First, private patrons can shape the aesthetic direction of public institutions. The relationship is not a straightforward one as suggested by the cases of Charles Saatchi and late nineteenth century Montreal collectors. In doing so, there is a material impact on our historical record of taste. Second, the role of the BCA, a lead American lobbying organization, is examined; a critique which draws on Hans Haacke offers a sharp reminder that the arts may be used as a social lubricant to enable business to be conducted. Third, the therapeutic value of the arts is gaining attention from business through promotion by the likes of Charles Handy and the UK's A&B. On the other hand, critics view this engagement as reactionary: it is based on conservative liberal humanist sentiments, and represents another form of social engineering to control workers.

5 Artistic leadership

Arts and cultural organizations need to emphasize a strong commitment to excellence and artistic integrity to be successful beyond the short term. Film maker Woody Allen works outside the world of the major studio system, yet he is not willing to tag along with the 'arty' independents who often fail to secure distribution. This means that Allen seeks distributors (in the USA and Europe) as a precursor to securing financing to see his projects to fruition. Henry Rollins sees his charged performances – over the last two decades as lead singer of Black Flag and, more recently, as a spoken word artist – based on a personal point of view. His success at producing motivated songs owes something to Rollins's decision not to set out to make music and art that is loaded politically.

Controversial ventures arise as non-commercial arts organizations attempt to balance a commitment to an aesthetic mission alongside cultivating revenue-generating projects. The museum shop or restaurant rather than the permanent collection is now the prime destination of a growing cadre of visitors. Consider the retail tentacles of two of London's more prominent fine art venues. Architect Eva Jiricna, who designed the Joseph clothing shop in the late 1970s, was commissioned by the Royal Academy of Arts to revamp its shop. This is not surprising if we think that Rem Koolhaas designs spaces for Prada (New York, Los Angeles, and San Francisco) and the Guggenheim (Las Vegas); likewise Herzog & de Meuron, architects of the Tate Modern, are also employed by Prada (Tokyo); and Renzo Piano, one half of the architectural team responsible for the Pompidou Centre, works with Hermes. These architects have strong signature styles which make shopping more exciting. Making the museum shop more seductive has advantages, according to the Tate Modern's shop manager, who recognizes the role of retail therapy alongside culture: 'We did our own market research and found that people were visiting the shop first, then continuing into the museum' (Rosey Blackmore in the *Financial Times*, 17/18 November 2001). Broadening the selection of merchandise is under way. For example, compact discs produced by MuseumMusic (motto: 'raising revenue with integrity') have been marketed to coincide with exhibitions at several large museums in the USA (including the Museum of Modern Art and the Guggenheim), with the claim that the CDs are related to enhancing one's understanding of the time period of the exhibition.

Aesthetic leadership is essential for conventional high art organizations (like a chamber orchestra); at the same time, the promoters of popular culture aiming at mass audience consumption (such as an entertainment conglomerate) need to consider the role of creativity. Likewise, aesthetic decisions whether high (as with a museum of modern art) or popular (in the case of a budding fashion label) may be charged with socio-political significance. Managing change is examined in two complementary ways: bifurcated management structures emphasize dual executive positions; and Gareth Morgan's term 'imaginization' suggests that the organization is a creative process.

Leading and managing artists

'In simple terms, the overriding priority in the commercial world is the need to make a profit and be good; in the subsidized one, it is the need to be good' (Eyre 1998: Foreword). Yet this seems to devalue the role of individual initiative and enterprise prior to the establishment of arts quangos during the last sixty years. Must artistic excellence and market forces be viewed as oppositional? Are there not distinct advantages for an organization to operate under the banner of private support and public access?

In many respects, the Walt Disney Company and the English Chamber Orchestra have very little in common. Though operating in different environments and on vastly different scales, both organizations offer insights into leading and managing artists. 2001 marked the one hundredth anniversary of Walt Disney's birth. He is celebrated as one of the major brand-builders of the twentieth century, yet the leadership of Michael Eisner, chairman of Disney since 1984, has been instrumental. Disney had been a faltering brand following the death of its founder in 1966. Indeed, Eisner assumed the helm by preventing the break-up of the Disney empire: it was being stalked by an unfriendly suitor, Saul Steinberg, one of the leading corporate raiders of the 1980s, who wanted to sell the studio and keep the theme parks. Disney's value of $85 billion at the end of the twentieth century needs to be viewed against $2 billion when Eisner took over. (Under Eisner, Disney has become a major film studio.) Part of this enhanced equity is due to a pragmatic approach to managing creativity, according to Eisner:

> We are always looking for creative solutions to problems – and solutions that cost less money. Remember we still run a business; art and commerce go together. I often quote Woody Allen saying, 'If show business wasn't a business, it would be called show'. Everything we do must not only be creatively responsible but also fiscally responsible, whether we are talking about an acquisition or a corporate financing or a scene in a movie. And in the end, the most creative and sound solutions will emerge. Finding a solution is, by definition, a creative act.
>
> (Wetlaufer 2000: 117)

With organizational roots dating back to the post-1945 surge in baroque music, the English Chamber Orchestra (ECO) presents an innovative case of artistic entrepreneurship throughout the latter half of the twentieth century. According to Leopold de

Rothschild, founding chairman of the ECO Music Society, 'It is an enterprise governed by market forces and reliant on public demand for the excellence of its musicmaking' (ECO 1983: 9). The vision and ethos of Quintin Ballardie, current artistic director, principal violist, and moving spirit of the ECO, remains steadfast to founding principles as the orchestra celebrated its fortieth year: 'We believe very strongly in free enterprise. It is up to us to make it work and make money, if possible, as well as making great music' (interview with the author). He champions that the ECO should remain 'privately-held'. (The 'private' nature of the ECO creates an obstacle in being eligible to receive public funding. The 'non-distribution' constraint is not maintained: a surplus, if any, may be divided amongst two uses: ploughed back as retained earnings to support the activities of the organization; and/or paid as a dividend to the shareholders. Ballardie draws an annual payment as 'director' equivalent to the salary of an assistant arts administrator; he adds that his main source of income comes as full-time player in the orchestra.) The orchestra has a particular orientation, according to Ballardie:

> It is run on a completely different basis from any other orchestra in the world. The four London symphony orchestras – London Symphony Orchestra, London Philharmonic Orchestra, Royal Philharmonic Orchestra, and The Philharmonia – contract their players and rely heavily on government subsidy. All our players are freelance; we have no such thing as a written contract, though it is understood that they will give the ECO work first call. There is no such thing as public money without strings. We have to produce the best product. I find that pressure stimulating.

Disney is a factory churning out things for people to buy, but surrounded by myth. Uncle Walt, in his studied avuncular persona, promoted himself as a big bee gathering pollen in order to spread it, flower to flower. He invented the job title, 'imagineer', to describe the multi-skilled workers who combined a creative force with engineering know-how to design the original Disney theme park in 1955. A similar perspective is adopted by Eisner who views senior managers as 'editors of other people's work':

> In fact, we consider that our job. We're editors of architects, we're editors of screenwriters, and we're editors of sports shows. We don't just come up with ideas. We listen to other people's ideas, and we tweak them, change them, refine them, and hopefully improve them.
>
> (Wetlaufer 2000: 116)

Eisner believes that the success of Disney owes much to institutionalizing an environment for directed creativity: 'Discipline is part of creativity. ... Discipline is good for the creative process, and time limits are good. An infinite amount of time to do a project does not always make it creatively better' (Wetlaufer 2000: 119). At the same time, Eisner emphasizes the role of 'common sense' (essentially akin to good judgement) but makes a concerted effort to differentiate it from 'audience research':

For some reason, a lot of people in the creative industries think that you should come up with lots of great ideas and then subject them to audience research. But most audience- or customer-research is useless. Exit research is fine, even helpful, and a good thing. Audiences are honest generally on what they have just seen, but prospective research is ridiculous. If you conducted interviews after the movie Titanic came out, everyone would have told you they wanted another movie about a love affair and a sinking ship. But common sense tells you that if you made another movie like that, everyone would say, 'Not again!'

(Wetlaufer 2001: 120)

Guarding the Disney brand is an underlying responsibility for Eisner. For example, animated films, from the era of *Snow White* (1937), have been resurrected with recent successes such as *The Little Mermaid* and *Beauty and the Beast*. So-called 'pencil mileage' may be garnered from animators; moreover, there is a huge windfall from product tie-ins (including theme parks and network and cable television).

Four leadership roles for Disney are identified by Eisner. First, *leading by example* 'also means showing a combination of enthusiasm and loyalty to the institution, and it certainly means demanding excellence in the organization', according to Eisner. Second, *being there* means having contact and exposure and being available. As the organization gets larger, a 'team of leaders' needs to help run the organization. Eisner focuses on the forty people on whom he has an impact every day: 'I'm very available to them. And I try to get out there as much as possible'. Third, *being a nudge* means that 'sometimes all good ideas or good people need is an advocate who won't shut up'. It is about avoiding ideas falling through cracks or getting mired in bureaucracy. Fourth, *being an idea generator* means that the 'leader in a creative business should be creative'. Eisner adds an instructive comment on leadership which places attention on situational analysis:

I have come to the realization that there is no right and wrong with leadership. There is no exact formula. The right style of leadership varies by industry, by person, by the people you are leading. It is unrealistic to think that one leader's way is necessarily the only way.

(Wetlaufer 2001: 124)

The ECO cannot be a role model for all arts organizations, yet there is a great deal to suggest that it offers an alternative path: the orchestra has managed to cultivate an enviable artistic record, with a paramount commitment to national and international excellence in performance, while being able to generate sufficient revenue (in lieu of public subsidy) to remain an ongoing concern. While other arts organizations have engaged in intense competition for arts council recognition and public grants, the ECO is proud to announce a certain independence: 'The orchestra receives no support from the Arts Council of England' (included as part of its programme notes). Through fiscal conservatism, the ECO has focused on staying in business by making great music for its audiences, including having recorded over 1,200 works.

Quintin Ballarie has been described as a 'benevolent despot' with 'incredible energy', 'absolute devotion', and 'fantastic ears for talent'. The role of the musician–entrepreneur is crucial to understanding Ballardie's position at the ECO. With the title of artistic director, he is modest in describing himself: 'I am basically a viola player and I suppose a very good fixer. Those are my real skills, and that is what I enjoy doing'. Ballardie's role as a player – he was the principal viola of the London Philharmonic Orchestra between 1963 and 1971 at the same time as principal viola of the ECO – means that 'there is no "them and us" feeling in the ECO: I am "them", I am the chap who runs the show, but I am also one of "us"'. It goes without saying – but needs noting – that the ECO cannot help but reflect some of the cantankerous entrepreneurial spirit, disposition, and independence of its founder. Indeed, Ballardie's strong views on running an orchestra run counter to many assumptions regarding job security, participatory decision-making, and government subsidies.

First, Ballardie is not a conductor. Unlike most chamber orchestras established and maintained by conductors to further their careers, according to Ballardie, the ECO does not exist to further his cultural ambitions as a conductor. (The performance record of the orchestra also indicates that the orchestra has not been used to highlight Ballardie as a solo violist.) Yet as an unabashed cultural entrepreneur, Ballardie takes credit for the overall success of the orchestra, including the appointment of players. (As part of its status as a full-time orchestra, the ECO has first call on a specific set of musicians, who are appointed by Ballardie.) 'A good ear at picking the talent', according to Ballardie, is his most important skill. Indeed Ballardie is 'old school', stressing that he has no management background; what he knows about orchestral management was learned on the job, including skills developed as a manager of orchestras for theatrical productions in London's West End.

Second, the players do not have full-time contracts with the ECO, which is to say that they are self-employed musicians. Whereas in many instances, the hand of the accountant forces such a decision, Ballardie recognizes the central role of the players: 'An orchestra is the sum of its musicians, and this applies especially to a small ensemble of the ECO's calibre. Many members of the orchestra are distinguished chamber and concert soloists in their own right'. This implies two things: that the ECO is an ensemble of possibilities, with the contribution of each player having an impact on the overall quality of the performance; and that the ECO is confident enough in its retention capability to support its players – independent of their association with the orchestra – in developing solo careers and forming small ensembles (such as woodwind quintets, trios, and the like). Even though the players are not bound to the ECO by contract – about thirty are needed for a typical performance – they are willing to allow the orchestra to have first call on loyalty. The payment of 'good fees' provides a financial incentive; performing with some of the world's finest musicians and conductors is also important. (According to Pauline Gilbertson, the ECO's administrative director, fees offered by the orchestra are not exceptional – the top end of the BBC Symphony Orchestra range is £30,000 per annum – but higher than the London average and well above the promulgated Musicians' Union rates for engagements.)

London's position as one of several international centres of music, essentially an issue of clustering, means that the ECO is able to draw on a rich pool of talent.

Third, the ECO is not democratic in that it does not operate with a player's board for collective decision-making. 'In an ideal world', according to Ballardie,

> it is right that an orchestra should be self-governing; however, there are just too many problems. After all, why should players, artists in their own right, be saddled with responsibilities many of which they are not trained to cope with. I find that they appreciate someone who will not only take care of them but also take the very difficult decisions which are needed from time to time. They want to be able to moan and groan and blame someone, and I suppose I fulfil that function. All I know is that I admire and respect beyond measure their collective ability.

Empathy is included in Ballardie's toolkit: as a player he feels confident in recognizing the particular problems facing fellow players; there is also the sense of a shared experience as he experiences the highs and lows with the other musicians on stage.

Fourth, the artistic direction has remained in the ECO's hands under the general direction of Ballardie. Artistic activities have to pay: owing to a lack of public subsidy, private sponsorship assumes greater importance. This provides a certain amount of commercial pressure but it also offers Ballardie freedom to see the orchestra develop in a way based on artistic possibilities offered by the players. For example, the orchestra has just started its third 'permanent' relationship with a conductor, Ralf Gothóni. Prior to his appointment, the music critic of the *Financial Times* (12 May 2000) noted the good fit:

> Gothóni first conducted the orchestra in Finland in 1997, and what began as love-at-first-sight seems to be developing into a long-term affair. Their London concert eighteen months ago suggested a partnership made in heaven, as the orchestra responded to Gothóni's inspirational direction with playing that transcended questions of style or authenticity.

Gothóni succeeded Jeffrey Tate, who was conductor between 1985 and 2000; and there was a brief relationship in 1961 with a young Colin Davis. During the period of three decades when the orchestra was without a principal conductor, the ECO relied on a succession of three leaders (Emanuel Hurwitz, Kenneth Sillito, and José-Luís García) who took an enormous amount of responsibility for maintaining and developing the orchestra's style and standards; at present, Paul Barritt and Stephanie Gonley serve as co-leaders.

Extra-aesthetics

Aesthetic choices may also include non-aesthetic concerns, which is to suggest that artistic production is never conducted in a vacuum. Art can get dragooned into cultural service. Two divergent New York 'brands'; Fubu (For Us By Us) and MoMA, illustrate how artistic decisions can represent wider socio-political concerns. Fubu was founded in the early 1990s by four African-American friends (Daymond John, Keith Perrin, Carl Brown, and J. Alexander Martin) as an urban sportswear label. The name refers to the core audience and the perception that it has largely been ignored. (Indeed, Fubu had to confront the belief of many financial organizations that black designers cannot design for a mainstream audience.) Like the rap group, Run DMC – but without an Aerosmith in the wings – Fubu is using aspects of 'black' popular culture to cross America's fraught colour divide. As such, Fubu is being described as the first black global lifestyle brand on a scale comparable to Calvin Klein, Ralph Lauren, and Tommy Hilfiger. Founded in 1929, MoMA is considered by many as the single most important institution devoted to the history of twentieth-century art. Yet an account of MoMA's administrative history cannot avoid its role in a wider ideological battle with communism. 'The American Century' was a phrase coined by *Time* publisher, Henry Luce, in a 1941 warmongering editorial. Though a journalistic conceit, it did support the American government's propaganda war interests. A case has been put forward that MoMA showed a readiness to create exhibitions – 'Road to Victory' (1942), 'Airways to Peace' (1943), and 'Power in the Pacific' (1945) were essentially extended magazine-style photo essays – to celebrate the military defence and the American way of life (Staniszewski 1998).

Some will read Fubu in contrast to Tommy Hilfiger. Hilfiger attempts to paint a multicultural American society dressed in clothing conventionally called 'preppy' (i.e. associated with rich East Coast families in the USA as depicted in Eric Segal's *Love Story*, or the photographs of Tina Barney). It has been suggested that Hilfiger represents a 'Mayonnaise Boy' attitude:

[A]n instant candidate for the White Studies canon, [Hilfiger's book] *All American* is one long 'Miles Davis wore khakis' ad, except Hilfiger would prefer Chet Baker modeling his chinos. Hilfiger is so white he earnestly offers Mister Rogers as a fashion plate for the American sweater.
(Andrew Hultkrans in Artforum's *Bookforum*, Spring 1998)

This is to suggest that replica clothing is offered, but none of the other trappings of a preppy lifestyle (including admission to an Ivy League university). In contrast, according to a profile in the *Financial Times* (weekend magazine, 5 May 2001), 'Fubu's strength is its authenticity. It has come from the street, both in design and business terms, and is driven less by corporate strategy than the needs of its consumers'. Guerrilla tactics (such as painting the Fubu logo, as a form of graffiti art, on store shutters) were used to generate attention in the early days. The endorsement of rapper LL Cool J was a crucial link to the music's hip-hop culture. (Celebrity endorsers include Busta Rhymes, Puff Daddy, Marieh Carey, Janet Jackson, Will Smith, and Lennox Lewis.) With an estimated turnover of $350 million in 2000, Fubu is appealing to a cool edge associated with black culture, according to the publisher of leading African-American-oriented magazines:

Daymond and the others have a passion for what they do and for their culture. But their skill is in seeing that as inclusive and understanding that aesthetic has widespread appeal. It's no understatement to say that they really are one of the greatest success stories for the black American brands. Fubu is up there with Motown, for instance. And as urban culture expands – it is being embraced worldwide, from sports to Eminem – it too will be embraced.

(Kieth Clinkscales in the *Financial Times*, 5 May 2001)

Fubu has to address what is a reversal of Hilfiger selling preppy wear to disaffected urban youth: Norman Mailer called it 'wigga', a somewhat vulgar term he coined in 1957 to describe the appropriation of African-American culture by white youths. (Jazz of 1920s Harlem represented an earlier signal of the allure of black culture. The pastiche character 'Ali G' was a late 1990s example of this phenomenon in the UK).

Extending the original urban sportswear line to include upmarket segments (e.g. Lady Fubu and Fubu Tuxedo) plus children's clothing, loungewear, and accessories (including perfumes) is only part of the ambitions of the co-founders. Fubu has grander sights on being an entertainment brand, namely co-producing television and music videos and establishing a record label. The vernacular phrase 'keeping it real' will be the most difficult challenge for a firm established with such high-mind ('for us by us') credentials. As John puts it: 'In terms of maintaining that Fubu intimacy, well that's going to be hard' (*Financial Times*, 5 May 2001).

There is the case that during the cold war, MoMA helped to articulate the deeply-cherished values defended by liberal democracies in the face of perceived communist attacks. In a revisionist interpretation, Serge Guilbaut (1983) examined the convergence of modernist painting – Abstract Expressionism, as the dominant style of the American avant-garde – and the propagandist requirements of a post-1945 American hegemony. His work was informed by the Marxist-inspired critique of Duncan and Wallach (1978) that MoMA may be viewed as a masculine museum space, given the focus on the artist as hero and that stylistic progression means that new artistic intentions require new methods. MoMA's story of modernism accentuates an eventual triumphalism: Cezanne is posited as the father of a properly internationalist, modernist painting; progress in painting is represented by the work of Picasso; and Jackson Pollock 'accomplished an extraordinary alchemy whereby drawing, pushed to an extreme of density and elaboration, crossed over (just) into painting' (Crow 1999: 94). MoMA's point is to emphasize Abstract Expressionism, an American product, as a heroic movement.

Superbly illustrative of the American ideals of the arts in support of freedom and democracy was the MoMA address by President Eisenhower:

To me, in this [twenty-fifth] anniversary, there is a reminder to all of us an important principle that we should ever keep in mind. This principle is that freedom of the arts is a basic freedom, one of the pillars of liberty in our land. For our Republic to stay free, those among us with the rare gift of artistry must be able freely to use their talent. Likewise, our people must have an unimpaired opportunity to see, to understand, to profit from our artists' work. As long as artists are at liberty to feel with high personal intensity, as long as our artists are free to create with sincerity and conviction, there will be a healthy controversy and progress in art. Only thus can there be an opportunity for a genius to conceive and to produce a masterpiece for all mankind.

But, my friends, how different it is in tyranny. When artists are made the slaves and tools of the state; when artists become chief propagandists of a cause, progress is arrested and creation and genius are destroyed.

(MoMA 1954: 3)

Eisenhower's words, an example of cold war propaganda, were grounded in a fundamental aversion to central authority and the belief that state intervention should be limited. As the country where capitalism is most ideologically secure, the model of a free enterprise exchange economy extends to the arts; and MoMA reciprocated with the 1955 exhibition, 'The Family of Man', a statement of the universality of the American-style family (Staniszewski 1998). Indeed, Pop artists like Andy Warhol, representing post-Pollock artistic production, were able to elaborate a faith in the openness of the American life in terms supplied by consumer culture. Of course, it is ironic that the American distrust of a closer relationship between the arts and politics has not excluded a direct and active part of the role of government in promoting American art abroad; indeed throughout the cold war, the arts were considered a valuable tool in foreign policy.

In response to a changed (political) environment, including the cultural franchising strategy of the Guggenheim, a competitor institution, MoMA has embarked on two complementary initiatives. MoMA has established a 'programmatic alliance' with P.S.1, New York's largest alternative space. The exhibition 'Greater New York' (2000) was the first collaboration between the two institutions: thirty curators attempted a detailed map of New York art life, with painting, video, photography, and new media side-by-side; moreover, invited artists were drawn from those who have gained prominence since 1995 and those who have yet to gain public recognition. The P.S.1–MoMA partnership invites two commercial analogies: it represents a form of backward integration by MoMA to gain greater control of the overall production process; it is not unlike a venture capitalist taking an equity stake in an innovative start-up. It signals MoMA's desire to show a commitment to contemporary art; moreover, it allows a multidisciplinary approach to be included in order to counter the increasingly problematic linear story of modernism, as told by MoMA. For its part, P.S.1 gets MoMA's fund-raising acumen. According to MoMA's director, the partnership with P.S.1 makes MoMA more competitive:

The atmosphere for museums has become extremely competitive and there is enormous pressure to find the resources to differentiate oneself. ... I believe in competition. It forces you to do your best. It's good for the public. It offers the maximum number of choices. But this is a unique moment. Logic says things have to shift. And any institution focusing on money rather than on a quality collection and programming won't survive.

(Glenn Lowry in *Art in America*, June 1999)

The current expansion project, to be completed in 2005, includes creating 50 per cent more gallery space. 'MoMA Builds' is about enhancing the institution's identity and reputation, according to the director:

> Throughout its history, [MoMA] has used architecture as a vehicle for self-renewal and regeneration. With this building project, the Museum undertakes the most extensive redefinition of itself since its founding over seventy years ago. The timing could not be more appropriate, for MoMA's mission demands that we traverse the twenty-first century with the same confidence and boldness that we did the twentieth.

Bifurcated management structures

Management structures can influence the direction of arts organizations. What values are represented? Bifurcated management structures exist in many diverse types of organizations. The French talk of 'co-habitation', when the president and prime minister represent political parties of different ideological stripes. University halls of residence in England often have a bursar in charge of management, with a warden responsible for welfare and pastoral care; if residents liken the bursar to an 'iron fist', the warden is the 'velvet glove'. To have dual executive roles is the assumed practice in many art music organizations. For example, Quintin Ballardie is artistic director of the English Chamber Orchestra; Pauline Gilberston is administrative director. The Metropolitan Opera has Joseph Volpe as general manager; conductor Joseph Levine is in charge of music. However, a paid president in the top administrative position working alongside a director with authority over aesthetic (i.e. curatorial) matters, has been interpreted as a fundamental reorganization of the museum hierarchy. Following the retirement of Thomas Hoving, as director in 1977, the Met decided to adopt a bifurcated management structure. At the time, a number of prominent museum people were opposed to bifurcation, arguing in the main that there ought to be *one* chief executive, who progressed through the curatorial ranks. According to the then director of the Cleveland Museum of Art:

> It's a misapplication of quite different thinking into an area that is quite different by philosophy and by purpose from a business enterprise. ... The fastest way to destroy art is to make it like everything else, homogenize it, make it part of the profit-making setup.
>
> (Sherman Lee in *Artnews*, October 1977)

The appointment of Philippe de Montebello, as director, has not seen populism materialize, given his views on museum management:

> We do not compete with Disney theme parks, with rock concerts. We would be silly to do so. There always has been a solid core audience for high culture.

I don't think it has diminished. Its expectations are different from those who enjoy popular culture, who seek quick fixes and instant gratification.

(*Financial Times*, 1/2 December 2001)

Indeed many do not realize that the Met even has a president.

With the notable exceptions of the Met, MoMA, and the Philadelphia Museum of Art (from 1982 to 1997) bifurcation has not taken root in the USA; moreover, there has not been a move towards turning over the top post to a 'corporate' business manager. Italy has given new legal status as foundations or nonprofit organizations to formerly state-controlled institutions. Pompeii is a case in point: the superintendent, a career professional charged with protecting archaeological heritage, now works with a city manager. There was a short-lived, albeit animated, attempt at the British Museum with a 'managing director' (Suzanna Taverne) hired to work alongside the director (Robert Anderson). Taverne, with substantial experience in merchant banking and media, was hired in 1999 to offer additional management and financial support to the director, but when it emerged, in 2001, that she would not be appointed director upon Anderson's retirement, she decided to leave the institution. Selective excerpts of an interview Taverne gave to the London *Sunday Times* (9 September 2001) have been quoted with relish: 'There is this priesthood of curators, who look after the relics. There's this notion that only they can be the intermediaries between the relics and the public. They carry this sacred flame of the institution – the museum'; she went on to comment on the photos of the British Museum's past museum directors, 'Look at them. All white males'. A manager-scholar, Neil MacGregor, director of the National Gallery, was appointed as the new director of the British Museum. Viewed as a talented museum curator, MacGregor has a record in raising money and mounting crowd-pleasing exhibitions.

Finding the right person for senior posts is increasingly difficult given the combination of skills desired by arts organizations. For example, it is a rare prize to find a major dancer with professional management training. In the museum world, the Museum Management Institute was established in 1978 (by the American Association of Museums and the University of California, Berkeley) to offer an intensive summer residential course designed for mid- to senior-level museum professionals to develop and apply their managerial capabilities and leadership skills more effectively. Admission requirements – including at least five years of full-time museum experience and currently in a position involving direct responsibility for planning, decision-making, and supervising staff and sponsorship by the candidate's museum as evidence of its commitment – are consistent with 'criterion for entry to management education' namely 'proven success in managerial work' gained by 'intensive experience within at least one industry, preferably one organization, so that the knowledge base is deep', as set by Henry Mintzberg (1989: 83).

'Imaginization'

Gareth Morgan adopts an anti-mechanistic approach to exploring organizations. What he labels 'imaginization' – a combination of 'imagination' and 'organization' (with no reference to Disney's 'imagineering') – encourages one to become a skilled interpreter of actual situations (a form of reflective practice), and serves as a mode of personal empowerment and an approach to change:

> [It] seeks to mobilize the potential for understanding and transformation that rests within each and every one of us. It seeks to challenge taken-for-granted ways of thinking and, in the process, open and broaden our ability to act in new ways.
>
> (Morgan 1993: 276)

'Imaginization' builds on the principle that people and organizations tend to get trapped by images that they hold of themselves and that genuine change requires an ability to see and challenge self-images in some way. Two images are striking: 'strategic termites' and 'spider plants'.

Strategic termites are managers who seek to generate major organizational change in difficult situations. Strategic termites have clear aspirations about what they would like to achieve, but work in an open-ended manner. Like termites, they are opportunistic in their approach to change; they are strategic in the sense that decisions and actions are always guided by an overall sense of purpose and direction. Strategic termites are viewed as valued managers within organizations as they 'create substantial change by making small, significant changes that attract interest and attention of those immediately involved, allowing the character of the new organization to emerge' (Morgan 1993: 52). Consider the example of (now Sir) Nicholas Serota, who was appointed as director of the Tate Gallery in 1988. Given his previous experience, based on exhibiting contemporary art (at Oxford's Museum of Modern Art and the Whitechapel Art Gallery in London) without responsibilities associated with a permanent collection, Serota's first major project was the re-hang of the permanent collection:

> It is important that when you come to the Tate and look at twentieth century art, you should be conscious of the fact that you are in London and not in Paris or New York: that is to say I think people come hoping that they will see how British art plays a part in the broad story of international twentieth century art. I think that the re-hanging has helped to reinforce the part that British artists have played, not so much in the sense of coming third in the race, but in the sense of the interchange of ideas across the Channel or across the Atlantic, or now back across the Channel. We are an island and it is very interesting to see how artists have reacted to what is happening in continental Europe and America.
>
> (Serota in Papadakis 1991: 92)

The now 'annual' re-hang of the permanent collection under the banner 'New Displays' was initiated in 1990 with sponsorship from British Petroleum. The aim was 'to break the rigid divisions between British and Foreign, Historic and Modern' which had formed. Space limitations were addressed in an innovative manner; Serota was afforded a marketing opportunity to re-launch the permanent collection each year (treating it like a temporary exhibition). Furthermore, the political purpose of the re-hang was recognized from the start by informed observers: 'By making such grand and generous use of available space, it argues the absolute necessity for the building of a new and separate gallery wholly devoted to modern art' (McEwen 1990: 61). The re-hang may be read as the opening salvo by Serota of his goal to have two Tate sites in London, which was realized in 2000: the Tate Modern at Bankside was opened; and the site at Millbank re-fashioned as Tate Britain. Serota suggested as much at the time of the first re-hang: 'Waiting for the new buildings would simply take too long ... ' (McEwen 1990: 46). (Not all attention is focused on the Tate Modern, given that the annual Turner Prize, to recognize contemporary British artists, remains at the Tate Britain.)

As an image, spider plants are used to represent the desire of organizations to be more flexible and innovative. The umbilical cord (like those of a spider plant) serves to reconcile the contradictory demands of creating decentralizations while supporting accountability and control. Decentralization offers local units power and autonomy for some kind of self-organizing activity; at the same time, a measure of central control is retained. Consider the example of the Pittsburgh Symphony Orchestra (PSO) which has adopted *hoshin* (the 'shining needle' that points the way), a management process from Japan designed to make decision-making more democratic (see the *Financial Times*, 27/28 May 2000). In 1997, the PSO faced a shortage of cash and the management found itself unable to accommodate a new trade agreement that the musicians found acceptable. A board member first mooted *hoshin* as a possible solution to money and management problems. With the support of the managing director, Gideon Toeplitz, and the then incoming music director, Mariss Jansons, a *hoshin* retreat was organized with the PSO's main constituencies: musicians, administrative staff, volunteers, and board members. Musicians gain input to board decisions; volunteers develop closer relations with staff and management; board members get to know the musicians they have been listening to; and management gets input from all sides. Essentially a process of democratization, the *hoshin* process seeks to bring together groups that would normally operate independently, to set common goals and to help each other work towards them. According to Toeplitz, 'Looking back, the biggest change we had to go through was giving up some control. For managers like us, this is very, very difficult to do'. Questions remain. Is *hoshin* part of a list of Japanese management techniques (e.g. *keiretsu*, just-in-time, quality circles, business process reengineering) adopted with varying degrees of success outside of Japan? *Hoshin* replicates aspects associated with the Japanese production system, namely a learning system that focuses on continual improvement with workers assigned to 'activity clusters' arranged to harness the knowledge of all in the organization. Are facets of the Japanese model appropriate at the start of the twenty-first century? How democratic can an orchestra be?

Artistic leadership emphasizes winning and awards success. Arts managers need to act as facilitators, conduits in the creation of cultural products. This includes working with artists. Disney's Michael Eisner describes it as editing other people's work, and puts across a case for discipline in managing creativity. Quintin Ballardie, of the English Chamber Orchestra, thinks of himself as a good fixer, someone who runs the show but is also one of the players. Yet even successful organizations may not be viewed as following a straightforward agenda. There are affiliations between cultural products and society; however, the process of creation is not a mirroring role. Fashion brand Fubu internalizes a black American aesthetic; this core focus has been widened like hip-hop music in order to attract more diverse audiences. MoMA as an influential institution, serving as a model of a museum of modern art and shaping the history of modern art, has been used in America's ideological battle against communism.

The management truism, 'change is the only constant', applies to arts organizations. An aesthetic leader with management skills is a coveted individual. Adopting a bifurcated management structure, with dual executive positions, is one alternative solution. 'Imaginization' concepts associated with Gareth Morgan are examined: the (now annual) 'New Displays' exhibition was initiated by Nicholas Serota, who sought to generate organizational change at the Tate Gallery; and *hoshin* represents an example of the Pittsburgh Symphony Orchestra's desire to be more flexible and innovative.

6   Strategic positioning and brand identity

There are four guidelines to communicating an effective campaign, according to adman par excellence, David Ogilvy (1983: 11–18). First, do your homework by studying the product (or experience) you are about to market. What business are you in? What is the basic character of the institution? How does the institution set itself apart from other organizations? The more you know about it and the positioning strategies of competitors, the more likely you can come up with the so-called 'big idea': something that consumers want that competitors do not offer. Second, 'what the product does, and who it is for' is the essence behind positioning. Third, image is associated with personality: 'Products, like people, have personalities, and they can make or break them in the marketplace'. Fourth, use the above steps to create the 'big idea' (or 'unique selling proposition').

In many respects, Ogilvy was addressing the intersection of strategy and marketing. Auction house Bonhams (www.bonhams.com) is, at the start of the twenty-first century, the brand created by the merger of Bonhams & Brooks with Phillips in the UK. The luxury brands firm LVMH, one of France's largest companies, purchased Phillips in 1999. Bernard Arnault wants Phillips to be on a par with Sotheby's and Christie's. (Of course, Arnault looks at his overall performance against how well LVMH is doing against Richemont, another French luxury brands house, which includes Cartier.) Bonhams in the UK has a reputation of being a British-oriented firm with a strong regional network of salesrooms handling low- and medium-priced antiques. Owing to traditional links to solicitors and estate agents, there has been a perception that estate sales of the middle classes form a core segment; this also means that the opportunity to sell a seven-digit oil on canvas is rare, with the two leading firms carving up the high-priced end of the market. Bonhams seeks to present itself as 'a fresh and highly credible alternative within the international auction market' (advertisement in the *V&A Magazine*, January/April 2002). Does that make a strong statement about Bonhams's personality? Is a big idea or positioning statement discernible from the following self-declaration: 'So, while we may currently be the third largest, we should be the first choice'?

Three points of reference are highlighted. Strategy as positioning, which is influenced by marketing, draws on the work of Michael Porter, who seeks to analyze the ways in which firms compete. Economic clustering encapsulates cities and creativity: issues of wealth creation are important, but innovation also enhances the social fabric of urban living. Branding is assuming what appears to be mythic power. The role of the identity premium is instructive. Recent ruminations at the V&A draw attention to the links between institutional identity and national identity.

Strategy as position

As a management function, strategy (e.g. corporate strategy, strategic management) stresses a senior management perspective. Military connotations (e.g. the slogan 'business is war'; and so-called tribal chants of high-wage earners like 'wonga, wonga, wonga') are rife, with particular reference to Sun Tzu's sixth century BC text translated as *The Art of War* and Carl von Clausewitz's *On War* (1816–30; original German). It is only since the 1960s, with the likes of Igor Ansoff (1965) and Alfred Chandler (1962), that strategy has been articulated within a management context. Like Ansoff and Chandler, Michael Porter is based at the Harvard Business School. Other contemporary management writers on strategy include Henry Mintzberg, Gary Hamel and C. K. Prahalad, and John Kay.

Strategic management textbooks contain Michael Porter's models, theories, and frameworks. Porter is one of the most recognizable figures associated with management strategy, with convenient 'decision-aids' like three generic strategies, five forces (for analyzing competition and industry structure), and the value chain. In many respects, Porter's texts, which are used to train management students, impress upon future managers the need to design competitive strategies that preserve organizational autonomy while keeping price competition to a minimum. In particular, Porter posits 'strategy as position'. This is most apparent in *Competitive Strategy* (1980), a watershed text that met the needs of academics and managers. It cut across many management disciplines – namely marketing but also production, control, and finance – to offer a relatively holistic view of the entire firm.

Three generic strategies available to firms in order to outperform industry rivals are: overall cost leadership (i.e. having a cost structure lower than competitors), differentiation (i.e. creating an offering that is perceived *industrywide* as being unique), and focus (i.e. serving a particular target very well), according to Porter. How should the firm position itself *vis-à-vis* competitors in its chosen market(s)? What audiences are to be served? According to Porter, firms unable to adopt one of the stated generic strategies will find that they are 'stuck in the middle'; at best they will 'muddle through', while being vulnerable and susceptible to better-positioned competitors:

> The firm stuck in the middle is almost guaranteed low profitability. It either loses the high-volume customers who demand low prices or must bid away its profits to get this business away from low-cost firms. Yet it also loses high-margin business – the cream – to firms who are focused on the high-margin targets or have achieved differentiation overall. The firm stuck in the middle also probably suffers from a blurred corporate culture; a conflicting set of organizational arrangements and motivation systems.
>
> (Porter 1980: 33)

This suggests that a clearly articulated position is a necessary first step to success.

Moreover, in *Competitive Strategy*, Porter proffers five competitive forces as an instructive introduction of how to consider micro-level factors shaping the competitive structure of an industry: intensity of industry competition, bargaining powers of buyers, bargaining power of suppliers, degree of substitutes, and entry and exit barriers. 'The underlying structure of an industry, reflected in the strength of the forces, should be distinguished from many short-run factors that can affect competition and profitability in a transient way' (Porter 1980: 6). Consider media and entertainment conglomerates such as Disney, AOL Time Warner, News Corporation, Pearson, and Bertelsmann. Capital costs to enter are relatively high and oligopolistic tendencies are prevalent so that most entertainment industry segments come to be ruled by large companies with relatively easy access to large pools of capital. Marketing expenditures per unit are high, which highlights the importance of marketing to generating revenue streams. Ancillary markets provide disproportionately large returns (e.g. the initial theatrical release of a film is becoming less significant a source for overall revenue when examined alongside revenue from cable and home videos, and merchandising associated with character licences). Strong popular appeal is crucial if a vehicle is to generate revenue. Searching for universal appeal helps to account for the abundance of action flicks starring well-known actors or actresses.

Within each industry, there are clusters or groups of firms competing in a similar manner. The firm's level of success is determined not only by the industry in which the firm operates, but also the strategic cluster in which it competes. The concept of 'positioning' becomes important as it implies a frame of reference, that of competitors and consumers. Positioning decisions are crucial: they can have an impact on perception and choice decisions. Positioning starts with a product, according to Reis and Trout (1981), and then focuses on what is created in the minds of customers. Positioning is about the image of the product in the minds of the selected target group *vis-à-vis* competing firms. Who are the primary and secondary competitors? How are the competitors perceived and evaluated? Are the differences significant and meaningful? Analyze customers by trying to get a deeper understanding of their perceptions. Selecting the position usually requires a segmentation commitment (i.e. it is necessary to concentrate only on certain segments). Monitoring is important: a positioning objective should be measurable; and it is important to track the positioning strategy over time in order to generate diagnostic information about future positioning strategies.

Positioning strategies operate on various dimensions. *The Producers*, a Broadway production based on the film by Mel Brooks, opened in 2001 with retail prices in excess of $100. The high price was a signal of quality, a correlation promoted by many branded products. David-to-Goliath positioning is used when a smaller competitor wants to promote itself as innovative. The English National Opera, with productions sung in English, cheaper ticket prices, and a more informal code of conduct, has been likened in the *Wall Street Journal* (10/11 September 1999) to the NASDAQ stock market (listing many fast-growing technology firms), in comparison to the New York Stock Exchange of its more established rival at Covent

Garden. As another opera example, Pegasus accentuates a particular feature as intimated by the subtitle 'harmony in diversity': it bills itself as the only multi-racial opera company in the UK.

Additionally, Porter (1985) proposes the 'value chain' as a tool to appraise the firm's capability to create a differential advantage. The value chain identifies nine relevant activities that create value and incur costs: *primary* activities represent the sequence of bringing materials into the firm (inbound logistics), converting them into final products (operations), shipping out the products (outbound logistics), marketing them (marketing and sales), and serving them (service); and *support* activities – procurement, technology development, human resources management, and infrastructure – sustain the ability of the firm to conduct its primary activities. The central task of management is to improve the firm's value chain by reducing the costs of these activities or improving their performance. The value chain is built on a traditional notion of industry with flows through various stages in a sequential process, each adding value until the consumer is finally reached.

The presumed value of Porter's work is that it forces senior managers to think about the overall competitive position of their firm. Yet the body of work on strategic planning (including Porter's contribution) has come under attack: it causes 'managers to confuse real vision with the manipulation of numbers. And this confusion lies at the heart of the issue: the most successful strategies are visions, not plans', according to Henry Mintzberg (1994: 107). Strategic thinking is about synthesis and involves intuition and creativity (Mintzberg 1994: 108). Many successful firms invariably began with ambitions that were well out of proportion to their resources and capabilities. The essence of winning, which is about establishing shared values beyond the short term, depends on 'managers with a committing style who engage people in a journey' (Mintzberg 1994: 109).

Asset and competence-based strategies gained popularity throughout the 1990s. Gary Hamel and C. K. Prahalad have taken a broad swipe at strategy writing of the 1970s and 1980s:

> As 'strategy' has blossomed the competitiveness of Western companies has withered. This may be a coincidence, but we think not. We believe that the application of concepts such as 'strategic fit' (between resources and opportunities), 'generic strategies' (low cost vs. differentiation vs. focus), and 'strategy hierarchies' (goals, strategies, tactics) have often abetted the process of competitive decline.
>
> (Hamel and Prahalad 1994: 100)

They have promoted 'strategic intent' and 'core competencies' as essential if a firm is to be competitive (see Hamel and Prahalad 1994). John Kay, one of the few European writers on management strategy to have reached the first rank, proffers 'distinctive capabilities' as characteristics other firms lack; moreover, distinctive capabilities are sustainable (i.e. persist over time) and appropriable (i.e. exclusively or principally benefit the company which holds it). Distinctive capabilities fall into three categories: innovation, architecture, and reputation. First, *innovation* is an obvious source but is often less sustainable or appropriable as imitation can be attracted. Interactive technologies (e.g. on-site devices or web-sites) are seldom proprietary. Second, *architecture* refers to the set of relationships with donors and sponsors, for example. The shift from fund-raising to fund (or friend) development places the stress on creating a constituency in which the donor sees supporting the arts organization as a form of self-fulfilment. Third, *reputation*, which is easier to maintain than create, may be viewed as the transformation of an initial distinctive capability based on innovation or architecture. Thus, distinctive capabilities derived from reputation are considered more enduring ones.

Positioning remains important to Porter's understanding of strategy even in light of criticisms that it is too static for today's dynamic markets and changing technology. He reiterates early pronouncements: 'The generic strategies remain useful to characterize strategic positions at the simplest and broadest levels' (Porter 1996: 67). Strategy is distinguished from operational effectiveness, with strong leaders willing to make difficult trade-offs crucial to successful positioning.

Creativity, cities, and clustering

City life remains one of the great cultural legacies of modernity. It goes without saying that each modern city has its own unique loci: one needs to explore the cultural depths extending beyond buildings and streets. A wide range of services 'once regarded as unserious and even effete' may be harnessed to serve as 'diverse sources of innovation', according to Peter Hall, in his preface to *The Creative City* (Landry and Bianchini 1995). The socio-economic argument linking creativity, cities, and clustering appears to be quite straightforward. The current usage of creative industries (in the UK) includes the conventional arts alongside advertising, architecture, design, film, publishing, software development, and television and radio. These knowledge-intensive sectors of the economy are often based in cities, such that the creative city 'emphasizes the new, progress and continual change' (Landry and Bianchini 1995: 11). Clusters are represented by 'critical masses – in one place – of unusual competitive success in particular fields' (Porter 1998: 78).

However, some disentanglement is needed. What does it mean to be 'creative'? Raymond Williams includes it as an original keyword having both 'serious and trivial senses':

> The difficulty arises when a word once intended, and often still intended, to embody a high and serious claim, becomes so conventional, as a description of certain kinds of activity, that it is applied to practices for which, in the absence of the convention, nobody would think of making such claims.
>
> (Williams 1983: 84)

Works of artistic activity, as a dominant reading of culture, include art music, literature, painting and sculpture, theatre, and film. At the same time, Williams cites, for example, that advertising copywriters officially describe themselves as creatives; however, this widening of the keyword is not unproblematic: ' ... a description of everything of this kind as creative can be confusing and at times seriously misleading' (Williams 1983: 84). This is a theme of advertising examined in a dictionary of modern thought: the creativity used by advertisers must be

> instant attention-getting, resulting in a glibness or lateral cleverness ... [and] is exposed as a new form of post-war sloganeering; [moreover, the advertising industry has established] a plethora of self-aggrandizing award festivals, locally and internationally, at which 'creatives' award each other glittering prizes to celebrate the quality of their creative thinking.
>
> (Bullock and Trombley 1999: 11)

Of course, commercial firms may be creative. Alessi views itself as one of the 'factories of Italian design' (Alessi 1998: 7). The blending of manufacturing and art at a high level of accomplishment means that Alessi is considered a leader in applied arts and industrial design. With particular reference to household articles, Alessi has had celebrated collaborations including Michael Graves, *Kettle with Bird* (1985); Philippe Starck, *Juicy Salif* (lemon squeezer, 1990); and Alessandra Mendini, *Anna G* (corkscrew, 1994).

'Proximity – the collocation of companies, customers, and suppliers – amplifies all of the pressures to innovate and upgrade', according to Porter (1998: 90). Why do more regions have more enterprise clusters than others? Clustering may develop naturally because of intrinsic advantages found in a region. Some regions may provide more fertile ground for enterprise development because of the presence of an enterprise culture or a more favourable institutional framework. The size of clusters is limited by the size of the market, which may be limited by the national market if there are barriers to international trade.

Clusters affect competition in three broad ways (Porter 1998). First, being part of a cluster increases the *productivity* of firms based in the area. Firms are offered better access to employees and suppliers. Second, clusters can help to drive the direction and pace of *innovation*, which underpins future productivity growth. The constant comparison with peers (other firms and individuals) is a source of competitive pressure. Third, stimulating the *formation of new businesses* expands and strengthens the cluster itself (e.g. individuals working within a cluster may more easily perceive gaps in products around which they build businesses).

Success breeds success is the received wisdom, according to informed opinion: 'The benefits of clusters may be cumulative in that once a cluster has developed, its advantage increases with the size of the cluster' (OECD 1997: 157); 'A cluster allows each member to benefit as if it had greater scale or as if it had joined with others formally – without requiring it to sacrifice its flexibility' (Porter 1998: 80). There is a commercial logic to art centres. A clustering of dealers enhances the reputation of a location; it also reduces the shopping costs of collectors, making it more likely that a buyer will turn to a dealer based there. If the dealers have differentiated works of art – as expressed by different stables of artists – there is less price competition. However, clusters can and do lose their competitive edge due to both external and internal forces. There is an 'interesting instability in art agglomeration' (Caves

2000: 31). Artists seeking affordable studio and living spaces are often the first to consider the potential of industrial warehouse spaces in so-called marginal areas of a city. Loft conversions for members of the professional classes and the opening of upscale eateries pose 'crowding out' problems. This is encapsulated by the graffiti slogan: 'Artists are the shock troops of gentrification'. As too many artists get pushed out, they will have to move all over again. New York's East Village went through this in the 1980s. By the late 1990s, London's East End had become a thriving location for contemporary artists. Artists living and working in close proximity – the creation of an artistic community – can help to raise the overall quality of work as artists criticize each other's work. West End dealers complaining about high rents in Mayfair and Knightsbridge, for example, were turning their attention to postal codes in areas marked by economic deprivation. The decision of the Tate Gallery to locate its museum of modern art south of the Thames, in the depressed London borough of Southwark, has served as a focal point. The opening of the Tate Modern, in May 2000, was an opportunity to showcase London's thriving contemporary art scene in the East End. Moreover, there is a possibility to redirect pedestrian traffic away from a crowded Covent Garden to the south side of the Thames: the Tate Modern, the Shakespeare Globe Theatre, and a redeveloped South Bank Centre (by Waterloo Station) serve as a catalyst to revive the Thames, which has been described by architect Will Alsop as 'one of the biggest holes in London'.

'The mere collocation of companies, suppliers, and institutions creates the *potential* for economic value; it does not necessarily ensure its realization' (Porter 1998: 88; emphasis in the original). A cluster of South Kensington's cultural and academic institutions – Royal Albert Hall, Royal College of Art, Royal Geographic Society, Royal College of Music, Imperial College, the Natural History Museum, the Science Museum, and the V&A – put a bid to the Millennium Fund and the National Lottery for approximately £100m. Albertopolis, the project name adopted by these eight institutions, was a proposal to create a sense of community, linking the arts and sciences, approaching what Prince Albert had in mind in the euphoric aftermath of the 1851 Great Exhibition. According to the V&A's head of public affairs:

> Albertopolis will not only celebrate 150 years of the site, not only underscore the sense of confidence with which we can approach a new age, but will re-equip national and international institutions of the Albertopolis to consolidate and expand their position as a centre of knowledge, inspiration, object-centred study and creativity into the next century.
>
> (National Art Collection Fund's *Art Quarterly*, Summer 1994)

The bid was rejected. Critics questioned the conceptual basis of such a Victorian-inspired project as a means to enter the twenty-first century. Would a different project name have made the main thrust: namely to create one of the great cultural quarters of Europe, more appealing?

City images can change. Within the state of Pennsylvania, Philadelphia and Pittsburgh are natural rivals in the realm of popular culture (including competition in three major categories of professional sports). On the other hand, in terms of historical significance, the traditional consensus is that Philadelphia has no rival within Pennsylvania; indeed in many respects only New York and Boston can compare. Yet there are suggestions that as Pittsburgh experiences a 'cultural renaissance', Philadelphia struggles to maintain its economic and cultural stature. For example, Philadelphia's changing milieu has been reported in the *Financial Times*:

> Like the city whose name it bears, the Philadelphia Orchestra seems happier to contemplate its past than confronting the future. Audiences are mainly white and older-generation in an area where blacks and other minorities are a growing presence. ... After decades of stability, the orchestra is struggling to adjust to a changing world.
>
> (11/12 March 1995)

Though the Philadelphia Orchestra is one of America's 'Big Five', the city has been marked by various bouts of economic sluggishness since the 1970s. The Pittsburgh Symphony Orchestra, like those in Los Angeles and San Francisco, is making significant aesthetic inroads. The visual arts in Pittsburgh received a boost with the opening of the Andy Warhol Museum (administered by the Carnegie Museum of Art). The emergence of Pittsburgh as a cultural powerhouse is an obstacle to the ambitions of the Philadelphia Museum of Art: the PMA is attempting to reposition itself as a state (Pennsylvania) rather than city (Philadelphia) institution, which harks back to the institution's founding as the Pennsylvania Museum and School of Industrial Arts. The impetus to be recognized as a state-level institution is largely financial in the face of cutbacks at the municipal level.

Branding's mythic power

'From cornflakes to cars, our daily lives are increasingly dominated by branded goods and brand names', according to the 'brand.new' exhibition at the V&A (Pavitt 2000: 16). Commercially successful brands like McDonald's, Absolut Vodka, Ralph Lauren, and Marlboro are viewed as possessing properties which transcend the physical attributes of the product. 'Just Do It' with Nike; Coca-Cola is 'The Real Thing'. 'The brand is the prefix, the qualifier of character. The symbolic associations of the brand name are often used in preference to the pragmatic description of a useful object' (Pavitt 2000: 16). This promotion of tacit values via branding raises questions about the societal role of business. As a caveat, it is necessary to note that the search for success and survival is a myth of the first order. If all firms adopted branding, none would be able to secure a competitive advantage. However, the promise of unequal power which is derived from specialist knowledge is located in promises.

'Building successful brands' is an apposite chapter title in a standard MBA text:

> Brands are at the heart of marketing and business strategy. Marketing is about decommoditising the company's offer. If a company's offer is perceived to be

the same as those of competitors, then consumers will be indifferent and will choose the cheapest or most accessible. Companies that are forced to compete on price rarely make satisfactory profits. The purpose of marketing is to create a preference for the company's brand. If customers perceive one brand as superior, they will prefer it and pay more for it. Brand equity is the value of these additional cash flows generated for a product because of its brand identity.

(Doyle 1998: 165)

The work of David Aaker (1991, 1995), who defines brand equity as 'a set of brand assets and liabilities linked to a brand, its name and symbol, that add to or subtract from the value provided by a product or service to a firm and/or to that firm's customers', is crucial to the discussion of brand equity. Research by McKinsey seeks to distinguish *names* from *brands* from *power brands*:

> Many companies think that they have a brand when what they actually have is name recognition.
>
> A name becomes a brand when consumers associate it with a set of intangible and tangible benefits that they obtain from the product or service. As associations grow stronger, consumers' equal loyalty and willingness to pay a price premium increases. Hence, there is equity in the brand name. A brand without equity is not a brand. To build brand equity, a company needs to do two things: first, distinguish its product from others in the market; second, align what it says about its brand in advertising and marketing with what it actually delivers. A relationship then develops between brand and consumer – a relationship arising from the consumer's entire experience of the brand. As alignment grows stronger, so does the brand. Power brands create a more emotional bond that grows out of their personality. ... Power brands generate relationships with customers that are measurably stronger than those achieved by ordinary brands. Moreover, power brands seem to be present at every turn, reinforcing their distinctiveness. Such presence usually derives from national or international scale.

(Court *et al.* 1997: 26–8)

Management writers like Doyle and Aaker and firms like McKinsey and Interbrand (see www.interbrand.com), which view marketing as contributing to national wealth creation, valorize the equity or value vested in the brand as an intangible asset. Along with the name and trademark and other proprietary elements, the strength of a brand depends on associations, namely the image created by marketing activities (e.g. advertising, sales promotions, design) and reception of the firm's message by consumers. 'A brand is a promise. Never make promises you cannot keep' is a pithy definition. Yet it is instructive to remember that intangible assets (like brand equity) are crucial to adding value to the firm. Intellectual property rights represent a growing area of interest.

But do power brands operating in the global marketplace curtail genuine consumer choice? Yes, according to Naomi Klein (2000), a leader of one strand of the anti-capitalist movement, who believes that branding initiatives by multinational enterprises devalue indigenous production and consumption in developing nations; moreover, there is an undemocratic shift in power from citizens to consumers. An advocacy group like Adbusters is dedicated to making us resist 'those who pollute our minds' (www.adbusters.org). A radical example of 'culture jamming' was performed by José Bové, a crusading French farmer, who, in 1999, vandalized a McDonald's restaurant that was under construction; Bové's protest against what he calls *la malbouffe americaine* (crap American food) and unwholesome agriculture has accorded him folk hero status. 'The world is not for sale' is a slogan used by Bové to champion French wine; this has included preventing the Californian winemaker Robert Mondavi from opening a vineyard in the Languedoc (even though France's appellation system can intimidate rather than entice many neophyte wine drinkers).

A somewhat broad and eclectic approach adopted by Wally Olins in *Corporate Identity* (1989) is instructive:

> In order to be effective every organization needs a clear sense of purpose that people within it understand. They also need a strong sense of belonging. People and belonging are two facets of identity. Every organization is unique, and the identity must spring from the organization's own roots, its personality, its strengths and weaknesses. This is true of the modern corporation as it has been of any other institution in history, from the Christian church to the nation state.
>
> The identity of the corporation must be so clear that it becomes the yard-stick against which its products, behaviour and action are measured. This means that identity cannot simply be a slogan, a collection of phrases: it must be visible, tangible, and all-embracing. Everything that the organization does must be an affirmation of its identity.
>
> (Olins 1989: 7)

He also acknowledges the value of alternative perspectives, citing *The Invention of Tradition* (1983), an edited collection by Eric Hobsbawn and Terence Ranger. This is a contrarian selection by Olins, which examines the creation of imaginary structures that give a new, but invented, continuity, permanence, and authority to the ruling elite.

Identity operates at different levels, including the nation and the institution. Products from particular nations continue to be influenced by stereotyped images for attributes like quality, price, and reliability. Though national images do change over time, the process is long and costly. For example, Spain represents one of the best examples of a concerted attempt to rebrand a country: to shed the shadow of Franco; to move upmarket as a tourist destination (and shed the 'costa' image); to provide a place for Spain's constituent parts, such as Catalonia; and to redefine Spain as a modern industrial nation: a serious European Union player and a democracy. The España picture by Miro became the national logo, symbolizing a bright, optimistic passionate Spain (in contrast to the buttoned dourness of the Franco years). Following the attacks of '9–11', Charlotte Beers, one of the leading figures in the advertising world, was appointed by President Bush, as a new under-secretary of state for public diplomacy and public affairs, with a brief to think about 'rebranding' America (see Richard Tomkins in the *Financial Times*, 20/21 October 2001). Not unlike the perception that the USA is a 'hyper power', which draws a host of criticisms and attacks, maybe Disney has become too much of a commercial success. Along with being the source of economic value, Mickey Mouse is also a term of disparagement (i.e. a Mickey Mouse operation); in a similar manner, Disney is a term of contempt, an abbreviation for American cultural imperialism. Accusations by detractors, that the USA spreads a culture of crass commercialization around the world, are gaining more attention. American-style consumerism is seductive, but can bring with it a tawdry element.

The identity of the institution is important in creating a vision of the values of the firm, thus many enterprises are concerned with controlling and enhancing their corporate identity. Given that even popular commentators are grappling with the contest of British identity, it would be odd if the V&A did not address issues of national identity. Indeed it is an opportunity for the institution to redefine its positions in the UK and internationally.

Writing an editorial in the *V&A Magazine* (September/December 1998), published by the Friends of the V&A, Alan Borg, the then director of the V&A, was thinking aloud about the institution's name:

> Is our name an asset or a handicap and do we need a new one? The Victoria and Albert Museum does not tell you much about what we actually do, and quite a lot of first-time visitors come expecting to find a museum devoted to the life of the Queen and Prince Consort, or perhaps one devoted solely to the Victorian age. Our short form of V&A is even more opaque, risking confusion with C&A [a downmarket retailer which has ceased operating] and even DNA. The question is whether this matters and whether we should be thinking of changing our name as part of the Museum's image. ... If there is one word which covers all our activities, it ought to be excellence – in design and in the collections, in their display, in our scholarship and in the service we offer to visitors. As we strive to make the Museum still better, perhaps we need not worry about our name. It is what we do that matters.

On first reading, Borg's desire to change, to consider 'a new name for the Museum', seems motivated by the concern that 'quite a lot of first-time visitors' are not entirely sure what the V&A has on display. (Yet it is instructive if the V&A is able to distinguish between first-time visitors: those who are tourists versus those who are resident in the UK. The former can be pitched by promotional efforts aimed at London hotels, for example. The latter are taxpayers who expect the V&A, as an institution in receipt of significant public funding, to operate to maximize public benefit.) If the issue is primarily one of barriers to first-time visitors, impediments including admission tariffs and perceived images of exclusivity need to be tackled as part of audience development.

On further reflection, it appears that Borg's editorial was influenced by discussions concerning the rebranding of Britain. A case has been put forward, particularly by Demos research, that national identity within Britain needs to be taken seriously by highlighting some of the economic benefits to be derived from the identity premium (Leonard 1997). Borg's opening paragraph shares affinities with the Demos thesis that Britain's identity is in flux. First, there is bad press from around the world that Britain's image is perceived by others as remaining stuck in the past: the country is seen as backward-looking, and British products are seen as low tech and bad value. Borg ponders whether the Museum's name is 'a handicap' owing to connotations to the 'Victorian age'? Second, within Britain there is some confusion, even embarrassment, concerning 'Britishness': for example, British Telecom, British Gas, British Home Stores, and the British Airport Authority all dropped 'British' from their names. In a similar vein, according to Borg, 'thinking of changing our name [is] part of changing the Museum's image'.

It goes without saying that ill-fated attempts by Borg's predecessors (now Sir) Roy Strong and Elizabeth (now Dame) Esteve-Coll to gain greater popular attention for the V&A were raised. Roy Strong was bold – some contend merely foolish – when he declared that the V&A 'could be the Laura Ashley of the 1990s'. The unabashed praise of the commercial prowess of the then retail success story served as the basis for the V&A shop; opened in 1986 it represents the most visible success of V&A Enterprises. The reference to Laura Ashley has been interpreted as symbolic of a 'return to Victorian ideals' given the perceived positioning of the retail chain as exploiting the 'new traditionalism' associated with the then Thatcher and Reagan administrations. Moreover, Strong's directorship (1974–87) ended with unsuccessful attempts at broadening the appeal of the V&A (such as exhibiting Elton John's collection of *objets d'art* before Sotheby's auctioned them and allowing two retailers, the Sock Shop and Burberry, opportunities to self-sponsor their own exhibitions). An infamous Saatchi & Saatchi promotional campaign, 'an ace caff with a rather nice museum attached', failed to attract the desired target market of 'twenty-something' Londoners, but did incense large sections of the V&A community. Elizabeth Esteve-Coll's directorship started with an attempt to initiate reforms that many agreed were long overdue; however, her critics seized upon the proposed restructuring as an attack directly inspired by Thatcherism on the world of learning. She was never able to put a line under the 1989 restructuring, such that 'beleaguered' remains a good characterization of her tenure.

Two important qualifying points are raised by Borg: the reputation of the institution, or being 'well enough for what we actually do', cannot be addressed merely by a change in name; and the importance of the permanent collection as a starting point to articulate 'what it is we do'. Borg's editorial should not be dismissed as reflecting yet another example of a tedious management imperative at the expense of curatorial mandates, or a radical attempt to reinvent a stagnant museum project. It seems that he was seeking to provoke an overdue discussion about the direction of the V&A. Indeed, Borg may have been revisiting an internal strategy document from the mid-1980s which sought to articulate the institution's subtitle, 'The National Museum of Art and Design'. The subtitle was an attempt to address the historical circumstances of the V&A: the diversity of the permanent collection, essentially a federation of a dozen or so first-rank museums pulling in different directions, and the constraints posed by architecture – artworks are displayed over twelve separate levels in two buildings with only one internal linkage point. How do you communicate that the V&A is a 'visionary treasure house' – essentially a nineteenth-century concept – at the start of the twenty-first century?

Changing an institution's name can represent wider shifts in how the institution desires to be perceived. First, founded in 1860, the Art Association of Montreal adopted a new name in 1949: the Montreal Museum of Fine Arts. The AAM was deemed by many as a private institution based on privilege, and catering to members who were overwhelmingly English-speaking. On the other hand, the MMFA was articulating a more comprehensive title and more easily understood by visitors. Yet even the official adoption of a bilingual title in 1960 did little to reduce perceptions that the institution was an Anglophone enclave. Ideology and economics helped in forging the partnership established in 1972 between the province of Quebec and the MMFA: the former agreed to become the latter's prime source of funds in operations; in exchange the province gained the right to appoint a minority number of trustees to the MMFA's board. However, the MMFA would remain independent of direct government control. First, the socio-political climate which inculcated the so-called Quiet Revolution – a revolution against corruption and archaisms within Quebec (associated with the role of the Roman Catholic Church) *and* American and English–Canadian economic and cultural domination – laid the foundation for the transformation of the institution. Second, a direct consequence of fourteen consecutive years of deficits up until 1971, the MMFA required assurances of stable ongoing financial support to ensure the institution's survival; that is, to suggest that there was a decidedly pragmatic reason underlying the partnership.

Following the re-opening of the Art Gallery of Ontario in 1993, public relations handlers started to raise concerns about the use of 'A-G-O'. Did prospective visitors read it as 'ago', associating the art museum with the dictionary definition of the adjective, namely 'past; gone by; long since', rather than as a vibrant, contemporary exhibition space bringing art and people together and supporting lifelong learning? Moreover, were other prospective visitors not even able to make the association between 'A-G-O' and the Gallery? The name 'Art Gallery of Ontario' has proven to be less useful for identity enhancement. The Gallery is attempting to forge a more prominent following outside of Canada, yet non-Canadians are much more aware of the city of Toronto as opposed to the province of Ontario. Other 'competing' organizations in Toronto have stronger so-called top-of-mind recognition with diverse audiences: the Royal Ontario Centre (i.e. a miniature combination of the British Museum and the Natural History Museum with ancient art and dinosaurs), the Ontario Science Museum (i.e. hands-on and interactive displays for children), and the Metropolitan Zoo; at the same time, Canadian and international contemporary art is well-served in Toronto by a series of artist-run centres (created since the 1970s) and three large exhibition venues (e.g. the Power Plant, a publicly-funded exhibition space; the privately-funded Ydessa Hendeles Art Foundation; and the Art Gallery of York University). The original name, Art Museum of Toronto, is much stronger, yet it would run counter to the partnership with the *provincial* government. The thrust to promote 'The Gallery' as an alternative to the

'AGO' was viewed by PR operatives as a way to emphasize that the Art Gallery of Ontario is the primary art gallery to visit.

The case that competitive positioning of an arts organization is crucial to overall success is enticing. So is the notion that creativity is a liberating force, central to understanding how successful organizations in the twenty-first century will conduct business. Branding has assumed clear economic benefits, such as building an attractive corporate identity. There is a compelling seductiveness associated with Michael Porter, David Ogilvy, Wally Olins, and Demos researchers: there is an argument for unique positions to be offered to customers based on making trade-offs and considering choices offered by competitors; and the value of clustering has a particular resonance for the arts. Case illustrations are cited: competition is not static as the case of music via the internet seeks to address; unlike the Tate (particularly with the opening of Tate Modern), the V&A continues to suffer from an identity crisis; and the MMFA and the AGO represent complementary examples of the complexities associated with articulating a strong brand name.

Much is about doing, yet there is also an opportunity to reflect. Raymond Williams's concern about the treatment of 'creativity' is an instructive corrective. The fictive element suggested by the phrase 'invented traditions' ought to make one take a more critical look at how and why arts organizations manufacture positioning statements and brand identities.

7 Arts marketing and audience development

Marketing Dilemma I: 'Marketing' is, according to a dictionary of modern thought, 'now widely held to be the most important of industrial and commercial disciplines' (Bullock and Trombley 1999: 504). In no small measure, this is due to the valorization of the consumer at the heart of marketing philosophy. Yet American humorist Dave Berry, writing in *Fortune* (7 July 1997), makes an apposite point about marketing in practice: 'My theory is that the most hated group in any company is the customers. They don't know company procedures or anything about what you do, which drives you crazy!'.

Marketing Dilemma II: Of the many symptoms endemic to a non-marketing mindset, few raise more hackles than the following assertion in the *Harvard Business Review*: 'One can learn the key characteristics of a product in a few weeks, but market awareness and marketing expertise take years to master. Once gained this expertise can be applied to many products or market contexts' (Andreasen 1982: 106). Marketing discussions often emphasize the role of the marketer, the person doing the marketing. Can 'skills-will-travel' marketers add genuine value to arts organizations? Or is there the belief by the likes of many curators, musicians, and dancers that marketers are *peacocks* (i.e. all show and no real substance), *penguins* (i.e. always well-dressed and not very intelligent), or *Irish setters* (i.e. very good looking but not very intelligent) (Morgan 1993: 24).

Are marketers the promoters of images rather than the creators of value? This is the type of question posed by the varying views expressed in the two preceding marketing dilemmas. The arts marketing literature adopts a position that marketers help to widen choices available to arts consumers and to enhance the overall quality of the arts experience. This has resulted in a backlash from interpretative marketing researchers: 'Certainly there is no shortage of marketing-made-easy books for the arts community' (Brown and Patterson 2000: 17). These critics believe that the current marketing position is not progressive enough. Interpretative marketing researchers shift the emphasis from 'marketing the arts' to 'the arts for marketing' (see Brown and Patterson 2000: 18–19). The latter includes engaging with the marketing content of artistic artifacts; representations of marketing and consumption-related phenomena can offer alternative perspectives on the principles and practices of marketing management. (Another 'arts for marketing' agenda applies the tools and techniques of artistic appreciation to marketing institutions and ephemera such as advertising and promotional campaigns.)

The 'national arts marketing project' of the Arts and Business Council – which is distinct from a fellow American organization, the Business Committee for the Arts, and the British organization Arts & Business – describes 'marketing as a *process* by which you come to understand the relationship between your *product* and your *customer*' (see www.artsandbusiness.org – emphasis in the original). Rather than replicating what is already available in arts marketing textbooks, there is a focus on interpreting the principles of marketing, particularly ones promoted as instructive to museums and performing arts organizations. Furthermore, attention is given to the complex relationship between marketing initiatives and audience development.

Marketing orthodoxy and the arts for marketing

Marketers, say those involved in sales, advertising, public relations, media, and consultancy, for example, have a double role: they represent a commercial system; and they become actors in a process of commodity exchange. Marketing offers firms an opportunity 'not just to experience the sweet smell of success, but to have the visceral feel of entrepreneurial greatness' (Levitt 1960: 56). Marketing orthodoxy, as such, suggests that this interplay between company and customer within the context of competition helps to generate national wealth creation. At the same time, in order to succeed, marketers need to be myth-makers: what fiction is to be created, what story needs to be told to get the customer to believe your proposition.

The work by pioneers in the field of marketing – including Peter Drucker, Theodore Levitt, and Philip Kotler – started to be articulated during the 1950s and 1960s in the context of rising consumerism in the USA. Marketing orthodoxy offers a 'positivistic view of the world' (Morgan 1992: 136) which is prefaced on the central role of the consumer in relationship to the organization. Fifty years ago, Drucker was advocating single-minded, if not quasi-spiritual observations, in *The Practice of Management*: 'There is only one valid definition of a business: to create a satisfied customer'; and 'The customer is the foundation of a business and keeps it in existence' (Drucker 1954: 52). In a celebrated *Harvard Business Review* article, Levitt posited that 'the organization must learn to think of itself not as producing goods and services but as *buying customers*, as doing the things that will make people *want* to do business with it' (Levitt 1960: 56; emphasis in the original).

How do you like your marketing? Soft and easy, or hard and masochistic? The use of sexuality in selling commodities is a well-known phenomenon. It is not surprising that sexual images are redolent in how marketing is presented in plays. Jack and Jenny, marketing consultants, in Michel Vinaver's *Overboard* (1997; the French original, *Par-dessus bord*, was completed in 1969 and first produced in 1973), use the language of private relations to discuss commercial transactions: 'The man of marketing and the consumer form a couple: the man of marketing is the male; the consumer is the female' (Movement IV: 81). Whereas Vinaver is coy, one might even say coquettish, David Mamet's representation of marketing is grounded in the ethos of masculinity. In *Glengarry Glen Ross* (1983; a film version was released in 1993), which is part of Mamet's wider studies on male companionship and competition, the word 'fuck' is used with gusto by the salesmen: ' … they want to be fuck the competition, fuck women, and fuck their jobs, but they do not want to be the ones who get fucked' (McDonough 1997: 99). The process of language is at stake, but the approaches adopted illustrate the flip-sides of the same marketing coin. Vinaver adopts a 'romantic discourse', whereas Mamet emphasizes marketing as an overtly masculine and aggressive language. The thrust in both cases is on those who *do* marketing.

Compare and contrast the following two treatments. On the one hand, 'The man of marketing and the consumer form a couple: the man of marketing is the male; the consumer is the female', according to Jack and Jenny, who espouse their laws of marketing: 'The number of man's needs is limited but his desires and fears know no number. Through marketing they may grow'; and 'The man of marketing is a priest and a soldier, a man of faith and of steel doubting nothing and defying all created of both fire and ice' (Movement IV: 81). The marketing man – for he is a man in Vinaver's heterosexual account – is everything all at once: a lover, a warrior, a creator, a destroyer, etc. The list gives an exaggerated importance to the subject under discussion (namely to increase sales of toilet paper) and produces a profoundly comic result. On the other hand, 'Always Be Closing' is used by Mamet as an epigraph. Characterized as a practical sales maxim, it suggests a persistent urgency. An excited salesman enters:

> *Levene:* Get the *chalk*. Get the *chalk* … get the *chalk*. I closed 'em! I *closed* the cocksucker. Get the chalk and put me on the *board*. I'm going to Hawaii! Put me on the Cadillac board, Williamson! Pick up the fuckin' chalk. Eight units. Mountain View.
> (Act 2: 36; emphasis in the original)

Roma's prompt, 'Always Be Closing' (Act 2: 41), is a signal for Levene to tell his war story:

> *Levene:* That's what I'm *saying*. The *old* ways. The *old* ways … convert the mother fucker … *sell* him … *sell* him … *make him sign the check*.
> (Act 2: 41–2; emphasis in the original)

It has been noted that Levene speaks of selling the customer, as if the customer is no longer a human being, but merely a commodity to be exploited. Levene, like his colleagues, emphasizes the need for force; the prospect must be converted, get the prospect to sign 'on the line that is dotted'.

Overboard and *Glengarry Glen Ross* are instructive works which highlight issues crucial to those exploring the 'theory' and 'philosophy' of marketing (see Enis, Cox, and Mokwa 1992, especially Part I for key components of corporate marketing management; for agendas associated with interpretative marketing research, see Brown 1995; Brown and Patterson 2000). Kotler's thesis – marketing is central to the analysis of human behaviour, and all relationships between people can be seen in marketing terms – is a point of reference. What relationships do marketers cultivate? How is sexual imagery represented in marketing? The focus is on those who *do* marketing; this perspective, though not unproblematic, remains dominant.

In both plays, the spectator/reader is offered 'insider' looks at the mechanics of marketing in constructing a particular view of human beings and society. *Overboard* presented an opportunity for the playwright 'to find a way of bringing together his two separate selves': Michel Grinberg was a senior executive with Gillette in Europe; his alter-ego Michel Vinaver (now a professor at the University of Paris VIII) was a writer. Like others, Grinberg/Vinaver was able to see that the impact of American business on French society was becoming an important issue by the late 1960s. American dynamism, via technology advances in manufacturing and aggressive marketing to widen market access, was viewed as widening the gap between American and European industry. In an 'author's note' to *Glengarry Glen Ross*, Mamet commented on his experience working in a real estate office in 1969:

> The office was a fly-by-night operation which sold tracts of undeveloped land in Arizona and Florida to gullible Chicagoens. The firm advertised on radio and television and their pitch was to this effect: 'Get on the ground floor ... For more information call ... for our beautiful brochure.' Interested viewers would telephone in for the brochure and their names were given to me. My job was to call them back, assess their income and sales susceptibility, and arrange an appointment with them for one of the office salesmen.
>
> This appointment was called a *lead* ... it may lead to a *prospect*. It was then my job to gauge the relative worth of these leads and assign them to the salesforce. The salesmen would then take their assigned leads and go out on the appointments, which were called *sits*, a meeting where one actually *sits down* with the prospects.
>
> The competition centres around the *leads*, with each man trying desperately to get the best ones.

In addressing the issue of competition in the marketplace, which is viewed as a mechanism by which standards are set, Vinaver's play revolves around the concept of *par-dessus bord*, or 'throwing overboard'. Ravoire et Dehaze throws overboard things it does not need (like traditional hierarchies) in order to survive against the American conglomerate UPC. The title, *Glengarry Glen Ross*, evokes positive associations: the land being sold by the salesmen sounds romantic and reliable, and represents hope and possibility for buyers. Yet Mamet's play centres around a tough, all-male milieu. A sales competition is drawing to a close: the top earner is to be rewarded with a Cadillac; second prize is a set of steak knives; the remaining two salesmen lose their jobs.

What do relationships mean to marketers? Using the notion of 'transaction', Kotler (Kotler and Levy 1969; Kotler 1972) has promoted marketing as a pervasive social activity. According to Kotler, marketing is specifically concerned with how transactions are created, stimulated, facilitated, and valued. He distinguished three levels of marketing consciousness. First, marketing is defined in terms of market transaction; namely, buyers and sellers meeting to exchange goods (see, for example, Bartels 1968; Baggozi 1975). Second, two parties may meet to exchange things which are of value to them (e.g. political parties and voters) so that every organization (whether market-based or not) should be conceived as producing something of value for a client or customer. Third, Kotler raised the stakes by arguing that a higher state of marketing consciousness exists: marketing applies to an organization's attempts to relate to all its publics, not just its consuming publics. The things-of-value are not limited to goods and services, and money; rather, they include other resources such as time, energy, and feelings. In what has become an iconic statement (see commentary by Morgan 1992; Brown 1995), Kotler went so far as to posit marketing 'as a category of human action indistinguishable from other categories of human action such as voting, loving, consuming, or fighting' (Kotler 1972: 52).

Kotler has not been alone in letting the rhetoric rip. Terms like 'relationship marketing' and 'customer relationship management' are cited as offering a new mindset about how firms are trying to engage with customers. By way of analogy, marketing orthodoxy acknowledges a shift from marketer as hunter (e.g. focusing on the immediate sale) to the marketer as gardener (e.g. cultivating relationships). So-called 'new' marketing treats each customer as unique and aims to match his or her requirements. There is an emphasis on engendering loyalty, to the extent that marketers talk about the 'lifetime value' of the customer accruing to the firm.

Jack and Jenny are introduced as marketing consultants from the USA. As the possessors and disseminators of a new and powerful language, they illustrate that marketing is the cultural phenomenon of our time:

Jack: With the advent of mass consumption ...
Jenny: ... Man finds solace in the companions of another kind.
Jack: More useful because they can also wash your clothes, your face, your dishes, go pretty fast on the highways.
Jenny: Or wipe your bottom.
Jack: Soon enough.
Jenny: Religion, literature, art will fade into the past.
Jack: Man's creativity will find refuge in marketing.

(Movement IV: 89)

Vinaver recognized that marketers need to diminish the original, functional use of goods by attaching romance, desire, beauty, fulfilment, even to the mundanities of a product like toilet paper.

In *Glengarry Glen Ross*, relationships exist only to facilitate commercial success and to establish which party is in control, as illustrated in the exchanges between Roma and the prospect, Lingk. Following an attempt to win Lingk's trust through a studied stream-of-consciousness on the nature of life, Roma comes around to his real intention of flogging real estate:

> *Roma:*   James. I'm glad to meet you. (*They shake hands.*) I'm glad to meet you,
> James. (*Pause.*) I want to show you something. (*Pause.*) It might mean
> nothing to you ... and it might not. I don't know. I don't know anymore.
> (*Pause. He takes out a small map and spreads it out on a table.*) What is
> that? Florida. Glengarry Highlands. Florida 'Florida. Bullshit.' And
> maybe that's true; and that's what I said: but look *here*: What is this?
> This is a piece of land. Listen to what I'm going to tell you now.
>
> (Act 1, Scene 3: 26; emphasis in the original)

Roma plays upon Lingk's desire to make a friend; what is merely a commercial transaction takes on a greater significance for the latter. The next day Lingk appears in the real estate office and admits to Roma, 'My wife said I have to cancel the deal' (Act 2: 48). Lingk's masculinity is questioned by Roma who holds him in contempt. The exploitative nature of human relationships becomes apparent. Roma attempts to convince Lingk that their commercial tie is more significant than Lingk's marital bond:

> *Roma:*   Forget the deal, Jimmy. (*Pause.*) *Forget* the deal ... you know me.
> That deal's *dead*. Am I talking about the *deal*? That's *over*. Please.
> Let's talk about *you*. Come on. (*Pause. Roma rises and starts walking
> toward the front door.*) Come on. (*Pause.*) Come on, Jim. (*Pause.*) I
> want to tell you something. Your life is your own. You have a
> contract with your wife. You have certain things to do *jointly*, you
> have a *bond* there ... and there are *other* things. Those things are
> yours. You needn't feel *ashamed*, you needn't feel that you're being
> *untrue* ... or that she would abandon you if she knew, this is your life.
> (*Pause.*) Yes. Now I want to *talk* to you because you're obviously
> upset and that *concerns* me. Now let's go. Right now.
>
> (Act 2: 54–5; emphasis in the original)

Lingk's role is better understood in light of how marketing techniques are often marked by an absence or silence of the voice of the customer.

Segmentation and targeting

'Managing heterogeneity' is the essential basis behind understanding the importance of market segmentation, which is a process by which the total market is divided into distinctive groups. According to the pioneer of market segmentation:

> Segmentation is disaggregative in its effects and tends to bring about recognition of several demand schedules where only one was recognizable before ... market segmentation ... consists of viewing a heterogeneous market (one characterized by divergent demand) as a number of smaller homogeneous markets in response to different product preferences among important market segments. It is attributable to the desires of consumers for varying wants.
>
> (Smith 1956: 3)

The conventional wisdom is that marketers must decide which market segments to enter and design a marketing programme – that covers elements of the marketing mix including advertising, pricing, and channels of distribution – to suit the requirements of the selected target segments. The benefits from market segmentation, better matching of customer needs, enhanced profits, enhanced opportunities for growth, retention of customers, targeted communications, stimulation to innovation, and market segmentation share (Doyle 1998: 68–70), seem too enticing to ignore. From a commercial perspective, only a limited range of products invite mass marketing, that is one message for the entire market. Yet it has been noted that misapplication of market segmentation may occur. There may be too much emphasis on demand level: by concentrating on the heavy user, the marketer ignores the potential for increased usage by light users or non-users. Developing demographic profiles (e.g. sex, age, race, family lifecycle stage, income, occupation) of alternative segments is not unproblematic: there may be missing variables (such as associated with lifestyle analysis); and it may be difficult to translate demographic profiles into actionable marketing programmes. Following the identification of segmentation variables, a firm must decide those segments it aims to target. This entails evaluating the relative 'attractiveness' of the segments: size of the segment, its growth rate, profit potential, and its fit to the core capabilities of the firm are some of the conventional factors marketers take into account. The aim is to choose groups of customers who will have a 'lifetime value' for the company.

Philip Kotler labels 'STP marketing' (cited in Drucker 1990: 58) as instructive to all types of arts organizations, by which he means segmentation, targeting, and positioning have a generic application. The current emphasis is on micromarketing; that is, looking at establishing more refined market segments. Segments-of-one is an extreme example of personalization: this 'customer intimacy' position is supposed to change what the firm does in response to customer input and past behaviour by the customer.

Marketing the arts

If we believe Briton Keith Diggle, 'arts marketing' was coined by him in 1970 (Diggle 1984: 19). However, there is much to suggest that the application of corporate marketing management techniques to American nonprofit organizations in health care, education, social welfare, and the arts was gaining support by the late 1960s (see, for example, Kotler and Andreasen 1975; Kotler 1979). By refining Kotler's notion that transaction is a core concept of marketing, Benson Shapiro (1973) helped to set the tone of marketing in non-commercial contexts. Shapiro identified two constituencies (i.e. customer segments): *donors* provide resources; *clients* receive resources. Some individuals are donors and clients, as is the case with arts patrons, yet Shapiro was right to recognize that facilitating the exchange relationships becomes more complex than the traditional buyer–seller transactions. Diverse sets of customers mean that the so-called 'bottom line' of the non-commercial organization requires a twofold process: serving client groups is a prime objective, yet this is only possible if mutually-satisfying exchanges exist with donor groups.

In the foreword to *Marketing the Arts* (1980), Kotler identified four major interrelated marketing challenges: attendance stimulation, audience development, membership development, and fund-raising (Mokwa, Dawson, and Prieve 1980). Attendance stimulation, cited as the first major challenge, has an immediate and direct impact on attendance figures, a main yardstick to measure organizational success. There is a choice, according to Kotler, between *broadening* (i.e. 'trying to bring serious art to more people') or *deepening* (i.e. 'developing a more coherent experience for those who are already interested in the arts') the audience base. Membership development served an important linking role; getting one to join as a member represents the first stage of a more formal and potentially stronger bond. Finally, revenue from fund-raising activities complement attendance and membership revenue. 'Awards for marketing institutional excellence' are awarded by the American Association of Museums in four categories: awareness building, attendance generation, crisis management, and merchandising excellence.

Ideas associated with Kotler, one of the seminal thinkers behind the formation of marketing management, have been adopted by arts marketers. Indeed, Kotler's publications list includes marketing for the performing arts (Kotler and Scheff 1997) and museums (Kotler and Kotler 1998). Other commentators who have authored 'marketing for the arts' textbooks include Danny Newman, Alvin Reiss, François Colbert, Elizabeth Hill, Fiona Combe McLean, and Bonita Kolb.

Early arts marketers who are grouped with Diggle include Americans Danny Newman and Alvin Reiss. Newman was an early advocate of promotion and price to stimulate demand; he believed that it was possible to increase the market by emphasizing activities associated with selling. *Subscribe Now!* (1977) was the emphatic and evocative title of Newman's handbook: performing arts organizations were encouraged to attract more subscribers with a downgrading of occasional ticket-wicket patrons. Reiss was equally bullish and vigorous in a practitioner-oriented text, *Cash In!* (1986), which bore the descriptive subtitle, 'funding and promoting the arts, a compendium of imaginative concepts, tested ideas and case histories or programs and promotions that make money'. (Perhaps such texts – not unlike school mailings to alumni – take on an insistently cheery, exclamation-mark-strewn tone because they are really about raising money, which does not invite irony.)

It was with a 'greater broad-mindedness … entrapping those slothful, fickle, single-ticket buyers who I may sometimes for haste give up on', according to Newman (Diggle 1984: 1), that Diggle sought to expand on his work. Like Newman, Diggle had a background as a performing arts marketing consultant, which helps to explain why he suggested that museums ought to consider selling advanced-entry tickets. Diggle believed it was possible to introduce a theatrical flavour to the experience of museum goers:

> if attendance at an art gallery or museum were defined by date or time, and even given a stated duration, it would take on the character of a performance – something that begins at a certain time and ends at a certain time – the idea of a limited capacity would be suggested and so there would be *something* to buy and a reason for buying it *now* ('If you don't buy it now, you might not get in').
>
> (Diggle 1984: 38; emphasis in the original)

Museum blockbusters are in character driven by sales. While the notion of spectacle is not new – think of the 1851 Great Exhibition held at Crystal Palace – the contemporary museum landscape is more indebted to the attendance-shattering success of the 'King Tut' exhibition (which toured the USA and Canada in the late 1970s and early 1980s). There was optimism and museum growth: capital expansion projects were deemed necessary in order to secure large-scale travelling exhibitions. The prospect of higher attendance figures would entice corporate sponsors; moreover, sales from ancillary services (e.g. shops, cafes, and acoustiguides) not to mention admissions revenue, would flourish. Museums hoped to become more financially self-sufficient; broadening the appeal to museums was also viewed as a benefit. Art market hyperactivity and expanding links between culture and tourism added grist to the museum mill of the 1980s and 1990s. There is nothing to suggest, at the start of the twenty-first century, a reversal in the rallying cry associated with building projects.

The general popularity of blockbusters as major cultural events with an accessible social cachet seems to suggest that the sales-oriented approach has some relevance. Promotional hype – or marketing communications – serves to raise expectations and heighten anticipation on the part of prospective spectators; it also allows the institution to gauge the sales potential. For example, London's Royal Academy of Arts wrote, at the end of August 1998, to announce that 'the dedicated 24 hour Friends booking line opens on 14 September' for 'Monet in the Twentieth Century' (sponsored by Ernst & Young), yet the exhibition was not scheduled to open until 23 January 1999.

In discussing culture in the marketplace, Paul DiMaggio strikes at a concern dear to marketers:

> We know rather little about why some art forms do well on the market and some do poorly. It is not enough to say that popular forms survive and unpopular ones fail: what this assertion ignores is *the power of market segmentation*. Markets are created by entrepreneurs; they do not exist in nature. Thus American popular radio became dramatically more innovative and diverse when the radio industry began segmenting markets by age, ethnicity, region, and race.
> (DiMaggio 1986b: 88; my emphasis)

'Where markets for an art form are highly segmented, pluralism and often innovation thrive' (DiMaggio 1986b: 88–9). Marketing analysis from retailing and other industrial sectors seems to suggest that art museums need to identify two distinct types of audiences: *potential donors* who often become members; and *the general public* who attend museums to be entertained and educated (Blattberg and Broderick 1991: 327). Maybe there should be two different museums to cater to two distinct audiences: a *mass marketing museum* designed to appeal to the public-at-large; and a *boutique museum* aimed at the donor and potential donor (Blattberg and Broderick 1991: 337). However, conventional market segmentation seems to be a solution fraught with difficulties when applied to arts organizations. One can appreciate the emergence of a clash of cultures, or confrontation of ideologies. For example, the director of a prominent art museum in the USA was 'disturbed' by 'the possibility or the necessity of museums addressing two very different kinds of audiences': it 'may possibly undermine the whole mission of a museum, which is to bring as many people as you can get in an art museum: direct contact with a work of art' (Anne d'Harnoncourt in Feldstein 1991: 36–7).

Limitations of marketing on audience development

Marketing attention tends to be in keeping with Diggle's contention that arts organizations 'are looking for audiences and the money that comes from audiences … drawing audiences from those already favourably disposed' (Diggle 1984: 43). Arts organizations grapple with the issue of audience development: how to balance up the socio-economic profile of their audience members in order to be more representative of the general population. Quotas are not viewed as being instructive (as they can emphasize the relativist position that equates cultural equity with merely valuing differences in race, sex, and class). Reducing the ability to cater to the needs of the well-informed (i.e. core or primary) spectator is not recommended. But how to respond more positively to the needs to other groups? Should arts organizations think about addressing two very different kinds of audiences? Such a segmentation strategy would mean that members representing a more diverse audience could be offered a separate product. But does changing the product to fit what the audience wants abrogate some of the responsibilities associated with the most successful arts organizations? Merely to cater to aesthetic taste preferences of current spectators would result in arts organizations becoming predictable and narrow in their breadth and perspective. Regular visitors (frequent attenders) are familiar with the institution and feel psychologically comfortable in the surroundings because it is part of their lifestyle. How to entice wider participation?

In its *Final Report* (1992), the Independent Task Force on the Future of the Art Gallery of Ontario cast significant doubt on the contribution of marketing practices to genuine audience development:

> After extensive consultation, the Task Force is of the opinion that although marketing may be of primary importance in increasing audience, it is not the key to broadening audience.
>
> In particular, the Task Force has been told time and time again that the only way the Gallery can broaden audience is to make a clear commitment to cultural diversity. This means not only multilingual devices, but strong educational opportunities for the young to interact with the Gallery's collections and with the attitudes and ideas which have shaped the making of that art, concerted efforts to exhibit and collect contemporary art which comes from non-majority cultures, partnerships with ethno-racial professionals who work out of a different aesthetic, special incentives for membership and volunteer involvement and an emphasis throughout the programming of the Gallery on providing access for non-traditional audiences as participants in the Gallery as a cultural institution relevant to their needs.
>
> (Independent Task Force on the Future of the Art Gallery of Ontario
> 1992: 26–7)

Cultural diversity is not an explicit theme raised by Pierre Bourdieu (see Chapter 2), yet it does strike at issues of real and perceived exclusion.

Audience development can be approached in two distinct ways (see DiMaggio 1986b: 88, which is based on ideas proffered by Augustin Girard). First, classical dissemination is aimed at democratizing institutions that have historically been supported by 'urban elites'. If a proactive education policy makes the arts more accessible, the continuing inroads of mass high education particularly in the USA, Canada, and the UK, should assist. Even usually rarefied organizations like Glyndebourne engage in touring opportunities to broaden the opera company's reach. The internet has the potential to reach possible new audiences, but few institutions think of using the internet as an alternative to an on-site visit; rather the current emphasis is on offering information and a 'taster' prior to making a visit. There is the case, though, that the social constituency for the distinction between high and popular culture, formed due to an elite desiring a prestigious culture they could dominate and call their own, is eroding. Second, access becomes less difficult by broadening the definition of the arts. Should efforts to support and develop creative industries be emphasized? There is a blurring of the distinction between nonprofit and commercial enterprises in the arts. Popular musicals like *My Fair Lady* and *South Pacific* may be staged at the subsidized National Theatre before being transferred to the commercial West End. Commercial galleries like Sandy Simpson, Sadie Coles, and White Cube mount exhibitions that rival what subsidized contemporary arts venues offer. Restaurants in art museums are reviewed with a 'sex and the city' flavour:

> The American habit of hitting on people in art galleries has never really caught on over here so much, long may it last; there's nothing more irritating than having to swat an annoying suitor while you're admiring the charms of Lady Hamilton dressed as Circe. If, however, you do pick someone up these days there's usually somewhere to go and get a meal or a coffee without feeling like you're in the school canteen.
>
> (review by Serena Mackesy, of what is now the Tate Britain restaurant, cited in the London *Independent*, 19 December 1998)

Barriers to effective access or entry operate on various dimensions. Physical barriers are being addressed in many jurisdictions, though there are limitations to renovations to older buildings (which is particularly pronounced in the UK with buildings of architectural or historical merit designated as 'listed'). Transportation is an issue. Disability is an obvious point, yet transportation also includes the distance one needs to travel and the associated costs. For example, the lack of affordable hotels and late night trains and buses in London did not help to encourage Britons to visit the Millennium Dome.

Price is a complex issue. Opera is expensive so that even £50 does not guarantee an unobstructed view at the Royal Opera House. On the other hand, the Wallace Collection – close to Selfridges and London's equivalent to New York's Frick Collection – is free. Possibly more important than price are the so-called 'emotional' barriers, if the institution is perceived to be threatening or unwelcoming. Viewing the building as exterior space, contemporary architects of art museums – building types in their own right – try to avoid imposing grandeur and monumentality. This reflects a changing aesthetic of how the art museum wants to be perceived. For example, the Philadelphia Museum of Art's building opened in 1926 and became known as the 'Philadelphian Acropolis'; the Griffin, a fabulous creature with an eagle's head and wings and a lion's body, continues to protect the institution. Yet there was a missed opportunity to exploit popular culture links to Sylvester Stallone's working class hero in *Rocky I* (1976), who makes a triumphant run up the stairs of the PMA, to widen the visitor base. The Pompidou Centre, on the other hand, which opened in 1977, stands out as 'a turning-point in the design of museums by stating the case for the *desanctification* of art' (Davis 1990: 42; my emphasis), with riding its elevator reputed to be one of the 'must do' activities for tourists visiting Paris.

'Market solutions will do nothing to address problems of access for persons with little discretionary income; problems of diversity and survival of art forms without large markets; or, indeed, most of the other values with which cultural policy is concerned' (DiMaggio 1986b: 89). The director of London's Theatre Royal, Stratford, Philip Hedley, attempts to adopt broad social mandates:

> My theatre is in one of the most deprived boroughs in the country where more than half the population are on benefit of some kind. Appropriately, we admit 60 per cent of our audience for only £3, the lowest concession rate in the country. One result of this is our audience is much praised by reviewers for its mix of age, race and class. This is not achieved without considerable sacrifice in artists' and staff salaries and artistic ambition.

Furthermore, he argues that there is a need for quangos and state funders 'to reward those organisations already making sacrifices in the cause of social inclusion' (London *Guardian*, 12 January 2002). A case is being advanced that arts organizations help to nurture a citizenry equipped to make informed choices in a democracy.

Does widening the audience base need to be at the expense of having an educated audience? Lack of knowledge of a particular art form raises interesting issues. Is there a responsibility on the part of arts organizations to provide background information to complete neophytes? What level of visual or musical literacy should an arts organization assume on the part of its visitors?

Acoustiguide, the leading firm in the supply of audioguides to museums, emphasizes its value in supporting interpretative goals, which may be important to making the experience of non-habitual visitors more rewarding. But is access enhanced? Moreover, are audioguide users given sufficient tools to develop their own appreciation of art? Or do they remain dependent on the museum's products for their knowledge and feelings of privilege?

> The true educational function of Acoustiguide and similar tours, then, is not a democratic one. Quite the contrary, as Pierre Bourdieu has demonstrated in the 'Aristocracy of Culture' chapter in *Distinction* and his earlier *L'amour de*

l'art. One learns to yearn and later to demonstrate the requisite Kantian disinterest of the true initiate. One learns to spend one's time looking, while listening, supposedly in pursuit of knowledge, all the while lusting for the chimera of privilege imparted by the voice on the tape.

(Greenberg 1987: 107)

This supports a belief that most visitors aspire less to professional competence than to what Bourdieu calls 'status-induced familiarity' with legitimate culture. Institutions like new products that find untapped markets; audioguides, as a mid-market gadget, fit this bill. Those who are unable (or unwilling) to spend that most luxurious of commodities – time – in pursuit of a passion, are addressed by the audioguide: 'highlights' can be covered in a reasonable period of time. As an ancillary service, audioguides generate cash in a more cost-effective manner than traditional methods (e.g. tours by education staff members or volunteers) by exploiting advances in technology; and, like other products driven by technology such as mobile telephones, audioguides continue to become more aesthetically appealing to users.

The regression of listening to art music – a theme Theodor Adorno (1973) raised in the 1930s and 1940s – continues to be addressed on complementary fronts. The artistic director of the London Philharmonic Orchestra emphasizes the fixed etiquette for listening to art music:

To the first-time concert-goer, the unwritten codes of music appreciation can seem as demanding as Tamino's initiation rituals in Mozart's *The Magic Flute* – get to your seat before the music starts, sit still, listen in silence without rustling the programme or tapping your feet, and don't on any account applaud between movements. If you have a music degree, you're off to a good start. If you haven't, and your motivation is pure pleasure, then you may feel that you are in the right place at the wrong time.

(Serge Dorny in the London *Daily Telegraph*, 5 October 2000).

Pianist Charles Rosen cites first principles of acculturation:

Learning to sing and learning to play the piano have been supplanted today by collecting records. This is a disquieting development that is already affecting the future. The audience for serious music has become increasingly passive, and there is no longer an important body of educated listeners experienced in the making of music that can act as a bridge between the general public and the professional.

(*New York Review of Books*, 20 December 2001)

The popularizing of art music may lead to accusations of aural wallpaper: 'listeners' tune in to classical music stations but do not really listen; 'arty' bookstores play classical music to add a bit of 'class'. On the other hand, dwindling audiences for art music has depressing consequences: the language of the classical and modern 'canon' (say from Beethoven and Bach to Schoenberg and Stravinsky) is so 'unpleasant' that it can be used to shift undesirables from unattended car parks and malls.

The application of marketing as presented in standard textbooks is fraught with difficulties, even though marketing the arts (or arts marketing) represents a growing sub-sector. As an inversion, 'the arts for marketing' represents an interpretative marketing to disentangle core concepts. As such, Vinaver's *Overboard* and Mamet's *Glengarry Glen Ross* help one to better understand the precepts of marketing orthodoxy. In particular, the rhetoric associated with 'relationships' in marketing, which bears the influence of Philip Kotler, is addressed in the two plays.

Early arts marketers like Keith Diggle, Danny Newman, and Alvin Reiss were consultants who emphasized promotional activities to increase audience figures. The direct hand of Kotler is noticeable in texts on marketing the performing arts and museums. Moreover, he has shaped the current band of 'academic' marketers who are interested in the arts. A controversial issue for many large and prominent arts organizations is market segmentation (an organizing principle for retailers and restaurants, for example). There is a concern that an explicit decision to have different offerings for different types of visitors would require a fundamental rethinking of the role of arts organizations in society.

That marketing practices have little genuine impact on audience development is often not disclosed. Widening the base of support, say as measured by socio-economic profiling, is a political issue of social inclusion. What are the barriers to effective access and entry? Some are identifiable, yet more complex is how arts organizations should communicate to their current and prospective audiences. Does the popularity of the audioguide, as an access and interpretative device, aid its users to develop critical skills to look at art? Where do the visually or musically literate fit in? Can arts organizations continue to think of programming geared at so-called educated audience members?

8   Management by numbers

'People like to converse about creative goods' (Caves 2000: 180). This helps to explain why wine is part of the weekend editions of the international financial press. Indeed, we are informed by the *Financial Times* (5/6 January 2002) of wine's continuing rise in social status: 'For America's rich and famous, wine is the hobby of the moment. Hollywood stars are buying wineries or spending a season in Napa Valley'. Promoted as an independent and experienced assessor, American wine writer Robert Parker is best known for his 100-point rating system (based on tastings done in peer-group, single-blind conditions). He views his numerical rating system as a guide to what he thinks of the wine *vis-à-vis* its peer group:

> Certainly, wines rated above 85 are good to excellent, and any wine rated 90 or above will be outstanding for its particular type. While some would suggest that scoring is not well-suited to a beverage that has been romantically extolled for centuries, wine is no different from any consumer product. ... Scoring wines is simply taking a professional's opinion and applying a numerical system to it on a consistent basis. Moreover, scoring permits rapid communication of information to expert and novice alike.
>
> (Parker 1996: 13)

Of course, he notes the limitations of relying on the headline figure:

> Scores do not reveal the most important facts about a wine. The written commentary (tasting notes) that accompanies the ratings is a better source of information regarding the wine's style and personality, its relative quality level *vis-à-vis* its peers, and its relative value and aging potential than any score could ever indicate.
>
> (Parker 1996: 14)

'People value nonpurposive conversation' (Caves 2000: 181), yet there are tangible benefits from our casual, albeit informed, communications with others.

Rules and prescriptions based on numbers have been central to understanding management and organizational performance. First, taste has been subject to surveys and ratings, essentially the use of numbers to assist the making of decisions. Second, reference is made to Baumol and Bowen's influential concept of the 'income gap' (e.g. the efficiency gains made by substituting capital for labour do not often apply to arts organizations), the implications of the cost disease for non-commercial arts organizations, and how new sources of revenue are being generated to help ensure the financial stability of the organization. Third, management control techniques based on auditing practices are examined. The limitations of performance management are real. Fourth, 'restructuring' is highlighted as a management keyword that is used without much sense of irony.

Taste and numbers

The production and consumption of art can be dictated by numbers. The Russian-born visual arts team of Komar and Melamid interpreted consumer research data (based on a telephone poll of 1001 American adults answering 103 questions, and interviewing by focus groups) compiled by a Boston market research firm, with sponsorship from the National Institute (an offshoot of *The Nation* magazine), as the basis for their exhibition, 'People's Choice: The Polling of America' (1994–5), about aesthetic preferences and taste in painting (see www.diacenter.org/km). Intending to discover a true 'people's art' by surveying popular taste in painting, they created two art works: a tiny (e.g. paperback-sized) abstract canvas entitled *America's Most Unwanted*, embodying the sharp geometrical forms, mostly mustard yellow and red, with a darkening to black around the edges, supposedly least appreciated by the general public; and *America's Most Wanted*, a medium-sized, blue-skied lakeside vignette populated with humans (including a central figure of George Washington) and two deers, all allegedly comprising the nation's most-favoured elements. Of course, the raw statistical data cannot dictate such images; rather, these paintings could only arise from a sensibility well-acquainted with pictorial conventions. For example, *America's Most Unwanted* makes reference to Russian Constructivism with its 'aura of godless geometric mysticism and socialist utopianism' (Vine 1994: 118), which is not perceived to be ideologically sound in the USA. The Hudson River School, including the theme of Manifest Destiny, is referenced by *America's Most Wanted*.

What is represented by this jocular meddling of art and marketing? Making art is one of the last areas of 'democratic-consumer' society to be subjected to opinion polls. Melamid has described the concept for the project:

> In a way it was a traditional idea, because faith in numbers is fundamental to people, starting with Plato's idea of a world which is based on numbers. In ancient Greece, when sculptors wanted to create an ideal human body they measured the most beautiful men and women and then made an average measurement, and that's how they described the ideal of beauty and how the most beautiful sculpture was created. In a way, this is the same thing; in principle, it's nothing new. It's interesting: we believe in numbers, and numbers never lie. Numbers are innocent. It's absolutely true data. It doesn't say anything about personalities, but it says something about one's ideals, and about how this world functions. That's really the truth, as much as we can get to the truth. Truth is a number.

(www.diacenter.org/km)

Polls have become ubiquitous markers of contemporary public opinion and taste in advanced economies. But is there only the illusion of dialogue? Can polls serve as an index of value? Polling is fraught with distortions, eliciting truncated opinions. Preferences are elicited only in the abstract. Moreover, there is the argument that polls serve as an escape from real understanding of complex issues. Cynical observers argue that polls now serve as a tool for the *seduction* of public opinion.

The methodology underpinning Komar and Melamid's paintings, based on 'scientific' viewer-demand information, has links with America's ideological war against communism during the 1950s and 1960s:

> Many modern polling practices are an offshoot of cold war computer war-games developed to simulate battle scenarios in accordance with shifting variables. Just as advertising has been touted as a consumer society's bulwark against communism and fascist perversions of mass psychology, so the market-probability research as emerged from anticommunist war-gaming came to be seen as a way of keeping the free world one future ahead of the evil empire. The depth of attitudinal polling that has led to today's virtually daily tracking of neighborhood psychographics is the very essence of cold war democracy. New management, corporate symbolism, spin surgery, deep agenda-setting – these are the PR tools that helped to preserve our sacred liberties in the struggle against totalitarianism.
>
> (Ross 1995: 76)

Komar and Melamid exaggerate the mechanics of cultural production by numbers to such a degree that its absurdity becomes devastatingly apparent:

> Long intimate with bureaucratic thought and practice, their work feeds off a withering familiarity with the arts of the modern state: its procedures for manufacturing consent, and its facility for squeezing every possible drop from the rhetorical fruits of communism and democracy while exhibiting little evidence of either ideal.
>
> (Ross 1995: 72–3)

A sense of wry humour and irony is apparent in their work. As Melamid has put it: 'There is a truth in every joke' (Meyer 1994: 142). Questions are raised and left unanswered. Is their approach to aesthetic value based on scientific truth different from one generated from cultural taste? Just how many other things – subjected to market research – get so drastically misrepresented? What kind of society is produced that lives and governs itself by focus groups and exit polls?

Lampooning the obsession with demographics and target marketing can no longer be directed solely at Americans. Komar and Melamid's project began on the web, in 1995, under the auspices of the Dia Center for the Arts, and has expanded to more than a dozen countries. Results of surveys in other countries are highlighted by similarities with the American polls. This broaches ideas about the universality of art. Can one talk about a homogenization of tastes and standardizing what is on offer, namely the globalization of markets?

Beyond the income gap

In the early 1970s, Kenneth Boulding remarked: 'It is clear that there is something, which now exists perhaps only in its embryo, which deserves the name of cultural economics. Because it has not yet taken an unambiguous form, it is obviously hard to describe' (Boulding 1972: 272). There was a general shift in mood about 'the arts' (in the USA):

> And it might seem odd to speak of 'the arts' as an economic sector, the notion that they constitute an 'industry' would have positively repelled most cultural leaders *before the 1960s*. With the advent of public funding, however, advocates of government aid lost no time in gathering industry statistics useful for constructing reports on the 'economic impact of the arts' and other instruments of political persuasion ... The concept of arts as 'industry' now seems increasingly natural and suggestive of an almost corporate gravity of purpose.
>
> (DiMaggio 1986: 6; my emphasis)

More specifically, Boulding had in mind the pioneering study by American economists William Baumol and William Bowen, *Performing Arts, the economic dilemma* (1966). Baumol and Bowen's text has canonic status (for a thirtieth anniversary commemoration, see Towse 1997). It represents 'a point of origin', according to David Throsby:

> For the first time a major branch of the arts was subject to systematic theoretical and empirical scrutiny. To those economists who cared to read it at the time, it showed the extent to which their discipline could illuminate a new and challenging area of interest, using familiar tools of economic inquiry.
>
> (Throsby 1994: 2)

The study, which focused on 'problems common to theater, opera, music, and dance', was recognized as ground-breaking. As the performing arts had already garnered the attention of foundations, the Baumol and Bowen study was well-timed; moreover, it helped to shape the pioneering arts management journal, *Performing Arts Review: the journal of management and law of the arts* (now the *Journal of Arts Management, Law and Society*).

Baumol and Bowen put across a compelling 'cost disease' thesis regarding macro-level aspects of unbalanced growth in the performing arts industry and the impact on the individual performing arts organization. Performing arts organizations, as 'patients', had severe difficulties in achieving productivity advantages as achieved in manufacturing industries, for example, from technological advances and exploiting economies of scale. Is the performing arts organization able to generate progressive increases in revenue to outpace relative cost increases, not least of all labour? In most cases, the answer is 'no'. Individuals, as performers, are key to the productive process; this is to say that the production is the product itself, hence limitations and difficulties associated with enhancing productivity. The labour-intensity of the performing arts and the lack of factor substitution results in 'productivity lags' which, in turn, leads to an 'income gap'. The 'income gap' represents the ensuing shortfall between earned revenues and total expenditures were attributed to structural deficiencies rather than being immediately attributed to inadequate management practices (though the latter would obviously aggravate an already bad condition). Either unearned incomes – public subsidies in the main – would make up the difference, or deficits would be incurred (i.e. the 'patient' is not able to cure the 'cost disease').

The factor price adjustments at the core of the cost disease hypothesis have not occurred to the full extent suggested: the realities of labour markets in the arts mean a gradual erosion in the relative earnings position of workers in the performing arts; rising consumer incomes have gone some way to offsetting the negative effects of ticket price rises forced through cost pressures; moreover, many arts organizations have become more sophisticated in marketing, resulting in higher attendance figures and income. As such, refinements to Baumol and Bowen's original thesis have taken place:

> Essentially it can now be said that, while the basic logic of the cost disease is, in its own terms, inarguable, the casual chain linking certain characteristics of production of the live arts to a widening income gap is by no means as inexorable as many have supposed.
>
> (Throsby 1994: 15)

'The evidence is conflicting', according to Alan Peacock, 'but the disease seems containable if not remediable through the offsetting rise in *value* productivity' (Peacock 1998: 293; my emphasis), which is about inculcating taste for improved quality in the overall experience.

There are complementary ways for performing arts companies to address the cost disease. Broadcasting and recording technology can extend consumption of a single performance. Sharing administrations, say by having the London Philharmonic Orchestra and the Royal Philharmonic Orchestra appoint the same managing director, is one way to lower costs; however, it is viewed by critics as a first step to a complete merger and job losses. During the redevelopment period of the Royal Opera House at Convent Garden, there was talk that the English National Opera could share the space with existing tenants, the Royal Opera and the Royal Ballet. Opportunities exist for adjustment in factor use such as performing plays with simpler sets or smaller casts. Of course, there is the risk of 'artistic deficits' resulting from initiatives like 'canned' music. Another sort of artistic deficit seems to be central to music critic Rupert Christiansen's concern about the use of cheaper labour from central and eastern Europe:

> Taxpayers contribute about £50 million a year towards subsidising a network of opera and ballet companies, as well as considerable amounts towards the training of singers, dancers and musicians. It makes no sense then to deny these performers opportunities to perform by importing third-rate equivalents who contribute nothing of significance to our cultural life. And the eastern

Europeans could well do better to look to Asia, where capital cities such as Singapore and Taipei have been busily building superbly equipped new opera houses without establishing the indigenous companies to house them.

(London *Daily Telegraph*, 27 February 2001)

British impresarios such as Opera and Ballet International or Artsworld appear to be central to these touring shows. Christiansen questions the contractual arrangements of the impresarios (e.g. the current basic rates of agreement negotiated between the Theatrical Management Association and Equity and the Musicians' Union), and asks whether 'eastern-European companies have drained audiences away from our subsidised companies'?

In mooting a 'structural deficit', the Boston MFA would appear to be making reference to Baumol and Bowen's thesis. Following a missed opportunity to host the 'King Tut' exhibition, the MFA embarked on an expansion and renovation strategy, from the mid-1970s for about a decade, in order to attract blockbusters. Yet the institution was without money-in-hand for the various capital projects amounting to approximately $60 million; moreover, by 1980, endowment income covered 40 per cent of the operating budget (compared to 60 per cent in 1970). The MFA borrowed money. Successful blockbusters (e.g. 'Renoir' and 'Monet in the 90s') meant that reserves were boosted; however, financial reserves were depleted by debt charges and operating deficits (which mounted in the fallow 'blockbuster-less' years). With hindsight, it is clear that the heady optimism of the go-go 1980s served to mask areas of weakness. As such, the 1990s were marked by greater attention to strengthening the MFA's long-term financial position. For example, prior to the endowment enhancement campaign, the income accruing from the endowment covered just 15 per cent of operating costs. As such the MFA identified what it termed a 'structural deficit' of $2 million per annum. Of course, it is a benefit to calling the deficit 'structural' in that it implies an in-built weakness which can only be addressed by an extraordinary effort. The endowment campaign, with a goal of raising $100 million, was a means to eliminate the structural deficit.

In *c*.1600, the union of poetry, music, and theatre into a form, known as opera, was first developed in Italy. Opera represents the clearest example of an expensive and labour-intensive form of art with limited capability to exploit technological advances and economies of scale. The exchange in the *Financial Times* (8/9 and 22/23 September 2001) between the paper's music critic Andrew Clark and opera patron Alberto Vilar is instructive. Clark puts forward the case that 'opera is an art form that was fully developed in the nineteenth century. It's not just hung up on the past, it's also tied to the economic equations of the past, which render it unacceptably expensive today'. He continues:

The high noon of opera was the late nineteenth century – the high noon of the European bourgeoisie. Aristocracy was still the leading patron: without King Ludwig of Bavaria, Wagner would have been lost. But without an educated middle class there would have been no audience to fill the large, elaborate opera houses that had been built to replace intimate court theatres.

Today, according to Clark, 'opera has become the opium of a rich and educated minority'. One has to learn the core 'repertoire' (say from *Kobbé's Complete Opera Book*, an authoritative reference work which includes just over 200 works); it is assumed that one attends well-versed with plot summaries, not least of all to be seen to participate in the interval quiz which is an integral part of the Metropolitan Opera's radio broadcasts. A seasoned opera-goer, who focuses on beautiful voices and elaborate stage décor, should be able to make aesthetic comparisons with previous productions. 'Opera may no longer be a living, pulsating entity but its well-preserved corpse will be worthy of inspection for decades to come', according to Clark. Vilar disagrees with Clark's pessimistic prognosis, yet also recognizes the economic dilemma faced by opera houses around the world:

> Opera is a very costly art form because of the considerable resources it requires: choruses, orchestras, costumes, sets, lights, stagehands, etc. Nobody has ever pretended that opera could expect to pay for itself through ticket sales, which is why public and private support, which I relentlessly campaign for, remains essential.

As an early investor in high technology firms, Vilar believes that private wealth – in a short period, since the late 1990s, he has become a leading patron of opera at the Kennedy Center, the Metropolitan Opera, Covent Garden, La Scala, the Kirov, and Bayreuth, for example – must fill the gap that governments and ticket sales cannot cover.

A high cost per patron is a defining characteristic of the performing arts. How to cover this cost is a key question. Two alternative solutions are examined: English country house opera and blockbuster musicals. Country house opera represents an art form peculiar to England, with Glyndebourne and Garsington as predominant examples. Both are examples of private initiative (in the absence of state subsidy): John Christie built a small opera house as an attachment to the manor house of Glyndebourne, with the first performances taking place in 1934; and in the late 1980s, Leonard Ingrams, a successful banker, decided that his manor house at Garsington could be a second Glyndebourne. Both may be viewed as bastions of privilege, with social exclusivity part of a shrewd commercial equation. For example, there are 7,500 names on the waiting list to join the coveted Glyndebourne Festival Society, and that list is now closed. Members of the Festival Society are offered first crack at tickets, with the corporate market limited to 30 per cent of capacity; the season is generally sold out by opening night, with standing place among the hottest tickets for the general public. Picnicking in the grounds is a key part of the country house opera experience – the interval at Glyndebourne is 85 minutes – and for many, eating and drinking is more important than the opera. The popping of champagne corks suggests a certain style of dress, which is made explicit for the uninitiated on Glyndebourne's website: 'During the Festival season, evening dress (black tie/long or short dress) is customary' (www.glyndebourne.com). With under 500 seats, Garsington is attempting to recreate an atmosphere reminiscent of Glyndebourne before the new theatre was built: this means that Garsington is an expensive affair, it represents impeccable style, remains aloof from issues of public art subsidy, and there is an absence of the corporate season populated by upwardly mobile executives.

Innovation is central to understanding the rise of high cost blockbuster musicals aimed at the mass market (see Caves 2000: 260–1). There is the potential for enormous audiences through touring opportunities and merchandising. Productions associated with Cameron Macintosh and Andrew Lloyd Webber, such as *The Phantom of the Opera* and *Cats*, resemble blockbuster films: the emphasis is on grand sets and dazzling special effects; a high concept (i.e. a storyline that can be encapsulated in one sentence and which can be 'translated' outside Anglo-American marketplaces) ensures less focus on character development or individual actors. The revival of touring companies and modern technology makes the special effects of these shows portable. Heavy promotion is used to gain cross-national reach; moreover, the associated media attention when a flashy new musical arrives in town (whether it is Toronto or Helsinki) helps to generate the buzz necessary for the production to develop 'legs'.

Is a sports management model relevant in the arts? Unlike ticket sales from stadium sports (e.g. both forms of football), the economics of golf are such that even a prestigious tournament may only generate about $1 million in ticket sales (see the *Wall Street Journal Europe*, 17/18 August 2001). Corporate sponsors and broadcasters pay most of the bills and purse money. Players, operating as freelancers, pay their own expenses to compete in tournaments. This has led to 'pro-ams': wealthy sponsors (who dole out perks to employees and clients) are able to play a round of golf with the professionals before the start of the tournament. Pro-ams, in other words, pay part of the bills. Contractual obligations are enforced for tournaments on the PGA Tour and the PGA European Tour so that even the best golfers cannot avoid participation without suffering penalties. It goes without saying that the calibre of golf can be poor.

Performance indicators

Performance management is being positioned as an integral part of the strategic management of any organization. It includes issues associated with quality, governance, and accountability, which are of interest to all types of arts organizations. The question 'how well are we doing?' is at the heart of performance measurement. The collection of performance indicators, namely 'statistics, ratios, costs and other forms of information which illuminate or measure progress in achieving aims and objectives of an organization as set out in its corporate plan' (Jackson 1991: 51).

There is a need to understand the context which is enabling auditing and performance management to be identified with securing institutional legitimacy. An excellent account of the implications associated with the extension of auditing into different institutional settings is made by Michael Power in *The Audit Explosion* (1994). Power challenges the conventional view of auditing, in terms of its technical and operational qualities, as a value-free exercise: 'Auditing has become central to ways of talking about administrative control … It has much to do with articulating problems, with rationalising and reinforcing public images of control' (Power 1994: 5). There is the view that audits thrive 'when accountability can no longer be sustained by informal relations of trust alone but must be formalized, made visible and subject to independent validation' (Power 1994: 11).

Public accountability has been reframed in relation to concepts such as vision and mission statements, aims and objectives, customer satisfaction, and market competition. The growth of interest of accountability stimulated the significance of performance measurement during the 1990s, not least of all in the UK. The 3Es of 'economy, efficiency, and effectiveness' are fundamental to the so-called value for money (VFM) framework which serves to evaluate performance. Two areas are key: the relationship between resource inputs and service outputs; and establishing whether or not the service outputs being provided are those valued by the institution's stakeholders.

The VFM framework 'prioritizes that which can be measured and audited in economic terms – efficiency and economy – over that which is more ambiguous and local – effectiveness' (Power 1994: 34). 'Efficiency' as it 'is inevitably put into operation' raises the hackles of Henry Mintzberg:

> It is not a neutral concept but one associated with a particular system of values – economic values. In fact an obsession with efficiency can force the trading off of social benefits for economic ones that drive an organization beyond an economic morality to a social immorality.
>
> (Mintzberg 1989: 331, 333–4)

Furthermore, according to Power:

> For all its proclaimed sensitivity toward context, VFM demands that effectiveness be quantifiable. It does this by standardizing measures of effectiveness (on the one hand) and/or by reducing effectiveness to standardizable measures of economy and efficiency. Either way there is a necessary drift towards 'management by numbers' which enables a drift towards centralised forms of control and displacement of concern about good management.
>
> (Power 1994: 34)

What actually occurs is a displacement from first-order experts to second-order verifactory activities monitored by overseers. At the same time, there 'is now almost no way reservations about audit can be articulated without appearing to defend privileges and secrecy' (Power 1994: 40).

Performance indicators (PIs) are said to offer numerous benefits to arts organizations. First, more objective benchmarks against which to measure progress are established in order to meet aims and objectives identified in the corporate plan. It goes without saying that PIs are of little value or interest until they are compared with something. The best comparisons are with the institution's past performance (i.e trend or longitudinal analysis) and targets established for planning purposes (i.e. budget versus actual). However, 'the question of benchmarks or other externally-derived standards (rules-of-thumb)' remains problematic; and there is the warning that 'too formal a system of performance management invites working towards good PIs results to the exclusion of pursuing those less tangible goals that were not so easily susceptible to measurement or quantification' (Weil 1994: 347). For example, if performance management is equated with ratio analysis, the backbone of financial analysis, the institution runs into the problem of what Hamel and Prahalad characterize as 'denominator management ... an accountant's short cut to productivity' (Hamel and Prahalad 1994: 8). Second, areas of relative strength and weakness are identified in order to aid the decision-making process as regards the allocation of resources. The 'real utility of performance indicators' (Jackson 1991: 43), it has been contended, derives from their diagnostic value, as opposed to measures of evaluation and assessment. This requires monitoring key indicators which serve as early warnings of impending problems. Third, indicators encourage and motivate staff: performance management may support organizational learning such as finding out what visitors find appealing about the organization. On the other hand, there is a worrying perspective: 'The audit explosion is characterized less by an opening up of organizations and more by reinvestment of trust in new bodies of audit expertise and its legitimation through such things as accreditation and monitoring systems' (Power 1994: 26).

'A great deal of care needs to be taken in constructing performance measurement systems. The first imperative is to ensure that the purposes for measuring performance are clear and accepted by everyone' (Flynn 1993: 123). Is it possible to recommend a range of performance indicators for any arts sector which could be used, *inter alia*, to make meaningful comparisons between institutions? There is the opinion that effectiveness indicators 'must always be specific to a particular institution and should never be based on some hypothetical benchmark or standard applicable to all museums or even to museums of a specific discipline, scale, or type of governance' (Weil 1994: 345). Even with efficiency indicators, 'more broad-based comparisons – except, perhaps, for something so generic as staff turnover rates or the total return on endowment – could only be misleading' (Weil 1994: 346). It seems that at best such a form of regulation establishes minimum and often crude standards of acceptable behaviour. To mitigate against the promotion of a rigid set of problematic indicators, reframe the boundaries of reference:

> In this instance the programme's focus has been on an exploration of the broader context for performance assessment and on examining the strategic issues surrounding the issue of PIs. In particular an objective of the programme has been to develop a *common framework for approaching indicators* rather than a common set of actual indicators.
>
> (KPMG for the Department of National Heritage 1994: 4–5)

Greater emphasis is placed on linking PIs more clearly to the corporate planning process.

Two conventional management models (or diagrams) may be proffered as an attempt to communicate how performance assessment fits in with other management practices and processes. Model I – illustrating the four-level hierarchical relationship between *mission, objectives, do-wells* (or critical success factors), and *performance measures* (for each do-well) at the corporate level – stresses that PIs 'should be an integral part of the setting and monitoring of strategic direction' (KPMG for the DNH 1994: 14). Linked to the first model, Model II seeks to develop a common framework for performance assessment by attempting 'to link the identification and use of performance indicators into the overall organizational mission and objectives' (KPMG for the DNH 1994: 19). Model II is 'both flexible enough to be customized and robust enough to satisfy government requirements' (KPMG for the DNH 1994: 19); it is made up of five concentric rings with *the mission* at the centre surrounded by *primary objectives, change objectives, resources* (e.g. people and space), and *financial resources*. Of course, it is recognized that conventional management diagrams often emphasize the manipulation of numbers at the expense of creating visions. More attention needs to be devoted to considering whether relying on management consultants represents an effective use of an organization's funds. It might be argued that developing management talent within the organization offers better results in the longer term.

The current state of performance management, with its strong auditing alignment, raises philosophical problems about the orientation of neophyte arts managers regarding their training and socialization: 'Audits ensure accountability to individuals as "clients" rather than citizens and it is no accident that the audit explosion has accompanied the displacement of old languages with that of markets, missions, and management' (Power 1994: 54). From a management consultancy perspective, McKinsey identifies the absence of clear performance measures. Rather than capturing the right data to track performance, there is often an emphasis on an 'ad hoc assortment of metrics' such as money raised, membership growth, the percentage of repeat visitors, or the ratio of such measures to the cost of a programme (Lowell *et al.* 2000: 153). Weaknesses are recognized: lack of inter-organizational comparisons; focus on process (e.g. administrative efficiency) and outputs (e.g. number of people served) rather than outcomes (e.g. impact measures focus on progress toward mission and long-term objectives that drive organizational focus); and emphasis on the percentage of donations and revenues spent on overheads, which is a crude measure of fiscal responsibility. Paolo Baratta, president of the Biennale di Venezia, sums up the problem if attention to detail obfuscates a view of what is important: 'More fundamental than public versus private is the divide between bureaucratic mentality and enterprise. And I mean enterprise not efficiency. Efficiency is a cost-benefit calculation. Enterprise aims at quality' (*Wall Street Journal Europe*, 16/17 February 2001).

It is instructive and whimsical to consider an earlier attempt to organize culture. Just as PIs are cited as a contemporary aid to good judgement, Roger de Piles, a French academician, amplified the concept of rule, in the first decade of the eighteenth century, by devising a comparative list of artists appreciated according to four specific criteria. Composition, line (*dessin*), colour, and expression served as domains for artistic judgement in de Piles's *Cours de peinture par principes* (1708) (see Barasch 1985: 310–77). In this number-driven approach, each artist in each of the four categories was evaluated separately, with scoring according to a scale in which '20' represented perfection. On the composition-design (or line)-

colour-expression domains, Dürer scored 36 (8–10–10–8); LeBrun scored 56 (16–16–8–16); Leonardo scored 49 (15–16–4–14); Michelangelo scored 37 (8–17–4–8); Poussin scored 50 (15–6–17–12); Raphael scored 65 (17–18–12–18); Rubens scored 65 (18–13–17–17); and Titian scored 51 (12–15–18–6). What de Piles attempted was to give new meaning to rules as an acknowledged criteria of judgement. Why, as regards purpose or motivation, we are not certain – possibly at the request of a patron, or for the sake of entertainment rather than for more serious purposes. Like PIs, which are provocative and suggestive, de Piles's distribution of scores makes us wonder what precisely the individual terms meant. Moreover, what does 'expression' mean if LeBrun scores 16, twice as much as Dürer or Michelangelo? According to Svetlana Alpers, de Piles offers a nuanced account of how painting is to be viewed:

> First, in making the distinction Rubens/colour and Poussin/design, de Piles contributed the essential element to a binary structure of taste for art in France. The contrast between a view of Rubens and Poussin effectively divided pictorial taste and practice in France. Second, de Piles's defense of a definition of colour as exemplified in the paintings by Rubens gives a new emphasis to the viewer's experience of painting, and it does this in eroticized terms.
>
> (Alpers 1995: 74)

Restructuring

Restructuring is a contested term used to capture a large number of processes incorporating organizational change. It is one of the major themes in the reshaping of work and organizations and took root during the last fifteen years of the twentieth century (see, for example, Powell 2001). The general causes of restructuring include technological advances whereby workers are replaced, as opposed to increasing their productivity by enlarging their skills base. In the case of subsidized arts, a general desire in most advanced economies to see decent public services without over-straining the taxpayer means getting by with fewer resources from the public purse. In theory, restructuring is aimed at carving away layers of corporate fat, jettisoning under-performing business units, and raising asset productivity. Yet there appears to be a predictable sameness to restructuring as it is applied: 'Masquerading under names like refocusing, delayering, decluttering and right-sizing (one is tempted to ask why the "right" size is always smaller), restructuring always has the same result: fewer employees' (Hamel and Prahalad 1994: 6). Managers in the 'middle' of the organizational hierarchy – formerly 'safe' white-collar employees – are particularly vulnerable to losing their jobs when organizations decide to restructure.

If 'intended reductions in personnel' is a working definition of restructuring, this raises the question of when to stop: 'where is the dividing line between cutting fat and cutting muscle?' 'Too few companies have made the transition from restructuring to building. Unless they do, it is only a matter of time before they will be restructuring again', according to Michael Porter. Restructuring in practice can be 'a means of dealing with the failure of past strategies' (Porter 1987: 22). For example, the Boston MFA had two significant attempts at restructuring during the first half of the 1990s: forty positions from a staff of 520 were eliminated in the light of a projected deficit of $4.7 million (total planned operations of $25.7 million) in the FY 1991/92; in early 1994 the new director, Malcolm Rogers, issued a memorandum to staff that 'restructuring and defining all aspects of the Museum's operations and programming in light of our financial situation' (e.g. a deficit of $4.5 million on an operating budget of $23.5 million), and then eliminated 20 per cent of staff, or 83 positions from a staff of 483. In such circumstances, it is difficult to view the institution's financial shortfall and restructuring as separate events. Indeed, given the labour-intensive nature of many arts organizations, there is a primary focus on labour costs as a way to reduce the overall budget.

As management reform, which involves keeping the same old departmental structure (more or less), but hoping to do more with fewer people, downsizing is fraught with difficulties:

> Downsizing belatedly attempts to correct mistakes of the past; it is not about creating the markets of the future. The simple point is that getting smaller is not enough. Downsizing, the equivalent of corporate anorexia, can make a company thinner; it doesn't necessarily make it healthier.
>
> (Hamel and Prahalad 1994: 11)

There are charges that all the talk about 'human capital' (as the management term for employees) does not square with what may appear to be indiscriminate axing of jobs. Critics of restructuring cite work intensification for those who remain in the organization. Plummeting morale, higher levels of stress, and job insecurity of the remaining employees (e.g. the so-called walking wounded or carping critics) are not uncommon results; there is also the risk that those with the best skills and knowledge may accept other opportunities in order to escape the organization. On the other hand, downsizing and restructuring can be about eliminating redundant skills and acquiring new ones. This means an emphasis on changing the functional requirements of the organization as opposed to cutting costs.

Clement Greenberg's essay 'The plight of culture' helps to organize issues associated with management by numbers: 'Once efficiency is universally accepted as a rule, it becomes an inner compulsion and weighs like a sense of sin, simply because no one can be efficient *enough*, just as no one can ever be virtuous enough' (Greenberg 1963: 31; emphasis in the original). First, Komar and Melamid seek to illustrate that distortions may result from too much reliance on data from marketing research. Opinion polling cannot be viewed as providing answers and solutions to important decisions. Second, Baumol and Bowen's 'cost disease' and resulting 'income gap' provided powerful metaphors for arts organizations seeking an explanation for deficit positions. In the ensuing three decades, the economic determinism associated with 'productivity lags' and 'structural' weaknesses has not crippled arts organizations. The high cost per patron for the performing arts has been addressed in two distinct ways: elite provision as with English country house opera; and blockbuster musicals to appeal to mass audiences. Third, the rise of performance indicators owes much to the inroads made by auditing, as expressed in the ethos of the 'new' public sector in the UK. Yet it is important to remember that auditing, and the so-called value-for-money framework, is not a value-free exercise. (The collapse of Enron and pointed questions to its auditors Arthur Andersen should help to dispel remaining doubts.) Fourth, in practice, restructuring is often viewed as a response to budgetary restraints which entail cuts in labour costs. The positive contributions associated with changing the skills mix of the organization's staff is often overshadowed by the impact of 'work intensification'.

9 Raising funds and financing

Two interesting stories were reported in December 2001 to represent growth and decline associated with financial instruments and the arts. First, the case of Stagecoach Arts Theatre: it was one of the companies added to the Alternative Investment Market (AIM) establishing a monthly record for this second-tier exchange. AIM was created in 1995 as a market for young and growing companies. Flotation on a public market like AIM is first and foremost an opportunity to raise funds for further growth. (Other second-tier exchanges which are larger than AIM include America's NASDAQ and Germany's Neuer Markt.) Founded in 1988, Stagecoach now has over 250 schools in the UK providing education in the performing arts to 4–16 year olds. Stagecoach has trained over 10,000 students and describes itself as 'the world's largest part-time theatre school'. Stagecoach, which helped to train Jamie Bell, star of the film *Billy Elliot* (2001), joined AIM by issuing an initial public offering (IPO). The principal investors in Stagecoach, according to Beeson Gregory, which was behind the floatation (as nominated adviser and broker), were venture capitalist trusts, a financial investment that shelters capital gains by deferring tax due and offers income tax to persuade investors to back small companies (*Financial Times*, 15/16 December 2001). Second, Andrew Lloyd Webber announced the closing of the London production of *Cats* following a final performance on 11 May 2002, its twenty-first birthday. Given its phenomenal success – the longest running musical in the history of either the West End or Broadway – one tends to forget how innovative was *Cats*. Traditional theatre investors and producers would not touch Lloyd Webber's project, based on T. S. Eliot's *Old Possum's Book of Practical Cats*; Cameron Macintosh, who agreed to produce it, had to seek investors at £750 per subscription to raise the £450,000 needed to open the show in 1981. Investors have been well rewarded: every pound invested has seen a return of £56.67, this means £42,500 for an initial subscription of £750.

Three broad topics are addressed: fund-raising, equity financing, and the property rights of individual artists. First, to help ensure financial stability, most nonprofit arts organizations rely on fund-raising activities to supplement subsidies and revenue from commercial operations; furthermore, capital funding (for building projects and to establish endowments) is becoming more topical. The philosophy of fund-raising is thus an instructive topic to examine. Second, notwithstanding the opening illustrations, equity financing is not a panacea for arts organizations. Indeed equity financing is not available to many arts organizations in receipt of public funding. Equity financing does not offer a guaranteed return to investors. It goes without saying that most plays do not have the popular appeal of *Cats*; 'angels' who provide private equity to finance theatrical productions are investing in a highly speculative financial instrument. Third, exploiting intellectual property rights may be one method for individual artists to secure greater financial returns from artistic creation.

The philosophy of fund-raisng

Peter Drucker and Henry Drucker are not related, but both offer foundational points on the philosophy of fund-raising. Fund-raising can help to safeguard an arts organization against future cuts in subsidies, yet Peter Drucker voices some concern about too much attention to raising money:

> Almost by definition, money is always scarce in a nonprofit institution. Indeed, a good many nonprofit managers seem to believe that all their problems could be solved if they had more money. In fact, some of them come close to believing that money-raising is really their mission.
>
> But a nonprofit institution that becomes a prisoner of money-raising is in serious trouble and in a serious identity crisis. The purpose of a strategy for fund-raising money is precisely to enable the nonprofit institution to carry out its mission without subordinating that mission to fund-raising.
>
> (Drucker 1990: 41)

What he seems to be tackling is 'goal displacement'. Artistic excellence is difficult; it can be displaced by goals such as fund-raising targets that can be achieved, or are easier to measure. One knock-on effect, as discussed in Chapter 10, is a disproportionate increase in fund-raising staff *vis-à-vis* professional arts-based staff. Fund-raising has become a continuous process. A major pitfall of relying on major donors is the undue influence they may have on programming choices. This has been mooted in the case of Alberto Vilar, who has emerged, since the late 1990s, as an international patron of opera. It has been noted that strings are attached to his largesse: 'he likes to see his name writ large' so that there is the Vilar Floral Hall at the Royal Opera House, the Vilar Grand Tier at the Metropolitan Opera, and the Alberto Vilar titles represent a new system of multi-language translation; and 'he has also argued that donors should get bigger programme billing than composers' (London *Daily Telegraph*, 23 May 2001). As merely the most recent entrepreneur turned arts patron, it is not surprising that his operatic investments – for this is the way Bourdieu and Haacke (1995) would view Vilar's engagement – are strategically interlinked and based on cultivating social relations with general managers of opera houses. That there are relatively few large patrons on Vilar's scale allows him significant – but not undue – bargaining power which has longer term repercussions for his favoured opera houses.

Fund-raising may be an instrument to engage and energize donors who can develop an emotional tie to the organization. Oxford Philanthropic was established in 1994 as a management consultancy that advises nonprofit organizations on developing strategies for major fund-raising programmes. Henry Drucker, Oxford Philanthropic's founder, discusses giving and fund-raising in spiritual terms:

> Fund-raising can liberate the donor; and
> The most successful fund-raisers in the world, measured by dollars raised, are American universities. But the vocabulary, the arguments, are all Protestant arguments. It's about inspiration, changing the world, and personal destiny. The language of fund-raising I teach is really a version of Protestant theology.
>
> (*Financial Times*, 6/7 December 1997)

Two points require further comment. First, most of the elite universities in the USA are private, nonprofit institutions. Endowments are crucial to understanding the sustainability of the best American universities. For example, more than forty universities have endowments of $1 billion or more. Fund-raising skills honed at places like Harvard, Brown, Princeton, and Duke are being transferred to the most prestigious arts organizations in the USA. Oxford Philanthropic is attempting to replicate this pattern in the UK: half of the consultancy's thirty organizational clients are universities; visual arts and art music organizations account for an additional one-third. Second, liberal humanism issues, as raised in Chapter 4, help in understanding the role of Protestant theology. Can the transformative value attributed to giving be viewed as a form of reification? Moreover, a subtle point has been mooted that the devotion of Americans to capitalism and religion is peculiar to the USA: 'it is religion in this country to refute Marx', according to Harold Bloom, who believes that the American religion 'is an indigenous religion with almost nothing in common with European Protestantism' (Coutu 2001: 68). Apart from taxation benefits, which influence charitable-giving in the USA, 'freedom of democracy' issues need to be considered. Unlike the situation in Europe, giving in the USA to self-selected 'good causes', represents a way for Americans to express themselves.

The pyramid is a powerful visual symbol for fund-raisers. It represents something to ascend such as a corporate organizational chart or mountain. Moreover, the pyramid is a marker signalling market segmentation. (As a quotidian example, Dell Computer uses a pyramid to distinguish multiple layers, from 'all customers' at base level to 'partners' at the apex.) The fund-raising pyramid encapsulates two principles. First, a small group of top donors provide the bulk of monies gifted. The so-called '20/80' rule is a benchmark emphasizing that a relatively small proportion of donors accounts for the vast bulk of the total funds raised. These high-maintenance givers are difficult to cultivate in any formulaic manner, which is to say that a personal touch is required. Second, fund-raisers need to find incentives to encourage individuals to ascend the pyramid. Asking for a specific gift in relation to the individual's ability to give improves the rate of return. Once a suggested donation has been received, the donor falls into a category that the arts organization should seek to cultivate: how to encourage the donor to upgrade the gift? A reworking of Abraham Maslow's psychological hand, from the 1940s, is in evidence; his basic 'hierarchy of needs' pyramid has five levels of need (ranging from lowest order to highest order: survival and safety; human interaction; love; affiliation, and self-actualization). One is deemed to become more spiritually enlightened at higher levels of the pyramid. This is similar to the three-stage pyramid posited by Charles Handy's 'search for meaning': those who do not strive for the apex, namely to make a contribution to society, sell themselves short; too many individuals who satisfy basic survival needs are content to remain at the middle stage of 'identity', which may accrue through a position in marriage or career (Handy 1997).

Cynics interpret the pyramid model as exploiting individual insecurities about being excluded or not belonging to a group: the tactics of television evangelists, with their mixture of bullying and coddling, provide an obvious example; all the leading luxury brand owners (such as LVMH and Richemont) understand the power of emotion. Additionally, the US Securities and Exchange Commission notes that 'pyramid schemes' are a type of fraudulent activity:

> Participants attempt to make money solely by recruiting new participants into the programme. The hallmark of these schemes is the promise of sky-high returns in a short period of time for doing nothing other than handing over your money and getting others to do the same.
>
> (www.sec.org.gov)

Money coming in from new recruits is used to pay off early-stage investors, but at some point the scheme gets too big, and the promoter cannot raise enough money from new investors to pay earlier investors – eventually the pyramid will collapse.

There is a need to identify and articulate the range of project packages for each campaign to raise funds. Notwithstanding this constant, there are noticeable trends. First, the shift from fund-raising to *fund development* is promoted as more than semantic. But is it in practice? Fund-raising is about asking for money because the need is so great (i.e. going around with a 'begging bowl'). On the other hand, fund development is about *people* development; that is, creating a constituency in tune with the organization's mission. As such, the ultimate goal of fund development is enabling donors to see their support of the institution as self-fulfillment. There is also the general educational benefit of strengthening the objectives of the enterprise. Second, an emphasis on generating funds to supplement an endowment recognizes that a properly managed endowment – invest in a manner to grow the capital and live off the interest – offers greater financial stability than a reliance on public subsidy (which is subject to changing political tides) or even commercial operations (which can fluctuate depending on the popularity of programming). A private source of income can offer artistic independence (as suggested by Virgina Woolf in the case of writers who are women). Third, seeking money from individual donors for operating purposes now competes with fund-raising for capital projects. The tendency to seek 'outside' money for special projects remains important. Yet more and more of the money required by nonprofit organizations is for operating purposes (e.g. covering staff wages through endowed positions, a common practice at elite universities with named chairs). More pressing as a practical matter is the need to coordinate an increasingly heady stream of activity that requires a constant 'pressing of the flesh'. Capital projects occur with greater frequency so that a decade is viewed as a long time between major building projects. Ongoing (e.g. year-to-year) campaigns are used to generate much-needed operations revenue; furthermore, they serve to remind individuals of the multitude of ways that the institution can benefit from one's generosity.

What unites Peter and Henry (the two Druckers) is a belief that much of humanistic service, which includes the arts along with education, health, and social welfare, is better due to private giving generated via fund-raising; this is viewed in opposition to reliance on public funding. This suggests that ideology may play a more significant role than tax concessions to explain giving in the USA and Canada *vis-à-vis* Europe. A requirement to raise funds means that those who give show a greater commitment to the institution; and institutions need to upgrade, improve, and innovate to remain attractive to donors.

The social capital associated with being a board member of a leading arts organization would appear to remain high. Some prestigious arts organizations in the USA are using 'contracts of giving' so that expectations of trustees are made explicit (see, for example, *Wall Street Journal*, 7 May 1999). It costs $100,000 per annum to join at the Whitney Museum of American Art; the New York City Ballet asks for $25,000 which is the admission tariff at the Boston MFA. Carnegie Hall is a reputed pioneer amongst arts organizations by examining the financial assets of prospective board members as part of the selection process. The general criticism that such a view of board members – essentially as walking wallets – emphasizes fiscal concerns of art organizations above all else. On the other hand, 'new money' Americans (say those who have become millionaires in their thirties from financial services or high technology) see no taboo in talking about money; however, they may lack the cultural capital associated with inherited wealth. One way to alleviate this source of discomfiture is to make unwritten codes more transparent: 'At various points in history, etiquette books were produced to show the newly rich appropriate table manners. This new openness is the institutional equivalent of showing where to find the dessertspoon' (Peter Dobkin of Yale University in the *Wall Street Journal*, 7 May 1999).

The first constituency in fund-raising is the institution's own board. Raising money is a social process that revolves around the fund-raising committee. A figurehead is appointed as patron. From a perspective of generating funds, there is a need for trustees to take an active part in raising money (by giving themselves and persuading others to give). A board member needs to be able to respond to the following when making a pitch: how much are you going to give yourself? It is important to cultivate pace-setting donations, which is done during the 'quiet phase'. This important stage ends when the monetary goal of the fund-raising campaign is released to the public. A 'public' campaign is often measured in people not money: this stage is about generating moral support from a wider constituency; however, it is accepted that only a relatively small amount of money will be received.

One illustration of how the stakes have been raised is that becoming a member or friend of an arts organization is about 'buying a service', not an act of philanthropy or making a donation. At basic level, benefits need to be explicit. The casual visitor, in considering an annual membership, may do a quick 'cost-benefit' analysis as part of the decision-making process. For example, with the opening of the Tate Modern in 2000, the Tate decided to revise its membership scheme along lines associated with purchasing a new motor: a base membership at £30 can be complemented with a guest pass (£12 for all four Tates), London private view pass (£15), St. Ives pass (£5), and Liverpool pass (£5). Patrons of New Art and Patrons of British Art represent higher levels of membership (i.e. where 'friends' become 'Friends'): one is assumed to be more in tune with the organization's core aims and enjoying concessions becomes less important. At the same time, personal contact with works of art and artists and 'insider access' to the institution become crucial. Various stages are visible at the Boston MFA. Governance is via a two-part structure: at the apex is the board of trustees (25–43 members); in order to talent-spot potential trustees, a second-tier, 'board of overseers' (maximum 120 members), was created. The MFA Council was formed for those in the intermediate stage of post-university and pre-middle age (e.g. 25–40); these so-called 'young associates', who are recognized by many arts organizations as 'tomorrow's trustees', are attracted to the social life and network potential of an elite arts organization.

Equity financing

The availability of risk capital is one reason for entrepreneurial activity. Private equity financing provides an opportunity for third-party financing to be made available to enterprises not quoted on a main market (like the New York or London stock exchanges) or second-tier exchanges (like NASDAQ or AIM). Venture capital represents an important form of private equity capital. Since the early 1980s, venture capital has gained importance as a source of funding for innovative new ventures (particularly technology-based firms). Venture capitalists can 'cash in' on their investments via private transactions, or through an IPO on the securities market. Much non-venture capital equity, including the role of so-called angel investors, is managed by partnerships; it has been used to provide funds for the expansion of medium-sized firms or leveraged buy-outs and investments in firms in financial distress.

Equity financing is not 'easy money': some degree of autonomy and control may be lost to investors. On the other hand, debt financing is essentially a loan (often from a bank): the loan has to be repaid (with interest within a stated period of time) and assets of some sort must be pledged. When a banker, venture capitalist, or angel investor is considering giving an arts organization money, financial indicators and ratios may be used as part of the decision-making process (see, for example, Vogel 2001: 354–7). However, many of the measures – cash flows and private market values; price/earnings ratios; price/sales ratios; and book value – are most appropriate for entertainment industry investments. One measure, debt/equity ratio, is a basic statement of the amount of debt the firm has compared to its level of equity. To investors or lenders, this ratio is important because it indicates the amount of money available for repayment in the case of default. The ability to service debt depends on projected cash flows, which can be volatile.

Motives behind the funding of theatre are 'much more speculative and entrepreneurial than in any of the other [performing] arts' (Vogel 2001: 328). The financing and development process resembles that used for films. Angel investors seek opportunities which support financial and personal objectives. For example, theatre angels usually have advanced interests in theatre, possibly even some professional knowledge. Investing in a theatrical production is one way to get more involved. 'Closeness' can play an important part in the decision-making process of angels. This can mean geography as angels will want to see the production at one of the touring venues. Moreover, angels want to know with whom they are dealing, thus attention is devoted to the track record of the director and lead actors; straightforward information on the producer, arguably the most important player in the equation, can sometimes be more difficult to secure. In order to spread risk, angel investors do not need to invest alone. An investment club, essentially a group of like-minded people who pool their money to make investments, can be established. Pooling funds with other investors is one way to diversify holdings and hence spread risk (e.g. if five angels each stump up £5,000 – often investments are available in £5,000 units – there is the possibility to invest in five different theatrical productions, whereas a lone angel could only back one production). Theatre investment clubs can operate with members studying different investment proposals, with a vote as to which ones to back. On the other hand, an investment 'fund' approach – analogous to investing in a mutual fund to get involved in the stock market, as opposed to trading on one's own account – can be used: members are not involved with the decision-making process, which is placed in the hands of professional investment managers (e.g. the Gabriel Fund in the UK represents a relatively modest way to enter the world of theatre angels).

The Society of London Theatres (SOLT, known as the Society of West End Theatres, SWET, until the current name change in 1994) is the trade association which represents the producers, theatre owners, and managers of the fifty major commercial and grant-aided theatres in central London. One of the services offered by SOLT is its 'angels list', which puts private individuals who have expressed an interest in investing in London theatre in touch with SOLT-member producers who are seeking investors for new productions. The angels list is important in helping to stimulate entrepreneurial activity; it is a result of SOLT being an entrepreneurial institutional set-up.

'An opportunity to invest in the proposed West End transfer' forms the basis of the following example. £150,000 is sought in investment units of £5,000. Any opportunity to invest, not least of all in the theatre, has substantial risk factors:

> Investment in theatrical productions is extremely speculative and carries a high degree of risk. Subscribers must be aware that there is *no market for the transfer of investments in theatrical productions* and accordingly the investment is unlikely to be saleable or capable of being valued, nor can the extent of risks to which the investment is exposed be reliably identified. If the production does not recover any of its costs the whole subscription will be lost; if only a portion of the costs are recovered only an equivalent proportion of the subscription will be repayable.
>
> (from a private placement memorandum, 2000; my emphasis)

Some terminology is useful: the *producer* intends to present the *play* at a West End *theatre* with a capacity of around 775 seats. The presentation of the play at the West End theatre is called the *production*. The *actors* are contacted to appear in the production. *Director*, *designer*, and *lighting designer* have agreed to work on the production. (Biographies of all of the above are attached.) The producer has been granted all necessary rights in the play to mount the production by a company who act as literary agents for the *author*. A copy of the agreement between the producer and the author (the *licence*) is available for inspection at solicitors by appointment. *Net profits* of the production refer to box office income available to the production after paying or providing for all *weekly running expenses*, including royalties due to the *royalty participants* will be applied as to 100 per cent towards repayment contributions until *recoupment of the costs of production*. After recoupment, the net profit of the production shall be divided 40 per cent to the producer and 60 per cent equally to the subscribers.

The private placement memorandum provided background details of the original production along with information of a current remounting on tour prior to the proposed West End transfer. A date for the intended preview in the West End is given. The only income to the production is income from the West End presentation. The production will be capitalized at £150,000 (the *capitalization*) with no overcall. (Press and marketing at £50,000 account for a substantial proportion of the total capitalization.) In the event that the production costs exceed capitalization, the producer shall be entitled to raise or contribute the additional monies required. Subscribers will have no liability for anything in excess of their agreed contribution to the capitalization provided. Investment is available in units of £5,000. This means that after recoupment a contribution of £5,000 will receive 2 per cent of any net box office after running costs.

Estimates are provided for illustration purposes based on a theatre capacity of 775 seats: at an average of 50 per cent financial capacity of the theatre, the capitalization could be recouped in 8 weeks; at 60 per cent, the capitalization could be recouped in 5 weeks; at 80 per cent, the capitalization could be recouped in 3 weeks. The weekly running costs are approximately 32 per cent of the projected financial capacity of the theatre, which means that the production will make a loss in weeks where income falls below this figure.

The producer is in active negotiation with a West End theatre management to enable a West End opening in a theatre of the capacity on which the above estimates are based. If no theatre is secured within the specified timetable, all subscriptions will be returned in full. The schedule is based on theatre capacity of 775 with a ticket price range of £10.50 to £29.50 and a maximum box office yield of £124,500 on the basis of eight performances per week. The theatre will receive a guaranteed fee of £5,000 per week and the contra is estimated at £11,137; however, these figures may change.

The producer will receive a management fee of £1,500 per week plus £250 office expenses two weeks prior to the commencement of the production until two weeks after the close of the production. The producer will receive a royalty of 1.5 per cent of net weekly box office receipts (net of credit card discounts, agency and library commissions, VAT, and other direct expenses and deductions) pre-recoupment rising to 2.5 per cent post-recoupment. The originating theatre receives a royalty of 1.5 per cent post-recoupment only. The total variable royalties (inclusive of the producer's royalty) are at 10 per cent of net weekly box office receipts pre-recoupment, rising to 15.5 per cent post-recoupment. Estimated weekly running expenses of £32,500 include salaries, production maintenance, press and marketing, administration, estimated theatre rent and contra, and contingency/recast reserve. Additional costs are variable royalties (10 per cent pre-recoupment and 15.5 per cent post-recoupment).

Though the private placement memorandum is approved for the purpose of the Financial Services Act 1986, this does not reduce the need for investors to scrutinize the proposed financial instrument. There is an important caveat about the estimates and schedules proffered in the private placement memorandum: *estimates are distinct from a forecast*. Moreover, these figures are current estimates based on current expectations and may vary when negotiations are complete. The *estimates may be different from actual outcome* so that investors recoup less quickly and the point at which profits become payable may come later *if at all*. The role of risk – and the commensurate reward potential – is what distinguishes saving from investing. Even the financially literate will have a difficult time reviewing theatrical productions: how to separate the shoddy, second-rate, and over-priced from genuinely attractive vehicles? How to compare the goods on *all* the stalls?

Artists and intellectual property

Competition in an industry goes beyond the established players. 'Competition in this broader sense might be termed *extended rivalry*', according to Michael Porter (1980: 6; emphasis in the original). The twentieth century has been described as 'a rich and provocative period in the history of American entertainment, one marked by persistent technological innovation, an expansion of markets, the refinement of techniques of commercial exploitation, and the ongoing democratization of American culture' (Sanjek and Sanjek 1991: v). With this historical scope in mind, Napster is one of the biggest controversies in culture and entertainment concerning the role of reproductive technology and intellectual property rights, during the final decade of the past century. By the late 1990s, the Internet was being used as a low-cost mass-communications medium. It was ideal for the distribution of music, with the potential to change the means by which entertainment products are distributed, produced, and promoted. First, disintermediation is about cutting out intermediaries in the distribution network. Direct selling via the internet, as expressed in the term e-tailing, removes the need for conventional 'bricks and mortar' retailers. Second, using MP3 technology to download songs from one of the many 'jukebox' sites (with Napster being the most recognized) offers a wide variety of music free-of-charge. This so-called 'public service' to internet users further erodes the traditional process of buying music. Yet it is 'theft', according to the copyright owners of songs.

Matt Black of Coldcut raises some misgivings regarding the spread of MP3 technology:

> I'm in an ambivalent situation. I'm pleased that more people are making their own music and that there are alternative forms of distribution, but as an artist and owner of my own record label (Ninja Tune) I make a living out of selling music. If all music can become instantly pirated and that becomes acceptable, how are we going to stay in business?
>
> (London *Times*, 12 March 1999)

In December 1999, lawyers for the Recording Industry Association of America (RIAA), representing seventeen record labels, filed a lawsuit against Napster claiming that the music-trading site was promoting and assisting copyright violation on a massive scale. Though it may be possible to sue illegal jukebox sites out of existence – essentially what happened to Napster – online music has made major inroads. Large numbers of relatively young users are in the habit of downloading and swapping music online. The major record labels want to get into the loop, such as establishing subscription services. In theory any artist can circumvent a distributor, maintain control of the master recording, and capture the margin taken by the various intermediaries (e.g. label, retail outlet). But in practice, established artists may be more successful in selling direct to their fans. Most musicians require the marketing clout associated with a record label to develop a fan base in the first place. 'Cyberlabels' may give music away for free in order to build fan loyalty: they will try to make money by selling merchandise and concert tour tickets. Retailers may also have much less to fear if issues of 'why consumers buy' are considered: many people may continue to enjoy the process of buying music from a 'bricks and mortar' store. Like other monumental changes in the music industry, technological advances have been exploited by commercial interests to profit from the work of artists; at the same time, however, forms of popular music have broadened making the musical canvas of the USA much richer. Napster is merely a recent example of how the music industry responds to technological change:

> Technological evolution has in turn necessitated that the laws respecting copyright undergo a similar transformation, although it is inescapable that the law will always lag behind the laboratory. Each time an invention increases the variety of means whereby composers or performers might earn royalties for their work, the law has had to determine how these royalties might be calculated and how that technology affects the concept of intellectual property.
>
> (Sanjek and Sanjek 1991: vi)

Visual artists may well argue that they have been mistreated by the art world including control over the use of their work and participation in its economics after they no longer own it. The French *droit de suite* system, of collecting royalties for artists on the sale of their art works in secondary markets, is the basis for a European Union-wide policy of resale rights for the benefit of the creator of an original work of art. Securing resale rights means a right of the creator – or the creator's estate for seventy years after the death of the creator – to receive a percentage of the sales price obtained from the resale of the work. It is proposed that royalties are payable when the sales price is equal or higher than €1,000 (with the following calculation):

- 4 per cent of the sale price between €1,000 and €50,000;
- 3 per cent of the sale price between €50,000 and €250,000;
- 2 per cent of the sale price above €250,000.

The royalty is payable by the seller.

Resale rights have not taken root in the USA, though a novel approach was mooted in 1971 by Bob Projansky, a New York lawyer, who drafted a three-page agreement after extensive discussions and correspondence with people involved in the day-to-day workings of the international art world. 'The artist's reserved rights to transfer and sale request agreement' is designed to give the artist certain economic benefits and aesthetic control:

- 15 per cent of any increase in the value of each work each time it is transferred in the future;
- A record of who owns each work at any given time;
- The right to be notified when the work is to be exhibited, so the artist can advise upon or veto the proposed exhibition of his/her work;
- The right to borrow the work for exhibition for 2 months every five (5) years (at no cost to the owner);
- The right to be consulted if repairs become necessary;
- Half of any rental income to be paid to the owner for the use of the work at exhibitions, if there ever are any;
- All reproduction rights in the work;
- The economic benefits to accrue to the artist for life, plus the life of a surviving spouse (if any) plus 21 years.

(Projansky 1971)

Projansky acknowledged that his proposed agreement would alter the existing relationship between artist and art owner principally by putting new obligations on the owners. However, Projansky sought to articulate benefits to art owners: chief was 'a certified history and provenance of the work'; the others, such as the establishment of 'a non-exploitative, one-to-one relationship' and 'recognition that the artist maintains a moral relationship to the work' (Projansky 1971), appear more idealistic.

Artists in the USA do not receive any financial gains from the secondary sales market which accrues to the collector-seller, yet Projansky's agreement does not appear to have been adopted by many visual artists. Alongside difficulties associated with monitoring a work's commercial migration, interesting points are raised. 'The collector who first purchases a work subject to rebated capital gains is willing to pay less than for the same work with an unrestricted title': this means that a discount is required if the artist desires to capture potential resale rights (Caves 2000:

282). However, it has been suggested that a 'superior way to lay claim on future capital gains' is for artists to retain ownership of some of their best works, or trade for works of admired peers whose prospects for capital gains are likely to correlate with their own (Caves 2000: 282). This is about artists treating their own work and that of their peers as financial instruments.

Sponsoring individual artists can take various dimensions. Corporate interests are usually involved. Jeff Koons's sponsorship arrangement with Hugo Boss, a German fashion label attempting to cultivate a less hard-edged image in the US market, is essentially that of a model. Koons has learned lessons from the top of the professional sports pecking order: someone like David Beckham rakes in over £9 million per annum: wages from Manchester United account for approximately £4 million, with the remainder earned from commercial deals including Adidas merchandise and Brylcreem hair products (London *Times*, 24 January 2002).

Maya Angelou and Fay Weldon are two different writers each with a distinct voice, yet both have been involved with promoting products. Angelou's 'Life Mosaic Collection' is a joint venture between the author and Hallmark, a company known for producing greeting cards. The collection extends beyond greeting cards to include bookends, pillows, journals, and mugs – essentially stationery products and household items on which an inspiring sentence or saying by Angelou (e.g. 'life is a glorious banquet, a limitless and delicious buffet'; 'the wise woman wishes to be no one's enemy, the wise woman refuses to be anyone's victim') may be inscribed.

Product placement has become a naturalized way of doing business in Hollywood. Is it entering literature? Fay Weldon's *The Bulgari Connection* (2001), commissioned by the Italian jewellers of the same name, was published in the UK by HarperCollins (see, for example, the *New York Times*, 3 September 2001). According to the blurb on the jacket cover: 'Take one wealthy businessman on his second marriage to an avid, successful young woman; one ex-wife who happens to be a saint; one artist, and portrait for sale; two women wearing Bulgari necklaces: add a touch of the supernatural, a big dose of envy, stir, and see what happens'. The writer, sponsor, and publisher are all happy with the 'novel' agreement. Weldon worked as a copywriter for Ogilvy & Mather in the 1960s, and describes her novel as 'a good piece of advertising prose'. Bulgari's chief executive defends the commercial relationship as a form of promotion: 'When you take out an ad in a magazine, you have a certain amount of space in which to speak. That is why product placement, whether you're talking about books, movies or Hollywood stars, is so important'. The publisher was ebullient about all the media attention: 'This is fantastic. It gives me a lot of ideas. What better way to spread the word than to have a commissioned book? And if you are going to talk about jewellery, you might as well talk about Bulgari'. Of course, there are critics such as the president of the Authors' Guild of America: 'It erodes reader confidence in the authenticity of narrative. It adds to the cynicism. Does this character really drive a Ford or did Ford pay for this?' (As a wry aside, consider how the art museum has been used as an automotive dealership. The Art Gallery of Ontario mounted a Canadian-built Chrysler LHS on a revolving display platform at its inaugural exhibition, 'The

Earthly Paradise: Arts and Crafts by William Morris and His Circle from Canadian Collections', in 1994. The AGO was taking its lead from the Montreal MFA: in 1992, the MMFA placed a Lexus on display as part of a sponsorship arrangement for 'The Genius of the Sculpture in Michelangelo's Work'.)

Fund-raising, equity financing, and the intellectual property rights of artists are three topics which address 'money' issues. The cry for 'money, money, money' in these cases is outside the state sector of subsidy. In many respects, it illustrates some of the benefits associated with private enterprise. At the same time, caveats are raised. First, the philosophy of fund-raising, as articulated by the likes of Peter Drucker and Henry Drucker, would appear to be straightforward. Yet in examining the dynamics which animate fund-raising, the 'pyramid' serves as a point of reference. Such a simple diagram contains complex and contested ideas when applied to fund-raising and business practices. Second, equity financing in the arts is examined with reference to a private placement memorandum for a proposed West End transfer. Investing in theatrical productions, a speculative financial instrument, is examined from the perspective of a potential theatre angel. An entrepreneurial environment is created by which risk capital is available. Third, how artists can claim the economic benefits associated with the fruits of their artistic labour, a form of intellectual property, is an ongoing concern. The case of Napster represents how technology and copyright have been linked for a long time in the entertainment industries. Securing resale rights for artists has not been raised as a pressing issue in the USA, yet the European Union advocates collecting royalties on capital gains based on the French *droit de suite* system. Various forms of sponsorship arrangements can be proffered: some artists act as 'celebrity' endorsers; Fay Weldon's 'product placement' deal with Bulgari breaks new ground in literature. The blurring distinction and cross-over activity between art and advertising makes it more difficult to cite transgressions of aesthetic integrity.

10 Organizational forms and dynamics

'The European Iceberg: creativity in Germany and Italy today' (1985) was a large-scale, interdisciplinary exhibition of German Neo-Expressionism and Italian Trans-Avantgardism, mounted at the Art Gallery of Ontario (AGO) by guest curator Germano Celant:

> The image of a 'European Iceberg' has several functions. It serves to indicate the enormous complexity of European culture, which cannot be shown in totality. And the metaphor also emphasizes that the visible part here – Italy and Germany – leaves all other countries hidden underwater. Furthermore, the portion of Canada is the one now emerging in the territory of the arts, and it must always bear this in mind because of its profound influences on the visible situation.
>
> (Celant 1985: 12)

The exhibition was a defining moment for the AGO. It provided the impetus for the then chief curator, Roald Nasgaard, to develop an impressive collection of international (i.e. non-Canadian) art. Lothar Baumgarten's contribution was *Monument aux nations indiennes de l'Onatrio / Monument to the Native Peoples of Ontario* (1984–5), a site-specific installation that set out to interact with the place of its display, as both architecturally and geographically defined. In particular, the German artist was responding to a society in which native culture was absent, thus he named native tribes (Huron, Algonkin, Ojibwa, Iroquois, Petun, Ottawa, Neutral, and Nippissing) in a manner of European heros of arts and sciences sometimes found carved in classical architecture. Following the reopening of the AGO, Baumgarten's installation was revisited by Robert Houle, an artist from Canada's First People community, in a three-part installation, *Anishnake Walker Court* (1994), which represented a wry commentary on the manufacture of 'Indianness' in which ethnic identity masks a critical intersection between ambivalence and intentionality.

'Organizations are many things at once!' (Morgan 1986: 339). This exhortation is instructive, and serves as a motivating theme to examine insight by seminal writers – namely Henry Mintzberg, Paul DiMaggio, Walter Powell, and Gareth Morgan – on the study of organizations from a management perspective. First, Mintzberg's question 'who should control the corporation' (i.e. salaried managers, trustees, shareholders, etc.) raises pertinent issues regarding the corporate governance of arts organizations. Mintzberg's structural configurations remain an important attempt to relate the description of 'structure' with the 'functioning' of the organization. Second, Powell and DiMaggio, who focus on institutional isomorphic change, contend that certain conditions result in the homogeneity of organizational forms and practices. Third, Morgan's concern is to illustrate how to 'read' organizations via the use of metaphor in order to offer a more rounded appreciation of the 'organization' of arts organizations. Fourth, the new logic of organizing is challenging careers as an institution at the start of the twenty-first century.

Structuring configurations

In asking 'who should control the arts organization?', reference is made to the work of Henry Mintzberg (1984). Mintzberg is interested in the private sector debate, from a managerial and organizational perspective, of 'who should control the large, widely held corporation, how, and for the pursuit of what goals?' The debate, according to Mintzberg, addresses fundamental issues of democracy. Control by the owners is weakened as shareholding became more dispersed. The current situation is characterized by 'trust it' to salaried managers, to balance social and economic goals. At the same time, it is recognized that the direct and concerted voices of outsiders need to be considered. This raises the polemical issue of having direct control of the corporation in the hands of specific outsiders: under nationalization the state can address social goals; on the other hand, with direct shareholder control, economic aims and objectives gain unreserved attention.

Mintzberg's conceptual framework raises issues pertinent to arts organizations. Due to mandated fiduciary obligations, trustees are likened to owners. The management of many large and established arts organizations is contested by two sets of salaried employees: the 'operating core' (i.e. those performing the basic work of the organization); and the 'support staff' (i.e. those who aid the functioning of the operating core outside the basic flow of the operating work). Other stakeholders – for example, funding bodies and arts activists – attempt to 'regulate', or to 'pressure' the arts organization.

All this suggests that arts organizations can be subject to fierce contestation over who controls the agenda. The forces of change are wide and not always limited to overtly political ones. Not just management issues are at stake, as the curator Bruce Ferguson makes clear:

> [T]he public museum, like the university and the church (all of which are what Althusser called 'ideological state apparatuses' like the family or the school), is under fierce and sometimes violent contestation over who controls its agenda and what its fundamental purpose is.
>
> This institutional and intellectual shift in the museum field is occurring both because of outside reforms like government agencies and philanthropic organizations whose economic and social priorities have changed and because of internal forces which have to do with the inconstant nature of contemporary

art in particular and the changing roles of participants in the artworld, including patrons and, in particular, curators.

(Ferguson 1996: 177)

Moreover, there is the case that the art museum – Ferguson's focus – is a proxy for many types of elite arts organizations.

Who has power and authority for arts organizations? There is a case for broadening decision-making, but how far to go before 'disinterested' scholarship (or musicianship) gets 'sidelined' by other interests (including corporate sponsors)? Three issues are explored: the role of trustees in addressing authority and decision-making; parallel administrative hierarchies; and arts organizations subject to external pressures from groups interested in widening participation.

Boards of trustees are crucial to the governance of arts organizations. Trustees, as the most privileged breed of volunteer, are situated at the top of the organizational chart (as part of the 'strategic apex', which also includes the most senior-paid members of staff). Major decision-making powers are vested in these individuals, subject, of course, to the institution's charter, by-laws and mission statement. Trustees are asked to exercise effective control in order to fulfil their role as policy maker, management overseer, and performance evaluator. In practice, a smaller 'executive committee' may decide major decisions for the full board to ratify.

It is not surprising that the dominant supervisory body in the USA, the business corporation, is a model familiar to invariably all trustees. Established to be self-perpetuating, such boards offer institutional stability. 'In the case of the nonprofit corporation … the purpose of the charter is primarily to protect the interests of the organization's *patrons* from those who control the corporation', according to Henry Hansmann (1980: 62; emphasis in the original). He continues by arguing that many boards in the USA are able to exert power in an uncontested manner:

> Thus a nonprofit corporation may have a membership that, like shareholders in a business corporation, is entitled to select the board of trustees through elections held at regular intervals. But the statutes typically do not make this a requirement, so that the board of directors may, alternatively, simply be made an autonomous, self-perpetuating body.
>
> (Hansmann 1980: 59)

One particular reason for self-perpetuating bodies is the legacy of patronage by monied families; critical to establishing many elite arts organizations, their support remains important: 'Elite patronage has changed very little over time. It is still the case, at least in the USA, that affluent individuals and wealthy donors continue to be the main source of unearned income for cultural institutions' (Blau 1991: 90). The '3G' adage of trusteeship – one 'gives money, gets money, or gets off' the board – strikes at the vital fund-raising role of trustees. Such a system, which is most prevalent in the USA, has several consequences: a certain (socio-economic) sameness exists among trustees; ordinary members are excluded from electing trustees; boards are large in size; and there are no incentives for autonomous, self-perpetuating boards to proffer different models.

In the UK, the trustees of national or prestigious arts organizations are often appointed from a pool known colloquially as 'the great and the good' (of minor royals, major aristocrats, and those first in line for knighthoods, namely ex-politicians, captains of industry, (retired) first division civil servants, and distinguished academics). Unlike the situation in the USA, trustees in the UK are not viewed as a source of unearned revenue. In the case of many appointments to national institutions, the Prime Minister is involved, which suggests that appointments can reflect the prevailing political climate.

Representative democracy is discernible in many Canadian examples of arts boards. The hybrid nature of board composition means that there are appointed *and* elected trustees. For example, a state funder may play a significant role in appointing a minority number of trustees. However, appointed trustees may be unclear about whose interests they are appointed to represent: the state funder, that of a 'disinterested' observer, or some concept of 'watchdog' for the so-called average citizen? There is also a nod to 'one member, one vote' democracy whereby ordinary members are able to elect trustees at an annual general meeting; in practice, however, individuals put forward by the board-level nominating committee are usually elected without substantial opposition.

Many arts organizations offer a good illustration of what Mintzberg describes as the emergence of 'parallel administrative hierarchies'. Specialist members of the *operating core* (e.g. curators in art museums) have power because of their expertise concerning 'professional operations'. The operating core is 'at the heart of every organization', according to Mintzberg (1979: 24), and is responsible for securing the inputs, transforming inputs into outputs, distributing outputs, and providing direct support to the input, transformation, and output functions. In the case of *support staff*, power resides in administrative offices, which suggests that 'one must practice administration, not a specialized function of the organization, to attain status' (DiMaggio 1986: 12). An organization's 'attempt to encompass more and more boundary activities in order to reduce uncertainty, to control its own affairs' is reflected in the size and scope of support units (Mintzberg 1979: 32). Historically and traditionally, the ethos of the art museum has posited the curatorial departments at the core of the organizational structure (not unlike academic departments in universities): this in effect invited many curators to manage their departments like separate medieval baronies. In lieu of curatorial cooperation, many were at the ready for turf wars regarding the display of the permanent collection and the schedule of temporary exhibitions. At the same time, one can cite substantive change within 'professional bureaucracies' (or 'collegial' organizations dominated by skilled workers who use procedures that are difficult to learn yet well defined), namely the rise of the power of the administrator or manager (i.e. fund-raiser, marketer, accountant, retail manager) who is not part of the operating core. Non-specialist professional managers – those bracketed by Mintzberg's support staff component – have grown in importance and influence owing to issues of funding and education mandates, which necessitates an attempt to disseminate the arts to wider segments of the population.

Power flows to those professionals who care to devote their effort to doing 'administrative' as opposed to 'professional' work. It has been suggested by Adorno that complex and prosperous environments will augment cultural bureaucracy:

> The dialectic of culture and administration nowhere expresses the sacrosanct irrationality of culture so clearly as in the continually growing alienation of administration from culture – both in terms of its objective categories and its personal composition.
>
> (Adorno 1978: 97)

The professional administrator derives power from serving key roles at the *boundary* of the organization, between members of the operating core and interested parties on the outside, including funding sources. For example, a 'managing director' (coming from a background in finance, law, accountancy, or management consultancy) may be hired to work alongside the 'chief aesthetic officer', with a mandate to 'open out the institution' and 'take a hard look at how money gets spent'.

Arts organizations are subject to external pressures to change by 'marginalized' groups opposed to what they perceive to be bastions of the 'liberal humanist tradition', which critics view as far from being classless and politically neutral. Associations with a wealthy, patron class – arts organizations as elitist playgrounds for the rich and powerful – can clash with demands for social relevance. The USA, more than any other wealthy nation, is marked by advanced social politics where issues of race and sex are vocal and often divisive; at the same time, there exists a (closed) system of corporate governance denoted by a self-perpetuating board of trustees. Two approaches to change are examined: to *regulate*, or to *pressure* the arts organization. Seeking to regulate means a reliance on the state to develop centralist tendencies (including nationalization). Yet the emphasis over the last two decades has been to encourage arts organizations to become more self-reliant. At the same time, the state can require arts organizations to address public policy issues like social deprivation as a condition of funding. Accountability thus enters the arts manager's lexicon so that educational outreach and serving under-represented communities become assumed priorities. The distinctively American position, as expressed by consumer advocacy groups (e.g. Nader's Raiders and Adbusters), is to pressure organizations to change. For example, artists can help to articulate pressing social issues. One of the signboards installed by Group Material on the West Wing of the Boston MFA highlighted the belief that the institution, a public art museum, remains 'private' and removed from the experiences of those living nearby:

> It's close to Roxbury and yet aesthetically, culturally, and politically it's the furthest point away. The building looks like a rich white person's house. The museum is irrelevant to Roxbury because Roxbury is a community that has been denied anything that is Boston. I think the museum as a concept is obsolete. So I don't go.

The Guerrilla Girls, a collective of artists who are women, 'use a rapier wit to fire volley after volley of carefully researched statistics at artworld audiences, exposing individuals and institutions that under-represent or exclude women and artists of color from exhibitions, collecting and funding' (Chadwick 1995: 7). Using the tactics of urban warfare, the Guerrilla Girls's first posters materialized in 1985 in lower Manhattan, signed as 'the conscious of the art world'. 'Do women have to be naked to get into the Met. Museum?' demanded one well-known poster, which depicted a reclining nude Venus wearing a gorilla mask. The answer: 'Less than 5 per cent of the artists in the Modern Art Sections are women, but 85 per cent of the nudes are female'.

Institutional isomorphism

Is there sufficient homogeneity of form and practice amongst opera houses to suggest that they represent a distinct institutional form? Can the like be said of television stations? This issue of institutional isomorphic change has been examined by sociologists Walter Powell and Paul DiMaggio. Unlike Max Weber, to whom an explicit reference is made in their 1983 essay, 'The iron cage revisited', Powell and DiMaggio contend that 'bureaucratization and other forms of organizational change occur as the result of processes that make some organizations similar without necessarily making them more efficient' (Powell and DiMaggio 1991: 64). They argue that bureaucratization and other forms of homogenization emerge out of the structuration of organizational fields. The desire is not to explain variation among organizations in structure and behaviour; rather Powell and DiMaggio seek to understand why there is such startling homogeneity of organizational forms and practices. Isomorphism 'is the concept that best captures the process of homogenization'; it is 'a constraining process that forces one unit in a population to resemble other units that face the same set of environmental conditions' (Powell and DiMaggio 1991: 66). Three mechanisms by which institutional isomorphic change takes place are identified: *coercive*, *mimetic*, and *normative*.

Coercive isomorphism results from both formal and informal pressures exerted on organizations by other organizations upon which they are dependent and by cultural expectations in the society within which they function. The greater the dependence of one organization on another (A–1) or the greater the centralization of an organization's resource supply (A–2), the more similar it will become to the dominant organization or resource supplier in structure and focus. Many conventional arts organizations, like art museums and opera houses, have internalized the external bureaucratic environment by incorporating in their structures administrators responsible for retailing, fund-raising, and marketing. This suggests that art museums and opera houses, for example, grow administratively and hierarchically in complex environments that are abundant in resources. Transactions within a complex environment increase the tendency of the organization to formalize and amplify its administrative functions. With reference to nonprofit arts organizations in the USA, sociologist Richard Peterson has described the internal and extra-organizational factors that 'typically operate in concert, mutually reinforcing the drive toward formal accountability and increasing the need for arts managers with the orientation and skills of art administrators' (Peterson 1986: 175). Internal factors – growth in size, increasing task complexity, organizational life cycle, and the income gap associated with Baumol and Bowen – have been working to encourage greater bureaucratization in individual organizations (Peterson 1986: 169). Extraorganizational factors are important because institutional funders (whether government bodies, private foundations, or corporate sponsors), private patrons, or the market (as regards earned income and audience figures) increasingly hold arts managers formally accountable for actions taken in the name of the arts organization.

The funding environment is the culprit, according to research by McKinsey: 'All organizations – for profit or not – are shaped by those who fund them' (Lowell *et al.* 2000: 148). For example, Internet start-ups reflect the complexion of the venture capitalists who provided capital funding. Non-commercial organizations have fared less well: 'Nonprofits typically rely on grants and donations' (Lowell *et al.* 2000: 148). Most donors take 'a project-based rather than an organization-building approach to philanthropy' (Lowell *et al.* 2000: 149); and corporate sponsors also tend to focus on specific programmes. This means that nonprofits are discouraged from investing in organizational infrastructure (e.g. IT systems, staff development processes, and adequate management capacity). Managers may spend too much time following the money by adding programmes to obtain a particular grant even if the fit to the organization's mission is not great. The availability of new funding in the UK from the National Lottery meant that arts institutions had to learn to apply for this money. Large amounts were directed into capitalizing public arts projects and events. Institutions without substantial reserves or income found it harder to apply, especially since no funding was set aside for maintenance or lost revenue.

Mimetic isomorphism results from standard responses to uncertainty, given that uncertainty represents a powerful force that encourages imitation. An organization will model itself after organizations it perceives as successful, the more uncertain the relationship between means and ends (A–3) or the more ambiguous its goals (A–4). For example, the institutional formation of the V&A (as the Museum of Manufacturers and later the Museum of Ornamental Arts), in the direct aftermath of the 1851 Great Exhibition, devoted attention to decorative and industrial arts; in Philadelphia, following the 1876 Centennial Exhibition, the Pennsylvania Museum and School of Industrial Arts (now the Philadelphia Museum of Art) was created with the British example in mind, namely with the value of the industrial arts deemed as educational and commercial. Likewise, the (English) Arts and Crafts movement was an important influence on decorative arts in Montreal. The MMMFA is explicit in acknowledging decorative arts alongside painting and sculpture.

Much of the homogeneity in organizational structures stems from the fact that, despite a search for diversity, there is relatively little variation from the pool of generally acceptable alternatives. Large arts organizations choose from a relatively small set of international accountancy and consultancy firms using a limited number of organizational models. Under the conventional wisdom that 'institutions trust institutions', corporate sponsors (as represented by Fortune 500 or FSTE 100 firms) tend to have similar aims and look for equally 'blue chip' art organizations for relationships. Hans Haacke criticized the alliance between the Metropolitan Museum and Mobil Oil, in *MetroMobiltan* (1985), by highlighting the multinational's commercial interests in South Africa under apartheid. It is not surprising that Ernst & Young sponsored popular exhibitions at the Tate Gallery (e.g. Picasso, Cezanne, and Bonnard) and the Royal Academy of Arts (namely Monet). Capital projects remain a catalyst for rejuvenation, galvanizing support, and serving as a rallying point for key supports. Endowment funding is viewed by some as offering more financial stability to arts organizations, hence a push to adopt the fund-raising practices associated with the wealthiest private universities in the USA.

Normative isomorphism stems primarily from two aspects of professionalization: one is the resting of formal education and legitimation in a cognitive base produced by university specialists (A–5); the second is the growth and elaboration of professional networks that span organizations and across which new models diffuse rapidly (A–6). Elite academic recognition still matters: from an anecdotal perspective, many art museum directors in the UK have studied at Oxbridge or the Courtauld; reading art history at Williams College has a similar significance in the USA. The result from the two aspects of professionalization is to

> create a pool of almost interchangeable individuals who occupy similar positions across a range of organizations and possess a similarity of orientation and disposition that may override variations in tradition and control that might otherwise shape organizational behaviour.
>
> (Powell and DiMaggio 1991: 71)

The filtering of personnel is an important mechanism for encouraging normative isomorphism. 'Many professional career tracks are so closely guarded, both at the entry and throughout the career progression, that individuals who make it to the top are virtually indistinguishable' (Powell and DiMaggio 1991: 71). Furthermore:

> The professionalization of management tends to proceed in tandem with the structuration of organizational fields. The exchange of information among professionals helps contribute to a commonly recognized hierarchy of status, of center and periphery, that becomes a matrix for information flows and personnel movement across organizations. This status ordering occurs through formal and informal means.
>
> (Powell and DiMaggio 1991: 72)

The case of Elizabeth Esteve-Coll, who left the V&A in 1995 during her second term as director to become one of the few women vice-chancellors in the UK, addresses gender imbalances; it also highlights an individual with a non-traditional background who became director of a major art museum. Esteve-Coll was educated as Darlington Girls High School and completed her BA at Birkbeck College (i.e. the University of London college which caters to mature students) in 1976. Her primary career experience before moving to the V&A, in 1985, as keeper of the National Art Library was in higher education (head of learning resources at Kingston Polytechnic and then university librarian at the University of Surrey). In 1988, Esteve-Coll was appointed director of the V&A; the first woman to head a 'national museum and gallery' in the UK. Media attention by those hostile to her appointment became even more barbed and aggressive following the proposed 1989 restructuring, which focused on her background as a librarian without significant art history and curatorial experience. The 'femme-to-femme' comparison made by Sir John Pope-Hennessey (former director of the British Museum and the V&A) was a classic case of vitriol:

> There is an excellent precedent for appointing a woman as director: one of the most efficient and successful is Anne d'Harnoncourt, the director of the Philadelphia Museum of Art. I do not know Mrs. Esteve-Coll personally, but she is clearly in an altogether different and inferior class. ... It would be generally conceded that there is a point beneath which no museum should debase itself. But not Mrs. Esteve-Coll, who with a crude publicity campaign and exhibitions like that of the collection of Elton John, has added a new meaning to the phrase, 'She stoops to conquer'.
>
> (*New York Review of Books*, 27 April 1989: 13)

Organizational metaphors

In *Images of Organization* (1986), Gareth Morgan poses a series of 'what if ... ?' questions based on eight metaphors: what if we think of organizations as *machines*? as *organisms*? as *brains*? as *cultures*? as *political systems*? as *psychic prisons*? as *flux and transformation*? as *instruments of domination*? This is part of Morgan's creative approach to exploring organizations. His belief in the role played by images and metaphors in the social construction of reality makes him prominent and somewhat unconventional amongst management writers.

Complementary and competing insights are created via the metaphorical frameworks, each with strengths and limitations. For example, the *machine* view, which remains a dominant metaphor, approaches the organization as outlined by classical management theorists like Fayol and Urwick, and along the scientific management principles of Taylor: 'set goals and objectives and go for them'; 'organize rationally, efficiently, and clearly'; and 'plan, organize, and control, control, control' (Morgan 1993: 33). The *political systems* metaphor emphasizes issues of interest, conflict, and power; this 'helps to explode the myth of organizational rationality' explicit in the machine view (Morgan 1993: 195). The *psychic prisons* metaphor examines 'how people in organizations can become trapped by favoured ways of thinking ... [and] how organizations can become trapped by unconscious processes that lend organizations a hidden significance' (Morgan 1993: 200). Organizations as *instruments of domination* is a metaphor that focuses on the (sometimes unintended) negative activities of organizations on their employees or their environment (e.g. patterns of inequality in global economic development), and is often viewed as articulating 'an extreme form of left-wing ideology, serving to fan the flames of the radical frame of reference and thus adding to the difficulties of managers in an already turbulent world' (Morgan 1993: 319).

Particular reference to the Louvre as a model is often used in a history of the modern, public art museum. A full account of the development of the Louvre requires a very complex bureaucratic history which begins with the French Revolution, as one of transformation from private (namely royal) collection to public institution. The Louvre was born out of a contestation: it is an 'institution which embodied a form of publicity that functioned to challenge the "representative" publicity of royal collections (in order to realize a conception of publicness opposed to the secret politics of absolutism)' (Ward 1995: 76). Morgan's instrument of domination metaphor is evident in the critique of New York's Museum of Modern Art by Duncan and Wallach (1978: 28–51), who viewed MoMA as a 'masculine museum space'. A similar theme was articulated by the director of the Detroit Institute of Arts, in the 1940s: 'The building of the National Gallery [of Art] in Washington is not only a triumph of capitalism but is in accordance with the buildings in its neighbourhood, an expansion of the growing world power of the USA'. (Valentiner 1944: 658).

Interventions by artists, like Brian O'Doherty (aka the artist Patrick Ireland), Marcel Broodthaers (d. 1976), and Andrea Fraser, have contributed to our understanding of organizational metaphors and museum fictions. O'Doherty has examined the ideology of the gallery space by arguing against the perceived neutrality afforded by the so-called 'white cube' (particularly popular for the display of contemporary art):

A gallery is constructed among laws as rigorous as those for building a medieval church. The outside world must not come in, so windows are usually sealed off. Walls are painted white. The ceiling becomes the source of light. The wooden floor is polished so that you click along clinically, or so carpeted so that you tread soundlessly … . Unshadowed, white, clean, artificial – the space is devoted to the technology of aesthetics. … Art exists in a kind of eternity of display … there is no time. This eternity gives the gallery a limbolike status.

(O'Doherty 1986 :15)

Morgan's organization as psychic prison, which results in a severely restricted physical, conceptual, and cultural arena, corresponds with O'Doherty's characterization.

Broodthaers's fictive or invented museum, *Musée d'art Moderne, Department des Aigles, Section XIXeme*, was opened, in 1968, in the artist's studio, in Brussels; it closed in 1972 at Documenta V. *Musée d'art Moderne* served as an adversary art practice: the artist raised pointed questions concerning the 'double stranglehold of the museum and the marketplace' while attempting 'to become engaged in the political struggles of its time'. Through a close reading of Broodthaers's press releases for his fictive museum, a leading critic was confident in concluding that the artist's 'suggestion that the museum might wish to seduce "customers and the curious" by employing the mock-Kantian formula "disinterestedness plus admiration" is perhaps the most elliptical yet precise critique of institutionalized modernism ever offered' (Crimp 1993: 212).

Adopting the persona of docent (i.e. education guide) Jane Castelton, Andrea Fraser 'performed' at the Philadelphia Museum of Art; the artist documented the tour, 'Museum Highlights', in an essay first prepared for publication in *October*. In part, Fraser offered an examination of the volunteer docent, who is invariably female and smartly attired in a late 1980s Laura Ashley manner:

[S]he is the museum's representative. Unlike members of the museum's non-professional maintenance, security, and gift shop staff that visitors come into contact with, the docent is a figure of identification for a primarily white, middle-class audience. And unlike the museum's professional staff, the docent is the representation of the museum's volunteer sector.

While docents are usually trained by the professional staff, I would say that they aspire less to professional competence than to what Pierre Bourdieu [in *Distinction*] calls the 'precious', 'status-induced familiarity' with legitimate culture that marks those to whom the objects within the museum belong(ed); an 'imperceptible learning' that can only be 'acquired' with time and applied by those who can take their time.

(Fraser 1991: 107)

Fraser continued by describing how she perceived the fictional docent Jane, in the language of women's work:

Jane is determined above all by the status of the docent as a nonexpert volunteer. As a volunteer, she expresses the possession of a quantity of the leisure and the economic and cultural capital that defines the museum's patron class. It is only a small quantity – indicating rather than bridging the class gap that compels her to volunteer her services in the absence to capital; to give, perhaps, her body in the absence of art objects. Yet it is enough to position her in identification with the museum's board of trustees, and to make her the museum's exemplary viewer.

(Fraser 1991: 107–8)

As the preceding art museum examples illustrate, the use of metaphor to engage in problems associated with 'reading' organizations has benefits. By going against conventional orthodoxy with subtle analysis, visual artists remind us that 'all images are man-made' and 'every image embodies a way of seeing' (Berger 1972: 9–10). Morgan is at pains to stress that 'any particular way of seeing is limited ... the challenge is to become skilled in the art of seeing, in the art of understanding, and in the art of interpretation and reading situations we face' (Morgan 1993: 281).

New logic in organizing

At the start of the twenty-first century, the changing economic organization is drawing attention to flatter hierarchies, more ambiguous job descriptions, and fewer rules. Research predicts that 'the career, as an institution, is in unavoidable decline'; and the 'social division of labour into discrete professions and careers is obsolete' (Flores and Gray 2000: 9, 18). At the same time, 'knowledge production' is promoted as essential if it can be used to build a sustainable advantage that can be leveraged across products (Powell 2001: 35). For those in the arts, related issues of professionalization and career mobility are raised. Discussions about professionalization can be interminable and often painful, yet they continue to be raised by some arts workers. Viewed from a sociological slant, professionalism concerns 'a form of self-organization that enables practitioners of an occupation to defend the importance of their contribution and the legitimacy of their decisions' (DiMaggio 1988: 52). Furthermore, according to Ehrenreich and Ehrenreich (1979), the 'professional-managerial class' has assumed the accoutrements of professionalism, with organizations to advance the interests of the field; more importantly, they have come to conceive themselves as possessing special skills, and their work as deserving professional respect.

Consider the apprenticeship recollected by John Murdoch, who was assistant director (collection) at the V&A before taking up his current position, in 1993, as director of the Courtauld Institute Galleries:

> In his last months [1974] as Keeper Graham instituted for me a twice weekly private session, two hours long, in which he systematically took me through the collection of miniatures, of which I had no previous experience. For each artist there was something distinctive, the shape of the ear, perhaps, or more often something more minute, such as the way in which the shadow under the eye was drawn, or the outlining of the nose, or the shading of the background. He used a hand-held lens and knew exactly what he was looking for in each object. ... It was only years later that I realized what Graham was doing, that I was being inducted into a specific tradition of connoisseurship, and that there was, within it, an apostolic succession at the V&A.
>
> (Murdoch 1993: 326)

Murdoch goes on to outline how Graham Reynolds, who had joined the V&A in 1938, was inducted into the 'specially difficult and arcane field of miniatures, which is studied only at the V&A' by Carl Winter (1906–66); in turn, Winter, a great connoisseur, had joined as an assistant keeper in 1931, when the towering personality of the department was Basil Long (1881–1937), who had been in the department since 1906 and had a string of major catalogues to his credit including 'the monumental *British Miniaturists* of 1929, which is still standard'. According to Murdoch, he came across a newspaper obituary of Long in the departmental library: it noted that after graduating from the University of Heidelberg in the late 1890s, Long went off to Milan, where he studied the methods of the great Giovanni Morelli (1816–91). The 'tradition of objective art historical scholarship to which I was inducted in my turn in 1974', according to Murdoch, can be traced back to Morelli, rightly considered as one of the progenitors of the discipline of art history, hence 'an apostolic succession at the V&A'. In many respects, Murdoch's induction and mobility at the V&A is not unusual for museum professionals of his generation. Duchamp scholar Anne d'Harnoncourt has spent virtually all her professional career at the Philadelphia Museum of Art, where she is director and chief executive officer; Philippe de Montebello has spent most of his curatorial life at the Metropolitan Museum of Art. Joseph Volpe, the current general manager, started at the Metropolitan Opera as a stagehand in 1964. But is this system of organizational work (marked by security, clear hierarchies, and routine pay increases) no longer available for those entering arts organizations at the start of the twenty-first century?

Is the role of the career, the binding together of phases of a working life to shape a coherent narrative from it, now fading from view? Walter Powell identifies three changes shaping organizations. Rather than jobs, projects become more important. Work is organized around a team or work group charged with responsibility for a project. There is merging of conception and execution (with design and production running on parallel tracks). From a positive light, 'workers are increasingly authors of their own work' (Powell 2001: 57). In order to make organizations more dynamic, Douglas Hague (1993) suggests a rule-of-thumb for senior managers: stay five years in the job; do not remain more than ten years in the organization. On the other hand, job or work intensification may be behind the language of participation. Is the 'new flexibility liberating or imprisoning'? (Powell 2001: 58). Of course, some workers will have grown accustomed to job structures heavy with unskilled positions, antiquated job titles, and an acceptance of high absenteeism.

Flattening hierarchies and the spread of networks make it more important to develop a latticework of collaborations with 'outsiders'. Creating a record of performance becomes even more important as a way to encourage people to trust you and collaborate with you. 'When you stop learning in a job, you begin to shrink', according to Peter Drucker (1990: 154), who recommends taking a volunteer job with an organization (as a way to repot oneself). Yet such collaborations are not uncontroversial in blurring the boundaries of the firm, 'making it difficult to know where the firm ends and where the market or another firm begins' (Powell 2001: 58). For example, laws passed throughout the 1990s in Italy sought to make all types of cultural institutions more responsive to users. Contracting-out services was one way to address problems associated with aspects of 'pork-barrel' administration of cultural heritage.

Cross-fertilization among industries means leveraging distinctive capabilities across fields. How to manage the relationship: 'the execution – compete or collaborate with a dazzling array of rivals and partners – is complex indeed' (Powell 2001: 62). The case of the Guggenheim Foundation with its growing tentacles raises issues associated with franchising a cultural brand. Musical theatre has learned a great deal from Hollywood in making a certain type of performing art attractive to mass audiences. Are developments that encourage cross-fertilization among industries harmful or positive for consumers, or creators?

In many respects, the management literature on organizations is dense. There is a premise that organizations are not 'neutral'. Indeed one recognizes the creation of highly problematic stereotypes in arts organizations, say critiques posed by the Guerrilla Girls and Andrea Fraser's docent, or John Pope-Hennessy's dismissal of Elizabeth Esteve-Coll's V&A directorship. Contestation over who controls the agenda of arts organizations is raised in terms of stakeholders. Henry Mintzberg's professional bureaucracy is an instructive term which helps to examine the rise of cultural bureaucrats (or arts administrators), often viewed at the expense of arts-based professionals. Walter Powell and Paul DiMaggio's institutional isomorphic change points to why certain arts organizations may be similar in different countries. Gareth Morgan recommends reading or scrutinizing arts organizations. The exploration of his general theme – arts organizations are merely social constructions of reality – accommodates contributions by visual artists.

Arts workers more than workers in other sectors of the economy will feel the impact of the decline of conventional career structures and the rise of knowledge-based production. Self-development, as promoted by leading business schools, may be viewed as enhancing three forms of capital. *Intellectual* capital is usually associated with formal education, but it ought to be considered more broadly to include acquiring new skills throughout a working career. *Personal* capital focuses on one's emotional growth as a person. *Social* capital emphasizes the developing of a network of personal relationships, best if such contacts are fostered by shared values and trust, which can be converted into commercial support.

Bibliography

The following list includes the works cited in the main text, apart from newspapers and magazines.

Aaker, D. (1991) *Managing Brand Equity: capitalizing on the value of a brand name*, New York: Free Press.

—— (1995) *Building Strong Brands*, New York: Free Press.

Adizes, I. (ed.) (1972) 'Administering for the Arts' [special section], *California Management Review*, (Winter): 99+.

Adorno, T. (1978; original German 1960) 'Culture and administration', trans. W. Blomster, reprinted in *Telos* (Fall): 93–111.

—— (1991; original German 1975) 'Culture industry reconsidered', trans. A. Robinson, reprinted in Adorno (1991a): 85–92.

—— (1991a) *The Culture Industry: selected essays on mass culture*, ed. and intro. J. M. Bernstein, London: Routledge.

Alessi, A. (1998) *The Dream Factory: Alessi since 1921*, Cologne: Konemann.

Alpers, S. (1995) *The Making of Rubens*, New Haven and London: Yale University Press.

Alsop, J. (1982) *The Rare Tradition: the history of art collecting and its linked phenomena*, [Princeton University Press] Bollinger Series 25, New York: Harper and Row.

Altshuler, B. (1994) *The Avant-Garde in Exhibition: new art in the twentieth century*, Berkeley and Los Angeles: University of California Press.

Alvesson, M. and Willmott, H. (eds) (1992) *Critical Management Studies*, London: Sage.

Andreasen, A. (1982) 'Non-profits: check your attention to customers', *Harvard Business Review* (May/June): 105–10.

Ansoff, H. I. (1965) *Corporate Strategy: an analytical approach to business policy for growth and expansion*, New York: McGraw Hill.

Appignanesi, L. (ed.) (1984) *Culture and the State*, London: Institute of Contemporary Arts.

Bagozzi, R. (1975) 'Marketing as exchange', *Journal of Marketing* (October): 32–9.

Bailey, G. (1989) 'Amateurs imitate, professionals steal', *Journal of Aesthetics and Art Criticism* (Summer): 221–7.

Bales, C. and Pinnavaia, S. (2001) 'Art for more than art's sake', *McKinsey Quarterly* 1: 59–67.

Barasch, M. (1985) *Theories of Art: from Plato to Winckelmann*, New York and London: New York University Press.

Barnouw, E. (1978) *The Sponsor: notes on a modern potentate*, New York: Oxford University Press.

Bartels, R. (1968) 'The general theory of marketing', *Journal of Marketing* (January): 29–33.

Bataille, G. (1986; original French 1930) 'Museums', trans. A. Michelson, reprinted in *October* 36 (Spring): 25.

Battcock, G. (1973) 'The Warhol generation' (1970), reprinted in Battcock, (ed.) (1973): 21–8.

Battcock, G. (ed.) (1973) *The New Art*, New York: E. P. Dutton.

Baumol, W. and Bowen, W. (1966) *The Performing Arts, the economic dilemma: a study of problems common to theater, opera, music, and dance*, Twentieth Century Fund Report, Cambridge, MA: Cambridge University Press.

Bayley, S. (ed.) (1989) *Commerce and Culture*, London: Fourth Estate in association with the Design Museum.

Bazin, G. (1967) *The Museum Age*, trans. J. van Nuis Cahill, New York: Universe Books.

—— (1969a; original German 1936) 'The work of art in an age of mechanical reproduction', reprinted in Benjamin (1969c): 217–51.

—— (1969b; original German 1950) 'Theses on the philosophy of history', reprinted in Benjamin (1969c): 253–64.

Benjamin, W. (1969c) *Illuminations*, trans. H. Zohn, ed. and intro. H. Arendt, New York: Schocken Books.

Bennett, O. (ed.) (1995) *Cultural Policy and Management in the United Kingdom: proceedings of an international symposium*, Coventry: Centre for the Study of Cultural Policy, University of Warwick.

Berger, J. (1972) *Ways of Seeing*, London: BBC and Harmondsworth: Penguin Books.

Bianchi, F. (ed.) (1993) *Cultural Policy and Urban Regeneration: the west European experience*, Manchester: Manchester University Press.

Blattberg, R. and Broderick, C. (1991) 'Marketing of museums', in Feldstein, (ed.) (1991): 327–46.

Blau, J. (1991) 'The disjunctive history of U.S. museums; 1869–1980', *Social Forces* (September): 87–105.

Blaug, M. (ed.) (1976) *The Economics of the Arts*, London: Martin Robertson.

Bois, Y.-A., Crimp, D. and Krauss, R. (1984) 'A conversation with Hans Haacke', *October* 30 (Fall): 23–48.

Boulding, K. (1972) 'Toward the development of a cultural economics', *Social Science Quarterly* (September): 267–84.

Bourdieu, P. (1984; original French 1979) *Distinction: a social critique of the judgement of taste*, trans. R. Nice, London: Routledge & Kegan Paul.

Bourdieu, P. and Darbel (1991; original French 1969) *For the Love of Art*, trans. N. Merriman and C. Beattie, London: Polity Press.

Bourdieu, P. and Haacke, H. (1995) *Free Exchange*, trans. R. Johnson, Cambridge: Polity.

Bower, J. *et al.* (1995) *Business Policy: managing strategic processes*, eighth edn, Homewood, IL: Irwin.

Brawer, R. (1998) *Fictions of Business: insights on management from great literature*, New York: John Wiley.

Brooke, J. (1989) *Discerning Tastes: Montreal collectors 1880–1920*, Montreal: Montreal Museum of Fine Arts.

Brown, S. (1995) *Postmodern Marketing*, London and New York: Routledge.

Brown, S. and Patterson, A. (eds) (2000) *Imagining Marketing: arts, aesthetics, and the avant-garde*, London and New York: Routledge.

Bullock, A. and Trombley, S. (eds) (1999) *The New Fontana Dictionary of Modern Thought*, third edn, London: HarperCollins.

Burnham, J. (1971) 'Hans Haacke's cancelled show at the Guggenheim', *Artforum* (June): 67–71.

Burrell, G. (1989) 'The absent center: the neglect of philosophy in Anglo–American management theory', *Human Systems Management* 8: 307–12.

—— (1992) 'The organization of pleasure', in Alvesson and Willmott, (eds) (1992): 66–89.

—— (1997) *Pandemonium: towards a retro-organization theory*, London: Sage.

Byrnes, W. (1999) *Management and the Arts*, Second edn, Boston and London: Focal Press.

Caves, R. (2000) *Creative Industries: controversies between art and commerce*, Cambridge, MA and London: Harvard University Press.

Celant, G. (1985) *The European Iceberg: creativity in Germany and Italy today*, Toronto: Art Gallery of Ontario and Milan: Mazzotta.

Chadwick, W. (ed.) (1995) *Confessions of the Guerrilla Girls*, New York: HarperCollins.

Chagy, G. (ed.) (1970) *Business in the Arts '70*, New York: Paul S. Erikson.

Chandler, A. (1962) *Strategy and Structure: chapters in the history of the industrial enterprise*, Cambridge, MA: MIT Press.

Clark, K. (1969) *Civilisation: a personal view*, London: BBC and John Murray.

Colbert, F. (1994) *Marketing Culture and the Arts*, Montreal and Paris: Morin.

Court, D. *et al.* (1997) 'If Nike can "just do it" why can't we', *McKinsey Quarterly* 3: 24–34.

—— (1999) 'Brand leverage', *McKinsey Quarterly* 2: 100–16.

Coutu, D. (2001) 'A conversation with literary critic Harold Bloom', *Harvard Business Review* (May/June): 63–8.

Cowen, T. (1998) *In Praise of Commercial Culture*, Cambridge, MA and London: Harvard University Press.

Crimp, D. (1993) 'This is not a museum' (1989), reprinted in Crimp, *On the Museum's Ruins*, Cambridge, MA and London: MIT Press: 200–34.

Crow, T. (1999) 'Moving picture', *Artforum* (April): 90–95, 143.

Czarniawska, B. (1999) *Writing Management: organization theory as a literary genre*, Oxford: Oxford University Press.

Czarniawska-Joerges, B. and Guillet de Monthoux, P. (eds) (1994) *Good Novels Better Management: reading organizational realities in fiction*, Chur, Switzerland: Harwood Academic.

Damisch, H. (1989) 'The museum device: notes on institutional change', *Lotus International* 35: 4–11.

Davies, S. (1994) *By Popular Demand*, London: Museums and Galleries Commission.

Davis, D. (1990) *The Museum Transformed: design and culture in the post-Pompidou age*, New York: Abbeville Press.

Diggle, K. (1984) *Guide to Arts Marketing*, London: Rhinegold.

DiMaggio, P. (1986a) 'Cultural enterprise in nineteenth-century Boston, part I: the creation of an organizational base for high culture in America' (1982), reprinted in DiMaggio, (ed.) (1986): 41–61.

—— (1986b) 'Can culture survive the marketplace' (1984), reprinted in DiMaggio, (ed.) (1986): 65–92.

—— (1986c) 'Cultural enterprise in nineteenth-century Boston, part II: the classification and framing of American art' (1982), reprinted in DiMaggio, (ed.) (1986): 302–22.

—— (1988) *Managers of the Arts*, Research Division Report 2, Washington, DC: National Endowment for the Arts.

DiMaggio, P. (ed.) (1986) *Nonprofit Enterprise in the Arts: studies in mission and constraint*, Oxford: Oxford University Press.

—— (ed.) (2001) *The Twenty-First Century Firm: changing economic organization in international perspective*, Princeton and Oxford: Princeton University Press.

DiMaggio, P. and Ostrower, S. (1990) 'Participation in the arts by black and white Americans' (1990), reprinted in Pankratz and Morris, (eds) (1990): 105–39.

DiMaggio, P. and Useem, M. (1978a) *Audience Studies of the Performing Arts and Museums: critical review*, Research Division Report 9, Washington, DC: National Endowment for the Arts.

—— (1978b) 'Social class and arts consumption: the origins and consequences of class differences in exposure to the arts in America', *Theory and Society* (March): 141–61.

—— (1980) 'The arts in education and cultural participation: the social role of aesthetic education and the arts', *Journal of Aesthetic Education* (October): 55–72.

Dorian, F. (1964) *Commitment to Culture: art patronage in Europe; its significance for America*, Pittsburgh, PA: University of Pittsburgh Press.

Doyle, P. (1998) *Marketing Management and Strategy,* Second edn, London: Prentice Hall.

Drucker, P. (1954) *The Practice of Management*, New York: Harper and Row.

—— (1989) 'What business can learn from nonprofits', *Harvard Business Review* (July/August): 88–93.

—— (1990) *Managing the Not-Profit Organization*, Oxford: Butterworth Heinemann.

Duchamp, M. (1973) 'The creative act' (1957), reprinted in Battcock (1973): 46–8.

Duncan, C. (1989) 'The MoMA's hot mamas', *Art Journal* (Summer): 171–8.

—— (1995) *Civilizing Rituals: inside public art museums*, London and New York: Routledge.

Duncan, C. and Wallach, A. (1978) 'The Museum of Modern Art as late capitalist ritual', *Marxist Perspectives* (Winter): 28–51.

—— (1980) 'The universal survey museum', *Art History* (December): 448–69.

Eagleton, T. (1983) *Literary Theory: an introduction*, Minneapolis: University of Minnesota Press.

Eells, R. S. F. (1967) *The Corporation and the Arts*, New York: Macmillan.

Ehrenreich, B. and Ehrenreich, J. (1979) 'The professional-managerial class', in P. Walker, (ed.) *Between Labour and Capital*, Hasscocks: Harvester Press: 5–45.

Elsen, A. (1989) 'Museum blockbusters: assessing the pros and cons', *Art in America* (June): 24–7.

English Chamber Orchestra [ECO]. (1983) *ECO: into the eighties*, London: Spencedata.

Enis, B., Cox, K. and Mokwa, M. (eds) (1991) *Marketing Classics: a selection of influential articles*, Eighth edn, Upper Saddle River, NJ: Prentice Hall.

Eyre, R. (1998) *The Future of Lyric Theatre in London*, London: HMSO.

Falk, J. (1998) 'Visitors: who does, who doesn't, and why', *Museum News* (March/April): 38–43.

Feingold, M. (1987) 'Philanthropy, pomp, and patronage: historical reflections upon the endowment of culture', *Daedalus* (Winter): 157–78.

Feist, A. (1997) 'Consumption in the arts and cultural industries: recent trends in the U.K.', in Fitzgibbon and Kelly, (eds) (1997): 245–67.

Feldstein, M. (ed.) (1991) *The Economics of Art Musuems*, Chicago and London: University of Chicago Press.

Ferber, R. *et al.* (1980) *What is a Survey*, Washington, DC: American Statistical Association.

Ferguson, B. (1996) 'Museum rhetorics' (1994), reprinted in Greenberg, Ferguson, and Nairne, (eds) (1996): 175–90.

Fineman, S. (1993) *Emotions in Organizations*, London: Sage.

Fisher, M. and Worpole, K. (eds) (1988) *City Centres, City Cultures: the role of the arts in the revitalization of towns and cities*, Manchester: Centre for Local Economic Strategies.

Fitzgibbon, M. and Kelly, A. (eds) (1997) *From Maestro to Manager: critical issues in arts and cultural management*, Dublin: Oak Tree Press.

Flores, F. and Gray, J. (2000) *Entrepreneurship and the Wired Life: work in the wake of careers*, London: Demos.

Flynn, N. (1993) *Public Sector Management*, Second edn, London: Harvester Wheatsheaf.

Fraser, A. (1991) 'Museum highlights: a gallery talk', *October* 57 (Summer): 103–22.

Galbraith, J. K. (1987) *A View from the Stands*, London: Hamish Hamilton.

Gardner, H. (1983) *Frames of Mind*, London: Heinemann.

Garnham, N. and Williams, R. (1980) 'Pierre Bourdieu and the sociology of culture', *Media, Culture and Society* (July): 209–23.

Goleman, D. (1996) *Emotional Intelligence*, London: Bloomsbury.

Gingrich, A. (1969) *Business and the Arts: an answer for tomorrow*, New York: Paul S. Erikson.

Ginsburgh, V. and Menger, P. M. (eds) (1996) *Economics of the Arts*, Amsterdam: Elsevier Science.

Greenberg, C. (1963) *Art and Culture*, Boston: Beacon Press.

Greenberg, R. (1987) 'The acoustic eye', *Parachute* 46 (March/May): 106–8.

Greenberg, R., Ferguson, B. and Nairne, S. (eds) (1996) *Rethinking About Exhibitions*, London and New York: Routledge.

Greenhalgh, P. (1989) 'Education, entertainment and politics: lessons from the great international exhibitions', in Vergo, (ed.) (1989): 74–98.

Grout, D. J. and Palisca, C. (1998) *A History of Music*, Fourth edn, New York and London: W. W. Norton.

Guback, T. (1970) 'Review essay of Gringrich, *Business and the Arts*', *Journal of Aesthetic Education* (July): 131–7.

Guilbaut, S. (1983) *How New York Stole the Idea of Modern Art: abstract expressionism, freedom, and the cold war*, Chicago and London: University of Chicago Press.

Haacke, H. (1981) 'Working conditions', *Artforum* (September): 56–61.

—— (1986) 'Museums, managers of consciousness' (1984), reprinted in Wallis, (ed.) (1986): 60–72.

Hadfield, C. (2000) *A Creative Education: how creativity and the arts enhance MBA and executive development programmes*, report commissioned by Arts & Business, London.

Hague, (Sir) D. (1993) *Transforming Dinosaurs: how organizations learn*, London: Demos.

Hall, P. (1998) *Cities in Civilisation: culture, innovation and urban order*, London: Weidenfeld and Nicholson.

Hamel, G. and Prahalad, C. K. (1994) *Competing for the Future*, Boston: Harvard Business School Press.

Handy, C. (1996) *The Search for Meaning*, London: Crane and Lemos.

—— (1997) *The Hungry Spirit: beyond capitalism*, London: Hutchinson.

—— (1999) *The New Alchemists: how visionary people make something out of nothing*, London: Hutchinson.

Hansmann, H. (1980) 'The role of nonprofit enterprises', *Yale Law Journal* (April): 835–901.

Harris, N. (1990) 'Polling for opinions', *Museum News* (September/October): 46–53.

Hatton, R. and Walker, J. (2000) *Supercollector: a critique of Charles Saatchi*, London: Ellipsis.

Heilbrun, J. and Gray, C. (1993) *The Economics of Art and Culture*, Cambridge: Cambridge University Press.

Hill, E. and O'Sullivan, C. and T. (1995) *Creative Arts Management*, Oxford: Butterworth Heinemann.

Hillings, V. (1999) 'Komar and Melamid's dialogue with art history', *Art Journal* (Winter): 48–61.

Hobsbawn, E. (1994) *Age of Extremes: a short history of the twentieth century*, London: Michael Joseph.

Hobsbawn, E. and Ranger, T. (eds) (1983) *The Invention of Tradition*, Cambridge: Cambridge University Press.

Holt, D. (1998) 'Does cultural capital structure American consumption', *Journal of Consumer Research* (June): 1–25.

Hood, M. (1983) 'Staying away: why people choose not to visit museums', *Museum News* (April): 50–7.

Horkheimer, M. and Adorno, T. (1973; original German 1947) *Dialectic of Enlightenment*, trans. J. Cumming, London: Allen Lane.

Hoving, T. (1992) *Making the Museums Dance: inside the Metropolitan Museum of Art*, New York: Simon and Schuster.

Impey, O. and MacGregor, A. (1985) *The Origins of Museums: the cabinet of curiosities in sixteenth- and seventeenth-century Europe*, Oxford: Clarendon Press.

Independent Task Force on the Future of the Art Gallery of Ontario. (1992) *Final Report*, Submitted to Ministry of Culture and Communications, Government of Ontario and the Board of Trustees, Art Gallery of Ontario. Toronto.

Jackson, P. (1991) 'Performance indicators: promises and pitfalls', in S. Pearce, (ed.) *Museum Economics and Community*, London: Athlone: 41–64.

Jenkins, R. (1992) *Pierre Bourdieu*, London and New York: Routledge.

Jordanova, L. (1989) 'Objects of knowledge: a historical perspective on museums', in Vergo, (ed.) (1989): 22–40.

Karp, I. and Lavine, S. (eds) (1991) *Exhibiting Cultures: the poetics and politics of museum display*, Washington, DC: Smithsonian Institution.

Karp, I., Kreamer, C. M. and Lavine, S. (eds) (1992) *Museums and Communities: the politics of public culture*, Washington, DC: Smithsonian Institution.

Kay, J. (1993) *Foundations of Corporate Success: how business strategies add value*, Oxford: Oxford University Press.

Kellaway, L. (2000) *Sense and Nonsense in the Office*, London: Financial Times.

Kirchberg, V. (1998) 'Entrance fees as a subjective barrier to visiting museums', *Journal of Cultural Economics* (February): 1–13.

Klein, N. (2000) *No Logo: taking aim at the brand bullies*, New York: Picador.

Klintsov, V. and von Lohneysen, E. (2001) 'Shall we dance?', *McKinsey Quarterly* 4: 6–8.

Kolb, B. (2000) *Marketing Cultural Organizations: new strategies for attracting audiences to classical music, dance, museums, theatre and opera*, Dublin: Oak Tree Press.

Kostabi, M. (1996) *Conversations With Kostabi*, Boston: Journey Editions.

Kotler, N. and Kotler, P. (1998) *Museum Strategy and Marketing: designing missions, building audiences, generating revenues and resources*, San Francisco: Jossey-Bass.

Kotler, P. (1972) 'The generic concept of marketing', *Journal of Marketing* (April): 46–54.

—— (1979) 'Strategies for introducing marketing into nonprofit organizations', *Journal of Marketing* (January): 10–15.

—— (1988) *Marketing for Nonprofit Organizations*, Englewood Cliffs, NJ: Prentice Hall.

Kotler, P. and Andreasen, A. (1975) *Strategic Marketing for Nonprofit Organizations*, Englewood Cliffs: Prentice Hall.

Kotler, P. and Levy, S. (1969) 'Broadening the concept of marketing', *Journal of Marketing* (January): 10–15.

Kotler, P. and Roberto, E. (1989) *Social Marketing: strategies for changing public behaviour*, New York: Free Press and London: Collier Macmillan.

Kotler, P. and Scheff, J. (1997) *Standing Room Only: strategies for marketing the performing arts*, Boston: Harvard Business School Press.

KPMG for the Department of National Heritage, Government of Great Britain (DNH). (1994) *National Museums and Galleries Performance Indicators Steering Group Report*, London.

Krauss, R. (1990) 'The cultural logic of the late capitalist museum', *October* 54 (Fall): 3–17.

Landry, C. and Bianchini, F. (1995) *The Creative City*, London: Demos in association with Comedia.

Larson, G. (1983) *The Reluctant Patron: the United States government and the arts, 1943–1965*, Philadelphia: University of Pennsylvania Press.

—— (1997) *American Canvas: an arts legacy for our communities*, Washington, DC: National Endowment for the Arts.

Leadbetter, C. (1997) *The Rise of the Social Entrepreneur*, London: Demos.

Leadbetter, C. and Oakley, K. (1999) *The Independents: Britain's new cultural entrepreneurs*, London: Demos.

—— (2001) *Surfing the Long Wave: knowledge entrepreneurship in Britain*, London: Demos.

Lee, M. O. (1999) *Wagner: the terrible man and his truthful art*, Toronto: University of Toronto Press.

Lee, S. (ed.) (1975) *Understanding Art Museums*, New York: American Assembly.

Leonard, M. (1997) *Britain: renewing our identity*, London: Demos.

Levitt, T. (1960) 'Marketing myopia', *Harvard Business Review* (July/August): 45–60.

—— 'Marketing myopia: a retrospective commentary', *Harvard Business Review* (September/October): 177–81.

—— (1983) 'The globalization of markets', *Harvard Business Review* (May/June): 92–102.

Lowell, S. *et al.* (2001) 'Not-for-profit management', *McKinsey Quarterly* 1: 147–55.

Lumley, R. (ed.) (1988) *The Museum Time Machine: putting culture on display*, London and New York: Comedia/Routledge.

McDonough, C. (1997) *Staging Masculinity: male identity in contemporary American drama*, Jefferson, NC and London: McFarland & Company.

McEwen, J. (1990) '"Past-Present-Future" at the Tate', *Art in America* (June): 61–5.

McLean, F. C. (1997) *Marketing the Museum*, London: Routledge.

McShine, K. (1999) *Museum as Muse: artists reflect*, New York: Museum of Modern Art.

Mamet, D. (1984) *Glengarry Glen Ross*, London: Methuen.

Markus, T. (1993) *Buildings and Power: freedom and control in the origin of the modern building type*, London and New York: Routledge.

Martin, D. (1998) 'Arts administration (arts management)', in *Encyclopedia of Public Policy and Administration*, four volumes, (ed.) J. Shafritz, Boulder, CO: Westview Press (1998): 128–33.

Merriman, N. (1991) *Beyond the Looking Glass: the past, heritage, and the public in Britain*, Leicester: Leicester University Press.

Mescon, T. and Tilson, D. (1987) 'Corporate philanthropy: a strategic approach to the bottom-line', *California Management Review* (Winter): 49–61.

Meyer, P. *et al.* (1994) [Interview with Alex Melamid] 'Painting by numbers: the search for a people's art', *The Nation* (14 March): 134–48, 326, 328–9.

Micklethwait, J. and Wooldridge, A. (1996) *The Witch Doctors: what management gurus are saying, why it matters and how to make sense of it*, Oxford: Heinemann.

Minihan, J. (1977) *The Nationalization of Culture: the development of state subsidies to the arts in Great Britain*, London: Hamish Hamilton.

Mintzberg, H. (1973) *The Nature of Managerial Work*, New York: Harper and Row.

—— (1979) *The Structuring of Organizations*, Englewood Cliffs, NJ: Prentice Hall.

—— (1984) 'Who should control the corporation', *California Management Review* (Fall): 90–115.

—— (1989) *Mintzberg on Management*, New York and London: Free Press.

—— (1994) *The Rise and Fall of Strategic Planning*, Oxford: Oxford University Press.

Mokwa, M., Dawson, W. and Prieve, A. (eds) (1980) *Marketing the Arts*, New York: Praeger.

Morgan, G. (1986) *Images of Organizations*, Newbury Park, CA: Sage.

—— (1993) *Imaginization: the art of creative management*, Newbury Park, CA: Sage.

Morgan, G. (1992) 'Marketing discourse and practice: towards a critical analysis', in Alvesson and Willmott, (eds) (1992): 136–58.

Mulcahy, K. (1986) 'The arts and their economic impact: the values of utility', *Journal of Arts Management, Law and Society* (Fall): 33–48.

Murdoch, J. (1993) 'Attribution and the claim to objectivity', *International Journal of Cultural Property* (September): 319–34.

Muschamp, H. (1987) 'Chez muse: the American museum scene', *Lotus International* 53: 11–16.

Museum of Modern Art [MoMA]. (1954) *Bulletin* 22/1–2.

Mysercough, J. *et al.* (1988) *The Economic Importance of the Arts in Britain*, London: Policy Studies Institute.

Netzer, D. (1978) *The Subsidized Muse*, Twentieth Century Fund Report, Cambridge: Cambridge University Press.

Newman, D. (1977) *Subscribe Now!*, New York: Theater Communications Group.

O'Doherty, B. (1986) *Inside the White Cube: the ideology of the gallery space*, San Francisco: Lapis Press.

O'Hagan, J. and Harvey, D. (2000) 'Why do companies sponsor arts events', *Journal of Cultural Economics* (August): 205–24.

Ogilvy, D. (1983) *Ogilvy on Advertising*, Toronto: Pan Books.

Olins, W. (1989) *Corporate Identity: making business strategy through design*, London: Thames and Hudson.

Oliva, A. B. (1988) *Superart*, trans. H. Martin and A. Asher, Milan: Giancarlo Publications Editore.

Organization for Economic Cooperation and Development [OECD]. (1997) *OECD Economic Surveys: United States 1997*, Paris: OECD.

Pankrantz, D. and Morris, V. (eds) (1990) *The Future of the Arts: public policy and arts research*, New York: Praeger.

Papadakis, A. (ed.) (1991) *New Museology*, London: Art & Design.

Parker, R. (1996) *The Wine Buyer's Guide*, London and New York: Dorling Kindersley.

Pavitt, J. (ed.) (2000) *Brand.new*, London: V&A Publications.

Peacock, A. (1969) 'Welfare economics and public subsidies to the arts', *Manchester School of Economics and Social Sciences* (December): 323–35.

—— (1998) 'Review of Ruth Towse, (ed.) *Baumol's Cost Disease*', *Journal of Cultural Economics* (November): 292–3.

Peterson, R. (1986) 'From impresario to arts administrator: formal accountability in nonprofit arts organizations', in DiMaggio, (ed.) (1986) 161–83.

Pick, J. (1980) *Arts Administration*, London and New York: E&FN Spon.

—— (1986) *Managing the Arts: the British experience*, London: Rhinegold.

Pick, J. and Anderton, M. (1999) *Building Jerusalem: art, industry and the British millennium*, Amsterdam: Harwood.

Pointon, M. (ed.) (1994) *Art Apart: art institutions and ideology across England and North America*, Manchester and New York: Manchester University Press.

Porter, M. (1980) *Competitive Strategy: techniques for analyzing industries and competitors*, New York: Free Press.

—— (1985) *Competitive Advantage: creating and sustaining superior performance*, New York: Free Press.

—— (1987) 'Corporate strategy: the state of strategic thinking', *Economist* (23 May): 17–22.

—— (1996) 'What is strategy', *Harvard Business Review* (November/December): 61–78.

—— (1998) 'Clusters and the new economics of competition', *Harvard Business Review* (November/December): 77–90.

Powell, W. (2001) 'The capitalist firm in the twenty-first century: emerging patterns in western perspective', in DiMaggio, (ed.) (2001): 33–68.

Powell, W. and DiMaggio, P. (eds) (1991) *The New Institutionalism in Organizational Analysis*, Chicago and London: University of Chicago Press.

Powell, W. and DiMaggio, P. (1991) 'The iron cage revisited: institutional isomorphism and collective rationality in organizational fields' (1983), reprinted in Powell and DiMaggio, (eds) (1991): 63–82.

Power, M. (1994) *The Audit Explosion*, London: Demos.

Prieve, A. (1993) *Guide to Arts Administration Training*, New York: American Council for the Arts.

Prince, D. (1990) 'Factors influencing museum visits: an empirical evaluation of audience selection', *Museum Management and Curatorship* (June): 149–68.

Projansky, B. (1971) 'The artist's reserved rights transfer and sale agreement', three-page agreement, manuscript format, New York.

Raymond, T. and Greyser, S. (1978) 'The business of managing the arts', *Harvard Business Review* (July/August): 123–32.

Raymond, T., Greyser, S. and Schwalbe, D. (eds) (1973) *Cultural Policy and Arts Administration*, Cambridge, MA: Harvard Summer School Institute in Arts Administration.

—— (1975) *Cases in Arts Administration*, Cambridge, MA: Harvard Summer School Institute in Arts Administration.

Reiss, A. (1979) *The Arts Management Reader*, New York and Basel: Audience Arts.

—— (1986) *Cash In!: funding and promoting the arts, a compendium of imaginative concepts, tested ideas and case histories of programs and promotions that make money*, New York: Theater Communications Group.

Reza, Y. (1996) '*Art'*, trans. C. Hampton, London: Faber and Faber.

Ridley, F. F. (1983) 'Cultural economics and the culture of economists', *Journal of Cultural Economics* (June): 1–26.

Ries, A. and Trout, J. (1981) *Positioning: a battle for your mind*, New York and London: McGraw Hill.

Ripley, D. (1969) *The Sacred Grove: essays on museums*, New York: Simon and Schuster.

Rockefeller Panel Report. (1965) *The Performing Arts: problems and prospects*, New York: McGraw Hill.

Rogers, R. (1997) *Cities for a Small Planet*, London: Faber and Faber.

Ross, A. (1995) 'Pollstars: Komar and Melamid's "The People's Choice"', *Artforum* (January): 72–7, 109.

Said, E. (1992) *Musical Elaborations*, London: Vintage.

Sanjek, R. and Sanjek, D. (1991) *American Popular Music Business in the 20th Century*, New York and Oxford: Oxford University Press.

Sawill, J. and Williamson, D. (2001) 'Measuring what matters in nonprofits', *McKinsey Quarterly* 2: 98–107.

Schafer, D. P. (1992) *Canada's Contribution to the International Practice of Arts Management*, Waterloo, ON: Centre for Cultural Management, University of Waterloo.

Schiller, H. (1989) *Culture Inc.: the corporate takeover of public expression*, New York and Oxford: Oxford University Press.

—— (1991) 'Corporate sponsorship: institutionalized censorship of the cultural realm', *Art Journal* (Fall): 56–9.

Schlesinger, A. (1990) 'America, the arts, and the future', in Pankrantz and Morris, (eds) (1990): 3–13.

Schuster, J. M. D. (1987) 'Making compromises to make comparisons in cross-national arts policy research', *Journal of Cultural Economics* (December): 1–36.

—— (1991) *The Audience for American Art Museums*, research Division Report 23, Washington, DC: National Endowment for the Arts.

Scruton, R. (1982) *Dictionary of Political Thought*, London: Macmillan.

Seltzer, K. and Bentley, T. (1999) *The Creative Age: knowledge and skills for the new economy*, London: Demos.

Serota, N. (1996) *Experience or Interpretation: the dilemma of museums of modern art*, London: Thames and Hudson.

Shanes, E. (1989) 'Chairman of the board: Mark Kostabi and art as an industrial process', *Apollo* (January): 35–9.

Shapiro, B. (1973) 'Marketing for nonprofit organizations', *Harvard Business Review* (September/October): 123–32.

—— (1988) 'What the hell is marketing-oriented?', *Harvard Business Review* (November/ December): 119–25.

Sheard, W. S. and Paoletti, J. (eds) (1978) *Collaborations in Italian Renaissance Art*, New Haven and London: Yale University Press.

Sheffield, M. (1976) 'Hans Haacke', *Studio International* (March/April): 117–23.

Sherman, D. and Rogoff, I. (eds) (1994) *Museum Culture: histories-discourses-spectacles*, Minneapolis: University of Minnesota Press.

Shore, H. (1987) *Arts Administration and Management: a guide for arts administrators and their staffs*, New York and London: Quorum Books.

Smith, W. (1956) 'Product differentiation and market segmentation as alternative strategies', *Journal of Marketing* (July): 3–8.

Staniszewski, M. A. (1998) *The Power of Display: a history of exhibition installation at the Museum of Modern Art*, Cambridge, MA: MIT Press.

Strum, D. (1985) 'Corporate culture and the common good: the need for thick description and critical thought', *Thought* (June): 141–60.

Taylor, P. (ed.) (1988) *Impresario: Malcolm McLaren and the British New Wave*, New York: New Museum of Contemporary Art and Cambridge, MA: MIT Press.

Throsby, D. (1994) 'The production and consumption of the arts: a view of cultural economics', *Journal of Economic Literature* (March): 1–29.

Toffler, A. (1967) 'The art of measuring the arts', *The Annals* [of the American Academy of Political Science and Social Science] (September): 141–55.

Towse, R. (ed.) (1997) *Baumol's Cost Disease: the arts and other victims*, Cheltenham and Northampton, MA: Edward Elgar.

Turner, J. (ed.) (2000) *From Rembrandt to Vermeer: 17th century Dutch artists*, London: Macmillan Reference.

Tusa, J. (1997) 'For art's sake', *Prospect* (January): 36–40.

—— (1999) *Art Matters*, London: Methuen.

Valentiner, W. (1944) 'The museum of tomorrow', in P. Zucker, (ed.) *New Architecture in City Planning*, New York: Philosophical Library: 656–74.

Vergo, P. (ed.) (1989) *New Museology*, London: Reaktion Books.

Vinaver, M. (1997) *Plays I: (Overboard; Situation Vacant; Dissent, Goes Without Saying; Nina, That's Something Else; A Smile on the End the of Line)*, ed. and intro. D. Bradby, London: Methuen Drama.

Vine, R. (1994) 'Number's racket', *Art in America* (October): 116–19.

Vogel, H. (2001) *Entertainment Industry Economics: a guide for financial analysis*, Fifth edn, Cambridge and New York: Cambridge University Press.

Von Berswordt-Wallrabe, K. (1995) *Marcel Duchamp: Respirateur*, Schwerin: Staatliches Museum Schwerin and Ostfildern: Hatje Cantz Verlag.

Wallis, B. (ed.) (1986) *Hans Haacke: unfinished business*, New York: New Museum of Contemporary Art and Cambridge, MA: MIT Press.

Ward, F. (1995) 'The haunted museum: institutional critique and publicity', *October* 73 (Summer): 71–89.

Waterford, G. (1991) *Palaces of Art: art galleries in Britain, 1790–1990*, London: Lund Humphries.

Weil, S. (1994) 'Performance indicators for museums: progress report from Wintergreen', *Journal of Arts Management, Law and Society* (Winter): 341–51.

Wetlaufer, S. (2000) 'Common sense and conflict: an interview with Disney's Michael Eisner', *Harvard Business Review* (January/February): 114–24.

Williams, R. (1980) 'Advertising: the magic system', (1960), reprinted in Williams *Problems in Materialism and Culture*, London: Verso: 184–95.

Williams, R. (1983) *Keywords: a vocabulary of culture and society*, revised and expanded edn, London: Fontana.

Wills, G. (2001) 'Film: the collaborative art', in R. Silvers, (ed.) *Doing It: five performing arts*, New York: New York Review of Books: 71–86.

Wood, J. (2000) *The Broken Estate: essays on literature and belief*, London: Pimlico.

Worpole, K. (2000) *Here Comes the Sun: architecture and public space in twentieth century Europe*, London: Reaktion.

Worpole, K. and Greenhalgh, L. (1996) *The Freedom of the City*, London: Demos.

Zolberg, V. (1994) 'Art museums and cultural policies', *Journal of Arts Management, Law and Society* (Winter): 277–90.

Index